CHILD REARING IN
THE HOME AND SCHOOL

CHILD REARING IN THE HOME AND SCHOOL

Edited by
Robert J. Griffore
and
Robert P. Boger
Michigan State University
East Lansing, Michigan

PLENUM PRESS • NEW YORK AND LONDON

Library of Congress Cataloging in Publication Data

Child rearing in the home and school.

Includes bibliographies and indexes.
1. Home and school—United States. 2. School children—United States—Family
relationships. 3. Community and school—United States. 4. Child rearing—United
States. I. Griffore, Robert J. II. Boger, Robert P. [DNLM: 1. Child Rearing. 2. Family. 3.
Schools. WS 105.5.C3 C536]
LC225.3.C47   1986   649′.1   86-22613
ISBN 0-306-42417-7

© 1986 Plenum Press, New York
A Division of Plenum Publishing Corporation
233 Spring Street, New York, N.Y. 10013

Printed in the United States of America

PREFACE

This volume is intended to address contemporary aspects of child rearing in the home and the school, as well as major dimensions of interface between the home and the school. The authors of these chapters have used varying styles and approaches, and the range of perspectives is very broad and inclusive. An essential notion integrating all chapters is that child rearing is a human ecological concern of dominant importance for the home, the school, and the community during the 1980's and that this will continue to be true in the future.

This volume is intended to be useful as a reference book, as a text, for researchers and for policy-makers. It is hoped that the volume also will be of use to parents, teachers, school administrators, child-care workers and others who are interested in child nurturance.

The editors wish to extend appreciation to many individuals who made this effort possible. Our colleagues, Hiram Fitzgerald and Marjorie Kostelnik, have been most helpful and encouraging. We thank them for their patience, support, and invaluable editorial assistance during the production of the camera-ready copy of the volume. We also thank Barbara Taylor for her assistance in typing the chapters, and Carrie DeMyers for typing the camera-ready copy. Carrie's good-nature and positive outlook helped to smooth over the many frustrations inherent in the assembly and production of anthologies such as this one.

We believe that child rearing is one of the most important enterprises of our culture. Further, we believe that the home and the school are linked as a team in accomplishing the objectives of quality child rearing for our children. In the 1980's and beyond, social, economic, and technological change will continue to place new demands on families and schools. This volume can be of assistance to all those who are concerned with increasing the holistic network of effective support for child rearing in the home and in the school.

Robert J. Griffore
Robert P. Boger
East Lansing, MI 1986

CONTENTS

Child Rearing in the Home and School

PARENT AS TEACHER: WHAT DO WE KNOW?

Robert P. Boger(1), Richard A. Richter(2), and
Beatrice Paolucci

Institute for Family and Child Study and the
Department of Family and Child Ecology
Michigan State University
East Lansing, MI 48824

The concept of parents as teachers represents a large and rapidly expanding volume of literature. The proliferation of research studies, reanalyses, and evaluations require extensive organization and integration to discover what is said. The problem is not a lack of information, but rather the ability to use the information we have. In addition, as Leichter (1974) has noted, "The family is a different subject for inquiry because it is so much a part of everyone's experience that it becomes hard to avoid projecting one's own values, beliefs and attitudes onto the experience of others" (p. 215). All of this nothwithstanding, the considerable face validity engendered by the concept of parents as teachers has been supported by powerful empirical evidence (Bronfenbrenner, 1974; Lazar, 1981) supporting the position that parent involvement in the education of the child improves the effectiveness of that education. What follows is not a comprehensive state-of-the-art paper nor a comprehensive review of the parent as teacher literature. It is, however, an attempt to respond to the literature, particularly integrative summaries, and further, to place these in a context that we interpret to be important to their synthesis. We hope by so doing to place them in proper introductory perspective to provide the foundation for what follows in other chapters of the volume.

Parent education is not a new area of inquiry. Goodson and Hess in their 1975 review noted that childrearing advice was communicated to mothers through pamphlets as early as the eighteenth century (pp. 8-9). Groups comprised of middle-class mothers called "Maternal Associations" (Sunley, 1955) were organized before 1820 to meet and discuss childrearing problems. The middle-class orientation of early parent education efforts is referred to in the *1928 Yearbook of the National Society for the Study of Education,* which noted that programs of this period were not remedial programs for disadvantaged families, but were "supported by parents giving thoughtful consideration to training" (p. 276). Brim (1959) reports that by 1920 there were over 75 major organizations conducting parent education programs. National private organizations, university-based research programs, teacher's colleges, public and private school systems, social agencies, child guidance agencies, health agencies, and religious groups all were providing parent education at that time.

Since the initiation of these earlier efforts to "educate" parents, the focus has shifted from the moral and religious development of children to an interest in emotional and personality development, physical health, mental health, and cognitive functioning. The inception of Head Start in the 1960's saw a shift toward programs designed to aid low-income families. The primary emphasis was placed on cognitive development and better early preparation that might lead to improved school achievement of the children as they progressed through the educational system. Many of the early Head Start programs sought not just to educate parents but to *involve* them in partnership roles with professionals toward bettering the potential development of their children (Boger, Kuipers & Beery, 1969; Bronfenbrenner, 1974) and this seems to be very much related to the long term impact of those efforts (Bronfenbrenner, 1974).

The federally funded Head Start and Follow Through models were premised upon the assumption that the deficiencies of the home environment could be compensated for by expanding downward the role of the schools. Beginning in the 1970's, however, there has been increasing debate and questioning of the real influence of the school. Gage (1977) states that "a measure of the pupil's scholastic aptitude or prior achievement, obtained before the beginning of instruction, correlates much more highly than teacher behavior variables with measures of pupil achievement obtained at the end of the teaching period" (p. 76). He estimates this correlation to be as high as .7 to .9. But what accounts for these preinstructional variations? Bloom (1976) feels that a large amount of the variation in academic achievement can be attributed to the influence of the home. More recently Walberg (1984) has pointed to effective home/school partnerships as having major impact on academic function.

What are the conditions in the home that account for these differences? When an attempt is made to look at education of children by parents, considerable similarity is prevalent in the use of concepts such as socialization, enculturation, development and education. The pervasive influence of parents on their children is described in muddled terminology across disciplines that inevitably involves questions of education even when the label "education" is not used (Leichter, 1974;

Paolucci, 1977). Indeed, one of the issues that becomes apparent upon review, is the need for educators to consider parents as educators in the broad rather than the narrow meaning of that term. Literature dealing with the effects of parental behavior on children has been primarily on cognitive dimensions, particularly aspects of school achievement. This is understandable based upon renewed cries for educational reform (National Commission on Excellence in Education, 1983) and the continued emphasis placed on educational outcomes, with limited attention being given to the complex relationship of the family to the system of the school. As Leichter (1974) has pointed out "There is a certain vagueness about the process by which parental behaviors are linked to educational effects. The process is often implicit and assumed rather than explicit and observed" (p. 186).

FAMILY FROM AN ECOLOGICAL CONTEXT PERSPECTIVE

Ecological perspectives can be an aid in understanding the family's needs and resources. Such ecological models allow for more holistic approaches to the study of the family. This affords the opportunity to view the family, the environments which act upon the family, and the impacts that the family makes on the environment. Parents and children do not exist in isolation. What affects one family member also affects the family unit. The family and the environment interact and are interrelated in specific events. The answer to questions about an individual family member, the interaction of family members, or the collective action of the unit, is dependent upon the analyses of intrafamilial dynamics within a holistic family context. The relationships of education occurring in various societal settings and the relationship of these settings to each other is extensively examined and synthesized by Leichter (1978). Paolucci (1977) has also examined the contextual dynamics of the home as a learning center. These dynamics are outlined in more detail in Chapter 3.

Through time and across cultures the family has been viewed as the first instructor and the home has been viewed as a primary setting for learning basic life tasks. The education of family members to assume productive and supportive roles within the family and in the larger society is a critical and, at specific points in the life span, a unique output of household production.[4] The pervasive influence of the family environment on its members, both young and old, has been widely documented (Aries, 1962; Baker and Paolucci, 1971; Carew, Chan and Halfar, 1976: Lamb, 1976; Rapaport & Rapaport, 1971; White & Watts, 1973; Lareau & Benson, 1984; Walberg, 1984). Family members actively respond to the environmental demands of the family setting and their own physiological needs and in so doing learn and develop over time. They simultaneously modify the environment by their responses. In this way family members learn, grow and develop through the activities that occur on a day-to-day level. For the child, transactions with the most significant family adults and an ongoing expanding linkage of these dyadic relationships to transactional relationships between child and other significant adults outside the home, is extremely important (Bronfenbrenner, 1979). Through these transactions, (Paolucci, 1977) children and parents, initially within the home environment, then in an ever expanding set of contacts in neighborhood, community, school, work and leisure groups, learn those expectations which define the boundaries of their repertoire of personal competencies (Paolucci, 1977). The school and the teacher are a part of this whole. Their impacts cannot be fully understood without viewing them within this broader context.

The family organizes and uses a complex set of resources--a mix of materials, "things," time, labor, talents, skills and space--to achieve its particular set of goals (Paolucci, 1977). In most families, some of these resources are invested in building the human resource of each family member; i.e., the capabilities of members so they can become productive and self-fulfilled persons. From this stance, it is appropriate to view the development of the human resource as an investment in human capital and the role of the family and its members as one of production. Hence, a major kind of household production becomes that of enhancing the productive capabilities of family members.

Recently, considerable research has focused on time use in families and investment in human capital based on the assumption that human capital is developed primarily through human interaction. Mincer and Polachek (1974) and more recently Becker (1981) have theorized that family influences the use of time; i.e., parent's educational level is linked to time allocated to childrearing.

Much of the research in the "new home economics" (Schultz, 1974) examines the conditions which affect the family (Paolucci, 1977). The impact of institutions in which family members are involved enhance or constrict the development of human resources. For example, economic constraints make it difficult to secure adequate food, clothing, or shelter and in effect place constraints on learning. Moreover, if adults are involved in the activity of earning a living, little time is left for family involvement and interaction. If interactions between and among people are the essence of the educative process as Bronfenbrenner (1979) suggests, this time for parents and children to interact is critical.

Parents as teachers are making investments in children through time spent with them. This investment in human resource development occurs both deliberately and incidentally. Much of the education that occurs in the family is informal and appears as incidental --a by-product- of other activities. Within the context of the home environment, the development of family members occurs through the informal transactions of family members with one another and with the materials in the home space. The learning is achieved largely through modeling; i.e., imitation, identification, and internalization of ways of behaving. This learning is embedded in everyday activities, thus it is often unconscious or at the edge of consciousness; hence, it is invisible and unrecognized.

Some development of family members in the home setting is deliberate; that is, particular efforts are made to teach and learn. This learning is more conscious and recognized. It occurs when a family member deliberately guides the behavior of another: teaches skills, disciplines, rewards or punishes given behavior. Much of this learning is a "passing of information" from generation to generation or the taking on of new ways acquired through inputs from outside the family system (i.e. peer and work groups, the formal school system, informal educational experiences) all of which is filtered into the family. The current parent as teacher movement reflects the efforts of professional educators to penetrate the home with deliberate learning and conscious reflection on the part of parents that will enhance the development of children and increase their life chances.

The report of Forum 15 of the 1970 U.S. White House Conference on Children placed considerable credence on the role of participation in everyday family activities as a means of developing human resources.

> A child learns, he becomes human, primarily through partici-
> pation in a challenging activity with those he loves and
> admires. It is the example, challenges and reinforcement
> provided by people who care that enables a child to develop
> both ability and his identity...and it is primarily through
> exposure and interaction with adults and children of different
> ages that a child acquires new interests and skills, and learns
> the meaning of tolerance, cooperation and compassion (pp.
> 241-42).

One can assume that some learning--some development of the human resource--is embedded in family interactions. But what that learning is, or what the quality of it is, is not known. Caution must be taken in drawing the generalizations that participation in an activity or interaction is an investment in human capital. Nonetheless, observations of participation in families aimed at discovering the teaching-learning process that occurs between adults and children should offer new insights into the development of human capital--its measurement, cost and worth. Although the need for understanding this learning is readily recognized much of the learning that takes place in the family remains invisible, unintended, and ignored. The system context of family function, then, becomes crucial to interpreting the more molecular data base we have about parent as educator and serves as the target for much of intervention.

EARLY FOUNDATIONS OF PARENT AS TEACHER

The foundation of parent as teacher begins very early. The transactional parent-child dyad of teacher and learner is at no time more important than the perinatal period surrounding the birth of the child (Boger, Richter & Weatherston, 1983; Klaus & Kennell, 1976; White,

1968).   The work of Spitz (1945), Bowlby (1952), and Ainsworth (1973) with institutionalized infants emphasizes further the transactional needs of the newborn.   Babies need intimate involvement with other human beings for their immediate survival as well as for their long-term emotional health.

Research (Klaus and Kennell, 1976) indicates that naturally organized patterns of transactional behavior in both neonates and parents have evolved to help ensure that this requirement is met. These studies suggest that maternal contact with the newborn in the immediate period following birth may be an important cornerstone for later attachments. In one study (Klaus & Kennell, 1976), two groups of low-income, primiparous mothers were assigned to different postpartum experiences. One group had routine contact with their infant every four hours for feeding. The other group was given up to eight hours of additional contact with their infant during the daytime. During a twelve to twenty-one month follow-up study, more of the infants who had contact only every four hours required hospital attention (nonorganic failure-to-thrive, abuse, neglect, or abandonment). Prenatal preparation for birth and institutional procedures may be important factors that can facilitate such early contact and the foundation for an ongoing, positive, transactional relationship.

The importance of maternal attitudes which predict maternal/-infant involvement in the neonatal period is suggested by a longitudinal study of developmental disturbances in healthy infants (Broussard & Hartner, 1970). After delivery and at the end of the first month, healthy mothers were asked to rate how much they thought normal babies cry, spit, feed, eliminate, sleep, and are predictable. The mothers were then asked to rate their own infants on the same scale. The mothers who perceived their infants as better than average had children with fewer later behavioral or emotional difficulties. Situations where infants were perceived as worse than average were predictive of problems as long as four-and-a-half to eleven years later.

Cremin (1974) has remarked that, "What is taught is not always what is desired, and vice versa; what is taught is not always learned, and vice versa. Moreover, there are almost always unintended consequences in education; indeed, they are frequently more significant than the intended consequences" (p. 201). Implicit in this research is the assertion that the infant does not play a passive role in mother-infant interaction (Rheingold, 1969). Indeed, these events are transactional and, although at first the responsibility for initiating behavior may rest principally with the parent, interaction is influenced also by the characteristics and behavior of the infant, even during the early neonatal period.   This neonatal behavior is feedback to the mother, so that one mother may respond differently to successive infants, although the mother's experience with previous infants may play a part in this (Ainsworth, 1973, p. 45).   Maternal and infant behaviors, matched or mismatched, interact, and this interaction helps to shape the transactional course of subsequent behaviors and interactions.

The importance of positive reciprocal interactions over time has also been well demonstrated in Gordon's work. Gordon and colleagues (1975) speak of two patterns of mother-infant interaction in teaching situations. One pattern, labeled "ping pong," consists of the mother initiating something and, within three seconds, the child doing something responsively; action and reaction being repeated. This fundamental pattern was found to be related to how well children do on intellectual tests of age one. The other pattern was labeled "professional." This pattern saw the mother talking at the child without paying attention to the child's response. Such transaction was related to poor performance on subsequent intelligence measures. An important dimension of these early patterns of interaction is their similarity to those seen as necessary for later early childhood and upper grade parent-as-teacher function (Gordon, 1975).

There is evidence indicating that early, positive parent/child transactions lead to increasingly positive parent-as-teacher functions, while extensive early difficulties tend to hamper later potentials for parent-as-educator functions (Bronfenbrenner, 1974).

The Perinatal Positive Parenting program was developed to meet the parenting support and informational needs of first-time parents (Boger, Richter, and Weatherston, 1983). A nationally recognized primary prevention program, PPP trains experienced parents to provide parent-to-parent support to new parents in-hospital and at-home during the perinatal period surrounding the birth of the first child. In addition, parent peer support groups, facilitated, but not lead by the experienced parent volunteer, are established for the new parent participants during the third to fifth week postpartum. Videotapes and written materials which focus on such topics as newborn capabilities, as well as parent/child and parent/parent transaction, have been developed by PPP for use in the program.

The Perinatal Positive Parenting encourages parents' self-confidence, helps them develop realistic expectations for their infant, assists them in becoming more knowledgeable about early child development and provides them with a support network for the very first days of parenthood. By focusing on this time of high readiness for learning surrounding the birth of the first child, the program aims to improve the quality of parent/child interactions and initiate a positive chain of child nurturing events very early in the parenting careers of those participating. Evaluations of the program utilizing direct observation of parent/infant transaction in the home at fifteen months postpartum indicate that PPP families have significantly better maternal involvement and child nurturing environments than do controls (Boger, Kurnetz, Richter and Haas, 1985).

PARENT AS TEACHER IN THE PRESCHOOL YEARS

Three excellent reviews integrating the efforts in early childhood since the early 1960's are of particular import in any summary of what we know about parent as teacher. The first of these, by Bronfenbrenner (1974) integrates much of the early work as it impacts on the interpretations of parent as educator in models of early childhood education. This was followed in 1975 by an extensive review of evaluative research particularly involving parents as teachers in programs for preschool children by Goodson and Hess. Finally the longitudinal, collaborative study of long-term efforts, by Lazar et. al. (1977) sets forth definitive evidence of positive longitudinal impact.

Bronfenbrenner (1974), in his work entitled *A Report on the Longitudinal Evaluation of Preschool Programs,* evaluated the follow-up data from preschool programs of two kinds: the traditional group setting outside the home, and programs involving a regular home visit by a project staff member who works with both parent and child. Some home visitor projects supplemented this with a group setting outside the home, others did not. Studies were included in the evaluation if: (a) there were systematic follow-up data for at least two years after termination of the project; (b) similar information was available for a matched control group; and (c) the data were comparable from one project to the next (p. 2). Only seven projects were found which met all these criteria but twenty additional research studies were included "which failed to fulfill one or another of our requirements but provided evidence that could be used to challenge, confirm or clarify conclusions drawn from the primary investigations" (p. 3). The effect of initial I.Q. level, the role of age, the degree of deprivation, the effect of requiring prior commitment and problems of comparability are all discussed by Bronfenbrenner as important contextual variables which have bearings on the interpretation of results (pp. 8-13).

Although long term gains were not substantiated, Bronfenbrenner arrives at several conclusions which support the importance and effectiveness of early home-based intervention efforts (pp. 52-54).

1. Preschool intervention in group settings shows children making substantial, initial I.Q. gains; that program children show a progressive decline in gains; and that the results point to factors in and around the home as critical.

2. That programs focusing on a home-based tutoring approach had similar results to preschool programs in group settings.

3.   That programs focused simultaneously on parent (usually mother) and child resulted in I.Q. gains still evident three to four years after program; the intervention benefited not only the target child, but also other siblings; and that gains were higher when the parent rather than a staff member assumed prime responsibility for the child's development.

In supporting these conclusions, Bronfenbrenner emphasized the work of Levenstein (1970). In her project the mother was treated as a colleague by a home visitor. The home visitor shared verbal interaction techniques with the mother, first demonstrating them to the child, then drawing the mother into the activity, and finally taking a secondary role as the mother repeated and elaborated the activities. The home visitor was told to, "Keep constantly in mind that the child's primary relationship is with his mother; do all you can to enhance that relationship" (Levenstein, 1970, p. 429). The significance of this project is that it did not target on mother or child, but on the two of them as an interactive system. This strategy using a focused, sustained, sequential and highly qualitative interactive approach involving the parent/child dyad is also seen in the intervention efforts of Gray and Klaus (1970), Karnes, et al. (1970), Weikart (1970), White (1973) and others and reflects directly on Bronfenbrenner's original (1958) and subsequent analysis (1968, 1972) bearing out the child's need for a consistent, quality interaction with a significant caregiver over time. Bronfenbrenner states:

> In the early years of life, the psychological development of the child is enhanced through his involvement in progressively more complex, enduring patterns of reciprocal contingent interaction with persons with whom he has established a mutual and enduring relationship (Bronfenbrenner, 1974, p. 26).

These findings are consistent with Bronfenbrenner's conclusion that the I.Q. gains of programs focusing on parent and child simultaneously, result in longer lasting gains than either home-based tutoring programs or group settings outside the home and that the intervention benefits not only the target child, but the other siblings as well (Bronfenbrenner, 1974, pp. 52-54). As he notes:

> Since the participants remain together after intervention ceases, the momentum of the system insures some degree of continuity for the future. As a result, the gains achieved in this kind of intervention are more likely to persist than those attained in group preschool programs, which, after they are over, leave no social structure with familiar figures who can continue to reciprocate and reinforce the specific adaptive patterns which the child has learned (Bronfenbrenner, 1974, p. 27).

Based upon the evaluation of these data Bronfenbrenner posed the following resultant principles he believed were warranted by the evidence:

General Principles[5]

1. *Family Centered Intervention.* The evidence indicates that the family is the most effective and economical system for fostering and sustaining the development of the child.[6] The evidence indicates further that the involvement of the child's family as an active participant is critical to the success of any intervention program. Without such family involvement, any effects of intervention, at least in the cognitive sphere, appear to erode fairly rapidly once the program ends. In contrast, the involvement of the parents as partners in the enterprise provides an on-going system which can reinforce the effects of the program while it is in operation, and help to sustain them after the program ends.

2. *Ecological Intervention.* The first and most essential requirement is to provide those conditions which are necessary for life and for the family to function as a childrearing system. These include adequate health care, nutrition, housing, employment, and opportunity and status for parenthood. These are also precisely the conditions that are absent for millions of disadvantaged families in our country.

An extensive review of preschool educational experiments was also conducted by Barbara Dillion Goodson and Robert D. Hess (1975) titled, *Parents as Teachers of Young Children: An Evaluative Review of Some Contemporary Concepts and Programs.* This review was stimulated by three questions:

1. What are the assumptions underlying the involvement of parents?
2. In what ways are parents being involved, and what roles are they expected to play?
3. Is there evidence that some parent involvement programs have more effect than others on the academically relevant performance of the children toward whom they are directed?

In examining twenty-nine such programs Goodson and Hess found the underlying goals to be uniform toward the establishment of a standard most likely to produce intelligent, well-adjusted, academically successful children (p. 10). The assumptions about parents common to most of the programs reviewed include:

1. The home is important as the environment preparing the child for entry into the public school.
2. The early years of a child are particularly important in setting the pace and direction of cognitive growth.
3. The impact of the family is not usually overcome by later schooling. (pp. 10-11).

As noted by Bronfenbrenner and others, educational intervention programs for young children have become noted for producing immediate short-term effects in "cognitive" areas which fade out when the children are tested well after the intervention is completed (White, 1973; Wolff & Stein, 1967). Of the twenty-nine programs Goodson and Hess reviewed, twenty-six tested the children when they entered and when they exited the program. Of these twenty-six, twenty-three produced significant gains for children on standardized intelligence tests by the end of the intervention showing that programs to train parents as teachers of their own children are successful in producing immediate advantages (p. 203).

Nine of the programs which Goodson and Hess examined included follow-up testing of program and control children as part of their evaluation design. The follow-up testing of children ranged from three months to five years after the end of the intervention (pp. 203-212). The data from these nine programs indicated that seven of the programs reported positive or significant differences on standardized intelligence tests favoring the program children over varying lengths of time (p. 208). The programs thus gave the children in the program an immediate advantage over control children in average I.Q. score, an advantage that was sustained into grade school. Both program and control children declined somewhat in scores over time, but program children usually continued to score consistently higher.

Three of the programs reviewed by Goodson and Hess assessed classroom grades or performance on standardized achievement tests and all showed positive results (p. 213). Not many of the programs looked at long-term differences in academic achievement of program and control children, but those that did found strong evidence for the value of helping the program children keep in school and out of special classes (p. 215). The conclusions drawn by Goodson and Hess give evidence that program children maintain their advantage for one or two years after the completion of the intervention, but that follow-up testing at longer intervals was inconclusive with both groups exhibiting declining I.Q. scores, with program children remaining superior.

When specific program features of parent components were examined in light of a program's immediate and/or long-term effects on children, it was found that the more a program focused on the parents, the more likely it was to produce significant and stable gains in children, favoring home visits alone or in combination with preschool classes; that no one content of the parent component was favored by the outcome criteria; that greater effects in immediate and follow-up testing were produced by a one-to-one parent/teacher ratio; and that high program structure was most often related to greater program effectiveness (pp. 226-228).

Immediate outcomes of the programs focused on parents. Immediate outcomes on parent/child interactions and changes in the siblings of program families were also examined by Goodson and Hess. Of those programs measuring changes in parent attitudes, it was found that parental sense of personal efficacy or control over their own file, as well as their attitude toward their child and his/her development, were found to be significantly changed most often (pp. 228-229). Changes in parent's patterns of verbal behavior toward their children through the use of language to reinforce or support the child's efforts and the use of more syntactically complex or varied language patterns with their children were also noted (p. 232). Goodson and Hess also found that these programs produced changes in parental behavior, which benefited the intellectual development of all the children in the home (p. 236).

In summary, the review of Goodson and Hess as regards this group of twenty-nine preschool intervention programs developed to help parents teach their own children, indicates that these programs consistently showed significant immediate gains in children's I.Q. scores, seemed to show long-term effects on children's I.Q. and school performance, and seemed to positively alter the teaching behavior of parents.

Perhaps the most important synthesis of long term program evidence supporting parent as teacher functions is that included in the recent review by Lazar and his colleagues regarding the longitudinal effects of early intervention. A national collaborative study of twelve research groups entitled *The Persistence of Preschool Effects* (Lazar et al., 1977), summarizes the findings of current analyses of longitudinal studies of low-income children, who participated in experimental infant and preschool programs initiated in the 1960's. These children ranged from nine to eighteen years of age at the time of the review (p. 1).

The problem faced in this effort, as in Bronfenbrenner's and Goodson and Hess's reviews, was how to pool data from twelve different investigators. The consortium chose to analyze the results of each project separately, and then pool the summary results from the various projects, using program within site as their unit of analysis (Darlington, 1978, p. 1-3). To ensure that the overall significant results were not caused by one exceptional program, the projects were rank ordered by degree of confirmation to the experimental hypothesis, and then deleted from the analysis one-by-one (pp. 3-4). This test allowed them to disregard a result if it evaporated with the deletion of one or two projects or programs.

The data discussed in the report included data collected indepen-
dently by each research group at the beginning of their program and
longitudinally over a number of years after the program ended.   In
addition, common follow-up data were collected in 1976-77 (Lazar, 1977,
p. 1).   The first question asked was "Does the evidence indicate that
early education improves the academic performance of program children?" With only two exceptions, the mean I.Q. of program groups was
higher than the mean I.Q. of control groups up to three years after
children had left the program (pp. 49-57).   This increase in skills
measurable by I.Q. tests lasted for several years but eventually faded.
A permanent increase in intellectual skills as measured was not substantiated (p. 61).

Indicators of actual school performance--the assignment to special
education classes or retention in grade--which may be a better measure
than a predictive instrument, were also examined.   The combined
evidence of five projects which looked at whether program children had
been assigned to special education classes shows that early education
significantly reduces the number of children placed in such classes (pp.
63-67). The same trend was found from seven projects which looked at
whether program children had been held back in grade more than control
children (pp. 67-69).   The findings of Woodman's Micro-Social Learning
System program, which had no control group, are quite impressive
because they indicate that high risk children who attended an early
intervention program, were able to meet the minimal school requirements as well as the general school population (pp. 69-72).

Included in the data which this group collected in 1976-1977 is
information from interviews conducted with former program participants
and their parents.   The preliminary findings from the youth interview
indicate that there is a slight tendency for more control than program
children to drop out of school, that control and program children have
similar educational aspirations, and that program children rate how they
feel they are doing in school higher (pp. 82-84).   The results of the
parental interviews was consistently positive with one hundred percent
of parents whose children had been in home based programs, 93.4 percent
of parents of children from center based programs, and 87.8 percent of
parents of children from combination programs answering that the
program was a good thing for their child (p. 86). The cognitive aspects
of the program that their child attended was most frequently chosen by
parents as what they liked best about the program (pp. 87-89). In sum,
the most important finding from this study is that low-income children
who received early education are better able to meet the minimal
requirements of their school. This study found no indication of the most
effective age or length of intervention on program children (p. 110).

Another long term research effort that has had impact on judge-
ments regarding parent as educator during the preschool period is that of
White (White and Watts, 1973). This extensive work observed children

between the ages of one and three in their homes in interaction with their mothers as an attempt to ascertain causal factors for complex early behavior. They found that those mothers who were most effective tended to

> interact more with (their children), engage in more intellectu-
> ally stimulating activities with them, teach them more often,
> encourage them more often (and) initiate activities with them
> more often (p. 199).

This is quite in line with the findings of Bronfenbrenner, et al. (1974) as well as the work of Gotts (1978) at the Appalachian Educational Laboratory.

Lazar, in summary of his landmark follow-up analyses of early intervention programs, indicated five interrelated program characteristics that were related to long term positive outcomes:

1. Age of intervention - the earlier the better
2. Adult-child ratio - the fewer children the better
3. Number of home visits - the more the better
4. Direct participation of parents - the more the better
5. Services for families, not just the child - the more, the better (Lazar, 1981, p. 305)

It is noteworthy that three of the five are related to parent and family interfacing with the early educational efforts. Lazar commented on this and emphasized the family change dimension of these early home/school efforts.

> It is my belief that the basic reason these early programs had
> such long-lasting effects is not curricular, but rather is a
> result of changes in the parent' values and anticipations for
> their children. A single shot of preschool seems hardly enough
> to produce a life long change. I believe that the increased
> participation of parents provided the value change that led
> them to encourage and reward their children's learning activi-
> ties. When the professionalization of education drove parents
> out of their children's learning, an essential condition for
> learning may have been severely damaged. Perhaps we can
> prevent that loss in the future by bringing parents back into
> partnership in the educational enterprise (Lazar, 1981, p. 305).

PARENT AS TEACHER DURING THE FORMAL SCHOOL YEARS

A weakness quickly noted in the initial Head Start program was the lack of designed linkage to the public school. Once a child left the preschool program there was little or no continued support offered by the school system. The Follow Through program was initiated to bridge this gap.   The Parent Education Follow Through model, developed by Gordon and his colleagues, was specifically designed to focus on the parent as educator function in an attempt to meet this need (Gordon & Breviogel, 1975).

> The emphasis of the program...stresses the parent's teaching role as being equal to, not subordinate to, the teacher's. Basic to the model is the recognition of the fact that parents are uniquely qualified to guide and participate in their children's education.   In addition to their key role as teachers in the home, parents contribute ideas for new home learning activi- ties and operations of the school.   They are viewed as "partners" with, rather than "clients" of the school (Gordon & Olmstead, 1978, pp. 74-75).

The Parent Education model received a highly critical and widely publicized evaluation from Abt Associates which concluded that models which emphasize cognitive or basic skills "succeed better" than other models including those focusing on parent involvement (Cline et al., 1975).   Further reanalyses of the Follow Through data indicated this conclusion to be erroneous (House, Glass, McClean-Walker, 1977).   The evaluation by House et al. suggests that academic achievement is not the sole guide to effectiveness of a program and that contextual factors are extremely influential.

If early educational efforts and enriched home environments are important in the early years, there is no evidence to indicate that they decline in importance after the child enters the formal school system. A major investigation of the effectiveness of schooling (Coleman et al, 1966) suggested that the variation among students in academic achieve- ment is more a result of differences in home background than differ- ences among schools.   Jencks et al. (1972) further confirms this, indicating that it is very difficult to identify specific characteristics of schools that influence student achievement.   Other investigations sup- port the same general conclusion.   The Rand report, *How Effective is Schooling* (1971) disputed the long held assumption that there is a link between the amount of money spent on education and the quality of schooling that resulted.   An international study of educational achieve- ment (1973) looked at nineteen countries and indicated that, all over the world, the nature of the home environment is the crucial factor, and as such is more important than the schooling in determining children's overall achievement.   For example, the number of books and magazines in a student's home had a greater impact on literary achievement than the income level of the student's family (Rich, 1976, p. 73).

The focus of much educational research since Coleman's study has centered on classroom interaction or teacher effects during the school hours (Gage, 1977). Based upon the literature research into exactly what parents do to reinforce, supplement, ignore or subvert school goals has not been as extensive a topic of research. For most public schools, the contact between the home and the school has been largely limited to yearly open houses, report cards, parent-teacher conferences, and homework. Even these contacts are usually one way: from teacher to parent.

These models suggest that factors in the home/school interface might be altered to expedite achievement in older children. In an attempt to discern what such factors in the home might be, Walberg and Marjoribanks (1976) reanalyzed the four year longitudinal survey of reading achievement among more than 3,000 English children. They found that adjusted gains in achievement were as closely related to measure of parental encouragement and stimulation of adolescents as the same measure of the parents of young children.

To assess the quasi-experimental effects of such evidence, Walberg (1980) analyzed the results of a school-based parental involvement program on reading achievement. The program involved an inner-city elementary school (K-6) located in one of Chicago's most economically depressed areas. The model for this program was the Smith (1968) project. The Chicago project originated in the school and was directed toward the entire school population: teachers, students and parents. Staff-parent committees were appointed to plan and guide the accomplishment of school goals. A contracts approach was used by the district superintendent, the school principal, the classroom teachers, the parents, and each child to work toward better performance (p. 4). Various social activities were carried out to promote school pride and determination to achieve. On the academic side, a booklet of school policies and academic activities was prepared for the parents to encourage their children's reading in the home. Some participants (parents and teachers) were more intensively involved in the project than others. Walberg indicates that students in classes where parents and teachers were intensively involved in the program, gained twice the grade equivalents on reading achievement scales as students in classes where parents and teachers were less intensively involved (p. 8). Such programs merit further consideration and research. The question of what gain can be sustained throughout a particular child's school career in an inner city environment remains to be answered. Continuation and replication with systematic evaluation is needed, but as Walberg notes, "What's terribly important about this project is that it shows a child is not a lost cause just because he's past 6" (Sheils & Monroe, 1976).

The parents as educators literature becomes even thinner as the child progresses into the middle and high school years. This ascent up the educational ladder coincides with a greater and greater degree of subject matter specialization by educators. Just as we would not expect a teacher to teach without adequate preparation, the involvement of parents as educators, in the more deliberate sense during these latter years, cannot be accomplished without careful and deliberate programming.

An effective involvement of parents at the elementary and secondary level has been as tutors of children. Although the supposition that
putting two people together and designating one of them as a tutor will
lead to a healthy, profitable, academically enhancing relationship, is
simply untrue (Harrison, 1967; Neidermeyer, 1969), the program Structured Tutoring (Harrison & Wilkinson, 1978) offers a relatively new
approach for parents to help in the formal instruction of low achieving
children. Harrison feels that this type of tutorial relationship can be
successful if it is structured to train parents to tutor their children by (1)
use of principles of learning and insure mastery of principles before
moving to the next step in the sequences; (2) being material specific; (3)
being task specific; and (4) including aspects of record keeping (p. 29). If
parents can be involved in such an effort as true colleagues a number of
possible advantages may occur; including increased parent/child transaction, increased home/school understanding, and conceivably, cost benefits to the overall instructional effort.

The basic conceptualization of the Parents Are Teachers Too
effort, a program of language intervention developed by Boger and his
colleagues (Boger and Kuipers, 1971) was also focused upon the
home/school process. Although the content of the educational effort
was initially language development, the major thrust of the model was
home/school process, particularly teacher/parent facilitation.   Like
Levenstein (1970) and Gordon (1972), the model attends to the careful
construction of a colleague relationship with the parent.   Unlike the
home visitation models, the Parents Are Teachers Too facilitates the
teacher/parent dyad specifically.

The first evaluation of the program, consisting of a rural sample
(Boger, Kuipers, Berry, 1969) found that language treatment groups
performed significantly better than the placebo group on the Verbal IQ
subscale of the WPPSI. The two language groups saw the mother use
significantly more specific language in the explanation of a task to the
child.   These two treatment groups also used more words and more
complex language patterns when telling a story to their children. The
program children increased in their positive perceptions of the mother's
view of them as well as their own self-concepts.

Another study of the PTT program focused on research questions
not directly related to the testing of the effects of the program, but
rather on the use of incentives to initiate and maintain parental
involvement in parent education programs (Boger, Kuipers, Cunningham
& Andrews, 1974). An important result of this study was that, although
attendance was stimulated by the provision of incentives, the children of
those parents who came *without* incentives evidenced the greatest
change in self-esteem.

The home/school process research of Schaefer is also extensive, as
is the work of Rich at the Home School Institute (Barletta, et al., Eds.,

1978).   Both of these models have evidence of specific programming toward the home/school interface. The HSI has expanded and refined the cost effective "recipe" type of home developed approach in the Home Educational Learning Program (HELP).   Like the Parents Are Teachers Too model, the HELP program is a teacher/parent interactive effort, with lessons or "recipes" for home learning being provided for the parent to facilitate home learning activities. The program has outstanding face validity and appeals to participants.   The authors have reported a significant rise in reading achievement (Mattox & Rich, 1978).

PARENT AS EDUCATOR: A PERSPECTIVE ON RESEARCH PROCESS

The family environment is pervasive and malleable. It is also a highly complex system, evolving through time in close relation to other complex systems, particularly the school. Glass observes that:

> No education problem admits a single answer. We study a system and a process too complex and too interactive to give up its secrets easily. The variance in our findings of studies is essential, largely irreducible. It should be viewed as something to be noted in its own right, not something that can be eliminated with "tighter" designs or sharper measures. When a hundred studies can be arranged to yield a half-dozen answers to a question, we can feel confident that we are nearer the truth" (1976, p. 6).

These realities are even more pervasive when studying the family system. It is particularly important, therefore, to build effectively on relationships that hold empirical validity not only for the short term but over time. Based upon the longitudinal evidence at hand, the relationships between parent and teacher in building a comprehensive environment for the effective nurturance and education of the child, would clearly seem to fall in this category.

An excellent summary of parent involvement and student achievement research was developed (Henderson, 1981) for the National Committee for Citizens in Education.   This summary, like that of Lazar, focuses on the generalizability of the parent involvement dimension as a critical factor in the long term effectiveness of the child's total educational milieu.

> Taken together, what is most interesting about the research is that it all points in the same direction. The form of parent involvement does not seem to be critical, so long as it is reasonably well-planned comprehensive, and longlasting. Even programs that just involve parents as reinforcers of what is being taught at school are effective (Barth).

What becomes very clear from reading the research is that families provide the most important learning environment of all. If parents are not encompassed in the learning process, schools -- and school children -- are being deprived of an essential source of support. If there is no continuity between home and school, it becomes difficult for a student to integrate the separate experiences ... (Henderson, 1981, p. 7).

SUMMARY

In summary then, the following conclusions appear warranted:

1.   Parent as educator functions in the context of a complex family ecosystem.
2.   Each parent and each child are unique. Each family is unique. Parents as educators functions for one family are not necessarily applicable to others. The most appropriate educational program grows as a partnership between culturally sensitive professional expertise and parent determined values, beliefs and attitudes.
3.   The parent as educator and home as a learning center function of the family system may account for more variance in child learning than does the system of the school alone.
4.   The interface of family systems with relevant school systems is not, overall, a highly efficient one in the United States. This reality is counterproductive to the role of parent as educator as well as the role of teacher as educator.
5.   Programs facilitating parent as educator at the preschool level result in substantial improvement in children's later cognitive functioning.
6.   There is evidence that the improved cognitive functioning as a result of parent/child programs within the educational system is cumulative and has lasting impact.
7.   Parent as educator functions during the perinatal period (Boger, et al., 1983) and throughout the first three years are highly important.
8.   There is evidence to support the inverse relationship of age of entry into parent/child programs and resultant gains.
9.   Programs facilitating parent as educator family functions are of benefit not only to the target child but all children within the family.
10. Programs facilitative of parent as educator functions can impact positively upon the parent's affective and cognitive functioning.

The importance of providing those conditions that are necessary for life and for the family to function as a childrearing system as necessary antecedents to all parenting functions including parent as educator can not be minimized. Such things as adequate income, adequate employment opportunity, adequate health care, nutrition and housing are included within such necessities. Building upon this foundation the concepts needed for more effective home/school interfaces are extensively expanded upon in the chapters that follow.

NOTES

1. Robert P. Boger is presently the Director of the Institute for Family and Child Study, and Professor in the Department of Family and Child Ecology, College of Human Ecology, Michigan State University, East Lansing.

2. Richard A. Richter, formerly a Specialist at the Institute for Family and Child, College of Human Ecology, is currently Project Manager, Michigan State University Health Promotion Project, College of Nursing, East Lansing.

3. Beatrice Paolucci, now deceased, was a Professor in the Department of Family and Child Ecology, College of Human Ecology, Michigan State University, East Lansing.

4. The definition of household production is defined by Margaret Reid (1934) in *Economics of Household Production* as "those unpaid activities which are carried on, by and for the members, which activities might be replaced by market goods, or paid services, if circumstances such as income, market conditions, and personal inclinations permit the service being delegated to someone outside the household group" (p. 11).

5. "The propositions stated in terms of parent rather than mother alone is in the belief that subsequent research will indicate that they apply as well to the father, or any other older member of the household who is prepared to assume a major and continuing responsibility for the care of the child" (p. 55).

6. Bronfenbrenner indicates the following in regard to the superscripts "i" and "r":

    "To indicate the extent to which each of the following generalizations are supported by research results, we shall label each one by a symbol. The superscript "i" denotes that the conclusion is *inferred* from the evidence; the superscript "r" means that the generalization is supported by *replicated results* obtained in two or more well-designed studies described in the main body of this analysis, but that there is need for further research designed specifically to test and refine the proposition in question" (pp. 54-55).

REFERENCES

Ainsworth, M. D. (1962). The effects of maternal deprivation: A review of findings and controversy in the context of research strategy. In *Deprivation of maternal care: A reassessment of its effects*. Public Health Papers No. 14, Geneva, Switzerland.

Ainsworth, M. D. (1973). The development of infant-mother attachment. In B. Caldwell & H. Ricciuti (Eds.), *Review of child development research, III*. Chicago: University of Chicago Press.

Aries, P. (1962). *Centuries of childhood: A social history of family life* (R. Baldick, Trans.). New York: Alfred A. Knopf.

Baker, G. & Paolucci, B. (1971). The family as environment for educability in Costa Rica. *Journal of Home Economics, 63*, 161-167.

Baltman, K., Weatherston, D. J., Boger, R. P., & Richter, R. A. (1983). Perinatal positive parenting: Parent support groups. *Infant Mental Health Journal, 4*(4), 316-320.

Barletta, C., Boger, R., Lezotte, L., & Hull, B. (Eds.). (1978). *Planning and implementing parent/community involvement into the instructional delivery system*. Proceedings from a Parent/Community Involvement Conference sponsored by the Midwest Teacher Corps Network, East Lansing, MI.

Becker, G. S. (1981). *A treatise on the family*. Cambridge, MA: Harvard University Press.

Bloom, B. S. (1976). *Human characteristics and school learning*. New York: McGraw-Hill.

Boger, R. & Andrews, M. (1975). *Early social development: Parent and child programs* (final report). East Lansing: Michigan State University, Institute for Family and Child Study, College of Human Ecology.

Boger, R. & Kuipers, J. (1971). *Parents are teachers too: A curriculum model for increasing positive parent-child, parent-teacher, and parent-school interaction* (Final report, Vol. II). East Lansing, Michigan State University, Institute for Family and Child Study.

Boger, R., Kuipers, J., & Beery, M. (1969). *Parents as primary change agents in an experimental Head Start program of language intervention*. East Lansing: Head Start Evaluation and Research Center, Michigan State University.

Boger, R., Kuipers, J., Cunningham, A., & Andrews, M. (1974). *Parents as primary change agents in an experimental head start program of language intervention* (Final report). East Lansing: Michigan State University, Head Start Evaluation and Research Center.

Boger, R., Kuipers, J., Cunningham, A., & Andrews, M. (1974). *Maternal involvement in day care: A comparison of incentives* (Final report). East Lansing: Michigan State University, Institute for Family and Child Study, College of Human Ecology.

Boger, R., Kurnetz, R., Richter, R. & Haas, B. (1985). *A follow-up of Perinatal Positive Parenting (PPP) treatment and control partici-*

pants (Final Report). East Lansing: Michigan State University, Institute for Family and Child Study, College of Human Ecology.

Boger, R., Richter, R. & Weatherston, D. (1983). Perinatal positive parenting: a program of primary prevention through support to first time parents. *Infant Mental Health Journal, 34*(10), 844-850.

Bowlby, J. (1952). Maternal care and mental health, *Monograph Series No. 2.* Geneva: World Health Organization.

Bowlby, J. (1969). *Attachment and loss* (Vol. 1). New York: Basic Books.

Brazelton, T. B., Koslowski, B., & Main, M. (1974). The origins of reciprocity in mother-infant interactions. In M. Lewis & L. A. Rosenblum (Eds.). *The effect of the infant on caregiver* (49-76). New York: John Wiley.

Brim, O. G. (1959). *Education for child rearing.* New York: Russell Sage Foundation.

Bronfenbrenner, U. (1958). Socialization and social class through time and space. In E. E. Maccoby et al. (Eds.), *Readings in social psychology* (400-425). New York: Holt.

Bronfenbrenner, U. (1968). Early deprivation: A cross species analysis. In S. Levine & G. Newton (Eds.) *Early experience on behavior* (627-764). Springfield, IL: Charles C. Thomas.

Bronfenbrenner, U. (1972). Is early intervention effective? A report on longitudinal evaluations of preschool programs, Vol. II. Department of Health, Education and Welfare, Publication Number (OHD)75-25.

Bronfenbrenner, U. (1974). Is early intervention effective? In F. G. Jennings (Ed.), *Teachers College record, 76,* 279-303. New York: Columbia University.

Bronfenbrenner, U. (1974). *A report on longitudinal evaluation of preschool programs, 2,* 767-87. Ithaca, New York: Cornell University.

Bronfenbrenner, U. (1978). Who needs parent education? In D. Sloan (Ed.), *Teachers College record* (Vol. 79). New York: Columbia University.

Bronfenbrenner, U. (1979). Contexts of child rearing: problems and prospects. *American Psychologist, 34*(10), 844-850.

Bronfenbrenner, U. (1979). *The ecology of human development.* Cambridge, MA: Harvard University Press.

Broussard, E. R., & Hartner, M. S. (1970). Maternal perception of the neonate as related to development. *Child Psychiatry Human Dev., 1,* 16-25.

Carew, J. V., Chan, I., & Halfar, C. (1976). *Observing intelligence in young children: Eight case studies.* Englewood Cliffs, NJ: Prentice-Hall.

Cline, M., Anes, N., Anderson, R., et al. (1975). Education as experimentation: Evaluation of the follow through planned variation model: Final Report. Prepared for the U. S. Office of Education.

Coleman, J. S. et al. (1966). *Equality of education opportunity.* Washington, D.C.: U.S. Government Printing Office.

Cremin, L. A. (1974). The family as educator: Some comments on the recent historiography. In F. G. Jennings (Ed.), *Teachers College record, 76,* 250-265. New York: Columbia University.

Danzberger, J. P., & Usdan, M. D. (1984). Building partnerships: The Atlanta experience. *Phi Delta Kappan, 65,* 393-396.

Darlington, R. B. (1978, March). *Methods, issues and some illustrative findings in analyzing the data of the Consortium on Developmental Continuity.* Paper presented at the American Educational Research Association, Toronto, Ontario, Canada.

Fels, C., & Lanston, B. (1982, April). *Spring into reading: A parent-child reading participation program.* Paper presented at the Annual Meeting of the International Reading Association, Chicago, IL.

Gage, N. L. (1977). *A re-examination of paradigms for research on teaching.* Stanford, CA, Stanford University: Center for Educational Research at Stanford.

Glass, G. V. (1976). Primary, secondary and meta-analyses of research. *Educational Researcher, 5*(10), 3-8.

Goodson, B. D., & Hess, R. D. (1975). *Parents as teachers of young children: An evaluative review of some contemporary concepts and programs.* Washington, D. C.: Bureau of Educational Personnel Development.

Gordon, I. J. (1972). What do we do about parents as teachers. *Theory Into Practice, II,* 150-156.

Gordon, I. J. (1975). *The Infant Experience,* Chapter 4, 46-65, Columbus, OH: Merrill.

Gordon, I. J. (1978). Rebuilding home-school relations. In Barletta, C. et al. (Eds.), *Planning and implementing parent/community involvement into the instructional delivery system* (1-9). Proceedings from a Parent/Community Involvement Conference sponsored by the Midwest Teacher Corps Network, East Lansing, MI.

Gordon, I., & Breivogel, W. (1975). *Building effective home-school relationships.* Boston: Allyn & Bacon.

Gotts, E. (1978). *Final report: Appalachian Educational Laboratory.* Charleston, WV: Appalachian Educational Laboratory.

Gray, S. T. (1984). How to create a successful school/community partnership. *Phi Delta Kappan, 65*(6), 405-409.

Gray, S. W. & Klaus, R. A. (1970). The early training project: The seventh year report. *Child Development, 41,* 909-924.

Harrison, G. V. (1967). *Training students to tutor* (Technical Memorandum 3686/000/00). Santa Monica, CA: System Development Corporation.

Harrison, G. V., & Wilkinson, J. (1978). Systematic use of human resources: Structured tutoring. In Barletta, C., Boger, R., Lezotte, L., & Hull, B. (Eds.), *Planning and implementing parent/community involvement into the instructional delivery system* (25-34). Proceedings from a Parent/Community Involvement

Conference sponsored by the Midwest Teacher Corps Network, East Lansing, MI.

Hattingh, D. L. (1978). *The place of the parent community in the education system.* (R. F. Purchase, Trans.). Pretoria, South Africa: Institute for Educational Research.

Henderson, A. (Ed.). (1981). *Parent participation -- student achievement.* Washington, D.C.: National Committee for Citizens in Education.

Hess, R. D. (1969). Parental behavior and children's school achievement - implications for Head Start. In *Critical issues in research related to disadvantaged children.* Princeton, NJ: Educational Testing Service.

House, E. R., Glass, G. V., McLean, L. D., & Walker, D. F. (1977). *No simple answer: Critique of the "Follow Through" Evaluation.* Urbana: University of Illinois.

Jencks, C. et al. (1972). *Inequality: A reassessment of the effect of family and schooling in America.* New York: Basic Books.

Jones, J. O. (1981). *Classroom directed home training activities. Preschool program: A regional demonstration program for preschool handicapped children.* (Grant No. G007800198). Washington, D. C.: Handicapped Children's Early Education Program.

Karnes, M. B., Teska, J. A., Hodgins, A. S., & Badger, E. D. (1970). Educational intervention at home by mothers of disadvantaged infants. *Child Development, 41,* 925-935.

Klaus, M. H., & Kennell, J. H. (1976). Human maternal and paternal behavior. In M. H. Klaus & J. H. Kennell (Eds.), *Maternal-infant bonding* (38-98). St. Louis: C. V. Mosby.

Kennell, J. H., Trause, M. A., & Klaus, M. H. (1975). Evidence for a sensitive period in the human mother. In *Parent-infant interaction, Ciba Foundation Symposium* (pp. 87-101). Amsterdam, The Netherlands: Elsevier Publishing.

Lamb, M. E. (1976). Effects of stress and cohort on mother- and father-infant interaction. *Developmental Psychology, 12,* 435-443.

Lamb, M. (1976). *The role of the father in child development.* New York: John Wiley.

Lamb, M. E. (1977). The development of mother-infant and father-infant attachments in the second year of life. *Developmental Psychology, 13,* 637-648.

Lareau, A., & Benson, C. (1984, February). The economics of home/school relationships: A cautionary note, *Phi Delta Kappan,* 401-404.

Lazar, I., Hubbell, V., Murry, H., Rosche, M., & Royce, J. (1977). The persistence of preschool effects: A long-term follow up of fourteen infant and preschool experiments (Final Report). *The Consortium of Developmental Continuity,* Grant No. 18-76-07843. Washington, D. C.: Government Printing Office.

Lazar, I. (1981). Early intervention is effective. *Educational Leadership, 38*(4), 303-305.

Leichter, H. J. (1974). Some perspectives on the family as educator. In F. G. Jennings (Ed.), *Teachers College Record, 76,*175-217. New York: Columbia University.

Leichter, H. J. (1978). Families and communities as educators: Some concepts of relationship. In D. Sloan (Ed.), *Teachers College Record, 79,* 567-658. New York: Columbia University.

Leichter, H. D. (Ed.) (1979). *Families and communities as educators.* New York: Teachers College Press.

Levenstein, P. (1970). Cognitive growth in preschoolers through verbal interaction with mothers. *American Journal of Orthopsychiatry, 40,* 426-432.

Lozoff, B., Brittenham, G. M., Trause, M. A., Kennell, J. H., & Klaus, M. H. (1977). The mother-newborn relationship: Limits of adaptability. *The Journal of Pediatrics, 77,* 1-12.

Marjoribanks, K. (1979). *Families and their learning environments.* London: Routledge & Kegan Paul.

Mattox, B., & Rich, D. (1978). Project help. In Barletta, C., Boger, R., Lezotte, L., & Hull, B. (Eds.), *Planning and implementing parent/community involvement into the instructional delivery system* (2-18). Proceedings from a Parent/Community Involvement Conference sponsored by the Midwest Teacher Corps Network, East Lansing, MI.

Mincer, J., & Polachek, S. (1974). Family investments in human capital: Earnings of women. In T. W. Schultz (Ed.), *Economics of the family.* Chicago, IL: University of Chicago Press, 397-429.

National Commission on Excellence in Education (1983). *A nation at risk: The imperative for educational reform.* Washington, D. C.: U. S. Government Printing Office.

National Society for the Study of Education (1929). *Twenty-eight yearbook: Preschool and parental education.* Bloomington, IL: Public School Publishing Company.

Niedermeyer, F. C. (1969, March). *The effects of training on the instructional behaviors of student tutors.* Southwest Regional Laboratory Research Memorandum.

Olmsted, P. P., Rubin, R. I., True, J. H., & Revicki, D. A. (1980). *Parent education: The contributions of Ira J. Gordon.* Washington, D.C.: Association for Childhood Education International.

Paolucci, B. (1977, January). *Invisible family production: The development of human resources.* Paper presented at the National Center of Scientific Research Roundtable sponsored by the National Science Foundation, Oise, France.

Paolucci, B., Bubolz, M., Rainey, M., Andrews, M., Boyd, V., Ferris, M. & Nelson, L. (1976). *Women, families, and non-formal learning programs.* East Lansing: Michigan State University.

Pugh, G. (1981). Parenthood: towards a framework for education and support. *Early Child Development and Care, 7,* 217-234.

Rand Corporation (1971). *How effective is schooling?* Washington, D. C.: Rand Corporation for the President's Commission on School Finance.

Rapoport, R., & Rapoport, R. (1971). *Dual career families.* London: Penguin Books.

Reid, M. G. (1934). *Economics of household production.* New York: John Wiley.

Rheingold, H. L. (1969). The effect of a strange environment on the behavior of infants. In B. M. Foss (Ed.), *Determinants of infant behavior IV* (137–68). New York: John Wiley.

Rheingold, H. L. (1969). The social and socializing infant. In D. A. Goslin (Ed.), *Handbook of socialization theory and research* (779–790). New York: Rand McNally.

Rich, D. (1968). *Helping parents become better teachers: Aids to teachers and children.* Washington, D.C.: Association for Childhood Education International.

Rich, D. (1976). The family as educator: A letter to principals. *The National Elementary Principal, 55,* 71.

Rich, D. (1976). *The relationship of the home learning lab technique to first grade student achievement.* Washington, D. C.: Ed.D. Dissertation, Catholic University.

Sandler, A., & Coren, A. (1981). Integrated instruction at home and school: Parent's perspective. *Education and Training of the Mentally Retarded,* 183-187.

Schaefer, E. S. (1968). *Progress report: Intellectual stimulation of culturally-deprived parents.* Washington, D. C.: National Institute of Mental Health.

Schaefer, E. S. (1970). Need for early and continuing education. In V. H. Denenberg (Ed.), *Education of the infant and young child* (61–82). New York: Academic Press.

Schultz, T. W. (1974). *Economics of the family.* Chicago: University of Chicago Press.

Sheils, M., & Monroe, S. (1976, November 15). A new kind of PTA, *Newsweek,* 105.

Sigel, I. E., & Loosa, L. M. (Eds.). (1983). *Changing Families.* New York: Plenum Press.

Smith, M. B. (1968). School and home: Focus on achievement. In A. H. Passow (Ed.), *Developing programs for the educationally disadvantaged.* New York: Teachers College Press.

Spitz, R. (1945). Hospitalism: An inquiry into the genesis of psychiatric conditions in early childhood. *Psychoanalytic Study of the Child, 1.*

Sunley, R. (1955). Early 19th century American literature on child rearing. In M. Mead & M. Wolfenater (Eds.), *Childhood in contemporary culture.* Chicago, IL: University of Chicago Press.

U. S. White House Conference on Children, 1970. (1971). Report to the President. Report of Forum 15. Washington, D. C.: U.S. Government Printing Office, 239-256.

Walberg, H. J., Bole, R. E., & Waxman, H. (1980, fall). School-based family socialization and reading achievement in the inner city. *Psychology in the Schools,* 509-514.

Walberg, H. J., & Marjoribanks, K. (1976). Family environment and cognitive development: Twelve analytic models. *Review of Educational Research, 46,* 527-551.

Walberg, H. J. (1984). Families as partners in educational productivity. *Phi Delta Kappan, 65*(6), 397-400.

Weatherston, D. J., Boger, R. P., Richter, R. A., & Bagchi, J. (1983). Volunteering for family strength. *Infant Mental Health Journal,* 4(4), 309-315.

Weikart, D. P. (1975). *Parent involvement: Process and results of the High/Scope Foundation's project.* Paper presented at the Biennial Meeting of the Society for Research in Child Development, Denver, Co.

Weikart, D. P. et al. (1970). Longitudinal results of the Ypsilanti Perry Preschool Project. Ypsilanti, MI: High Scope Educational Research Foundation.

White, B. L. (1968). Informal education during the first months of life. In R. D. Hen & R. M. Bear (Eds.), *Early Education* (143-169). Chicago: Aldive.

White, B. L., & Watts, J. C. (1973). *Experience and Environment* (Vol. I). Englewood Cliffs, NJ: Prentice-Hall.

White, S. (1973). *Federal programs for young children* (Vol. II). Cambridge, MA: Huron Institute, Department of Health, Education and Welfare, Publication No. (05), pp. 74-101.

FAMILY AS EDUCATOR, PARENT EDUCATION, AND THE PERENNIAL FAMILY CRISIS

Steven Schlossman

Staff Historian
The Rand Corporation
Santa Monica, California

This essay attempts to provide historical insight on two themes that are central to any discussion of parents as educators: first, the capacity of modern-day families to provide stable and vital educational settings for children; and, second, the nature and prospects of programs in parent education for improving parenting skills and enhancing child development. I approach these subjects as a historian, educator, and policy analyst. My research interests center on the evolution of child and family life during the past four centuries, and the creation of public and private institutions to integrate the young, especially poor, minority youth, into the cultural and economic mainstream. In the last few years I have focused particularly on the emergence of the juvenile justice system and the genesis of the fields of child development and parent education. I have appraised policies in both fields rather critically, as poorly designed, clumsily implemented, sex biased, and often inappropriate to the problems they were designed to alleviate (Schlossman, 1976, 1977, 1978a, 1978b, 1983; Schlossman and Wallach, 1978).

I write, however, not simply as a critic but as a concerned participant in current programmatic innovation in both fields. Under the sponsorship of the National Congress of Parent and Teachers, for example, I helped design, coordinate, and edit a self-instructional pamphlet series, *Today's Family in Focus*, to help parents better understand the role of the family in the modern world, and to facilitate their access to and control over resources directly related to family goals (National Congress of Parents and Teachers, 1977).

The essay is in three main parts. Section one seeks to lay a foundation for assessing the capacity of modern-day families to educate by suggesting that we are witnessing today only the latest outburst of an enduring malaise in American social commentary on the family, which I

31

dub the "family-in-crisis syndrome."   The issues here are terribly complex, the role of historical scholarship in illuminating them highly problemmatic and controversial.   My primary object is to stimulate dialogue and justify additional research.   In section two, I elaborate the concept of "family as educator" by demonstrating its heuristic value for studies in educational history.   And in section three, I offer an overview of the early years of American parent education in order to spotlight basis issues which, in my judgment, remain largely unresolved in the field today.

The Perennial Family Crisis

The family-in-crisis motif pervades both professional and popular commentary on the contemporary American family.   In reviewing this vast literature, I was surprised by the close convergence, in tone and content, between the observations of scholars and pundits of the popular media.   Perhaps this should not have been surprising: if the family is falling apart as rapidly as many commentators think (if it has not disintegrated already), then the current spate of jeremiads may indeed be in order, and woe to the nay-sayers.   But I remain skeptical.   As a historian of education and of juvenile justice, I recognize a familiar ring in much of this discussion, and feel a sense of deja vu, of redundancy.   I would draw a parallel between the twentieth-century "family-in-crisis syndrome" and the course of nineteenth-century evangelical religion-periodic outbursts of unusual religious fervor which stand apart but whose significance can be appreciated only as part of an ongoing spirit of religious revivalism throughout the century.   Similarly with the rhetoric of family-in-crisis: it has long been with us but, caught up in the latest fervor, the latest rediscovery of forces of evil in our midst, we put aside and selectively forget our earlier experiences, curse our fate, exhort our leaders (now likely to be social scientists rather than ministers) for cures, and pray for revitalization of basis values and institutions.

I know that there are many who regard any attempt to downplay a sense of crisis in the family today as somehow ethically bankrupt and socially irresponsible.   But this misses the point: if there are powerful continuities in our *perception* of family crisis, these continuities inevitably cast a different light on our present predicament, and should not be ignored or interpreted as evidence of callousness or blindness to harsh reality (Lasch, 1977).   While I have read to the point of exhaustion what statistical indicators show about recent trends in the structure and context of family life, it is essential to point up the obvious: statistics, no matter how balefully presented in the raw, never speak for themselves but only through interpreters.   Historical perspective may provide a buffer to fears easily induced by our national mesmerization with DATA, our characteristically American fascination with evidences of decline, and our nostalgic attachment to the family of yore.

Let me make three separate points about the statistics on family decline often cited as self-evident truths by many commentators. First, the data presented are often incomplete, can be rearranged to suggest different conclusions, and can be allied with other relevant data to lead to nearly opposite interpretations--tactics Mary Jo Bane has employed ingeniously in her book, *Here to Stay* (which I shall comment on again shortly). Second, it is in actuality remarkably difficult to determine the point at which fluctuations in long-term processes of social change merit the adjective "radical"; whether demographic indicators can ever be used to explain psychological distress in real-life parents and children; whether people themselves actually perceive "social change" as bearing directly on them and inducing "crisis" in their family lives; and whether, perhaps, initial sharp breaks from social norms, even if seemingly "small" in retrospect, better warrant descriptions as "crisis situations" than later increases in magnitude of the same phenomena (I am thinking, for example, of the large *relative increase* in the proportion of women entering the work force in the early 20th century, which was widely cited then--in terms that would make us blush for their naivete--as portending moral and social chaos).

These analytical problems have always intrigued me, but I recall becoming particularly attentive to them after reading *Future Shock* (Toffler, 1977). In the introduction to the book, Alvin Toffler appears to show considerable awareness of how difficult it is to compare, qualitatively, the impact of social change on human beings from one generation to the next: But then, throwing caution to the wind, he spends the next five hundred pages doing just that, assuming everyone can agree on the "critical point" at which people no longer adapt to change but are merely numbed by it. I find a similar problem in a more relevant book, Kenneth Keniston's *All Our Children*. After a bow to the family crisis experienced by second generation Puritans in seventeenth-century Massachusetts, he writes: "What is new and very American is the intensity of the malaise, the sense of having no guidelines or supports for raising children, the feeling of not being in control as parents, and the widespread sense of personal guilt for what seems to be going awry" (Keniston, 1977, p. 4). Well, how do we really know this? Certainly statistics alone cannot sustain the argument--"malaise," "guidelines," "supports," "guilt," "not being in control": these are obviously subjective perceptions and, whether accurate or not, clearly have their counterparts in the laments of earlier generations. And, not to belabor the point, let us recall Margaret Mead's marvelous insight in her essay on grandparents, where she suggests that the current generation may actually be experiencing less disruptive changes than previous ones, and many consequently be less well off for it (Mead, 1977).

The third and final point is simply a more systematic presentation of what I have been saying all along: I see little novelty in today's perceptions of family crisis, either in tone or in content. Not only have social commentators on the family traveled this road before but, in fact, they have been traveling this very road virtually without interruption for quite some time. Indeed, I can think of no decade in the twentieth century when, to experts and popular writers alike, the family did not appear either on the verge of collapse (the pessimists) or of radical readjustment (the optimists). The vast majority of writers on the family have always seen its Armageddon just around the historical corner.

Certainly this was the case in pre-World War One America, when the nation's leading social reformers bewailed the demise of traditional family life and created numerous new social institutions--juvenile courts, visiting teachers, social workers, compulsory education laws, mothers' pensions (welfare), for instance--to cope with the changes. Certainly this was true of the 1920s, when moral disintegration and the triumph of a hedonistic culture, led by self-satisfied parents and self-indulgent children, seemed imminent (recall Nancy Milford's *Zelda*). Certainly this was true of the 1930s, when economic deterioration jeopardized family foundations as never before, and when widespread joblessness attenuated traditional definitions of sex roles and severely weakened the authority of fathers in the home. Certainly this was true of the 1940s, when families were shaken by war-time separations and postwar adjustments, and when the plague of juvenile delinquency struck many commentators as a new bolt on the American landscape, symbolic testimony to and literal retribution for the decline of parental, especially paternal, authority. Certainly this was true of the 1950s-if only we could cast aside the haze of nostalgia about the period now befogging our recollection--when gang delinquency reached all-time prominence among lower-class youth, and when the peer group usurped primary socialization functions (so it was commonly alleged) from the moribund family. And certainly--how can we forget!--this was true of the 1960s, when it became fair sport to blame the family for producing rudderless, nihilistic youth seeking only the latest high.

In brief, counterparts to today's forebodings have appeared again and again during the course of the 20th century; moreover, dire statistics have always been available to "prove" the case. Why this has been so I shall not attempt to explain now, although it may have much to do with a vested interest among social scientists--the principal successors to ministers as sources of authority in childrearing--to call attention to and diagnose social ills which only they, presumably, possess the expertise to cure. But whatever the underlying causes, the lament is a commonplace of modern experience. If there is a family crisis, it appears to be perennial. Dare I suggest that one group of priorities in family research be to chart with some precision the various ways Americans have perceived the family, to assess the impact of changing perceptions on social policies, and to attempt to understand, with the advantage of hindsight, which perceptions were more or less accurate and why.

As noted earlier, Mary Joe Bane has tried to buck the tide of the family-in-crisis literature, and in the most "modern" way possible, i.e., via sophisticated statistical analysis.   Without underestimating the originality of Bane's contribution, let me offer three observations about Here to Stay to better comprehend its place in the historical stream of commentary on the American family.

First, Bane's work is clearly not the first to counter the prophets of family doom.   Several sensitive writers on family readjustment in the early years of this century, Jane Addams most prominently, were certain that family attachments were irreplacable and would remain central to human experience, however much family forms changed.   This was also true of the family sociologists who came to prominence in the 1920s and 1930s, led by Ernest Burgess, who argued that ties of affection had replaced economic necessity as the lynchpin of family identity, and that nostalgia concerning the old-time family overlooked the sources of contemporary family strength.   Second, Bane's conclusions rest largely on statistical evidence, brilliantly manipulated and analyzed, but "mere" numbers nonetheless.   There are, to be sure, a number of ethnographic studies which sustain Bane's broad argument--especially Laura Lein's Working Family Project, which examined dual-worker families of moderate means in Boston and revealed the lengths to which they would go to maintain traditional family values under difficult circumstances (Lein, 1974).   But the methodology of Here to Stay still raises a basic doubt: how confidently can we infer states of mind about millions of people, their intimate feelings about family relationships, from the data of demographic analysis?   Bane is surely sensitive to this difficulty, but it nonetheless places a serious restriction on the reliability of her family portrait.   Here, especially, subjective experience is at least as central as "objective," statistical description in analyzing social reality.

This leads to a third and final point.   Bane relies heavily on very recent historical research, nearly all of which employs sophisticated statistical indicators to "reconstitute" family structures.   There is obviously much virtue in this interdisciplinary borrowing, and Bane is quite right to spotlight such revolutionary studies as those by Peter Laslett, which make it doubtful that extended families ever existed in Western culture on a large scale.   But interdisciplinary borrowing often brings problems as well, and Bane may be more willing than most historians to generalize with an air of finality from limited research still at a beginning stage of development.   In reading Here to Stay, I was reminded of the sensation created by Margaret Mead's early studies of Samoa and New Guinea, and how quickly popularizers and scholars from other disciplines latched onto her work in order to disprove all prior research dealing with biological imperatives in human development. Likewise with Bane: the historical studies she cites are indeed relevant to her conclusions on the state of the family today, and her arguments certainly reinforce my own.   But, in my judgment, the available historical data are probably not substantial enough to merit such broad and definitive comparisons of past and present (for example: "there has been no significant emancipation of teenagers from their families," or "the data on marriage and divorce suggest that the kind of marriage Americans have always known is still a pervasive and enduring institution" (Bane, 1974, pp. 19, 35). What Bane's imaginative scholarship does demonstrate unequivocally is the potential of historical research to illuminate current policy issues, and the need for increased financial support to such basic and, in the best sense, relevant scholarship.

Families as Educators: The View from Educational History

I turn now to the theme of "family as educator" and its promise, as a new conceptual orientation, for the study of American educational history (Cremin, 1977a, 1978).

Concern for understanding the family's role as educator is not now in the mainstream of American educational history. Most educational history focuses on the public school, paying minimal attention to relationships between schooling and children's prior and later life experiences. Attempts to broaden this focus date back to the early 1960s when Bernard Bailyn and Lawrence Cremin sharply criticized the tendency to equate schooling with all of education, but their efforts to reorient the field--at least in my judgment--have largely failed (Bailyn, 1960; Cremin, 1965). One obvious reason has to do with the political climate. Just as Bailyn and Cremin began to urge historians to examine the wide range of institutions which educate, radical new interpretations of the origins of public schools appeared which seemed more immediately "relevant" to ongoing political battles surrounding the schools. While the so-called "radical revisionists" expanded our comprehension of school origins, structures, and functions, they, like the writers they attacked, were guilty of tunnel vision in simply assuming the omnipotence of schooling in children's overall educational experience, and in slighting the family's role as educator (Ravitch, 1978).

Other strands of historical research, however, do suggest the centrality of familial education in children's overall development and point the way to new historical understanding of families as educators. Surely the most flamboyant recent scholarship to call attention to families as educators--if not the most persuasive--is that of the psycho-historians, who argue, a *priori*, that family experience has always been the critical variable in explaining personal development and perhaps even social change as well, and who employ a variety of psychological theories to evaluate the dynamics of those processes (Quitt, 1976). In immigration history, to give a more conventional example, the tendency is away from the stress of an earlier generation of historians on the "uprooted," disoriented paterfamilies upon arrival to this country, and instead on the continuing strength and vitality of family experiences in the process of personal and social adjustment. Timothy Smith, Josef Barton, and John Briggs have done especially resourceful research in demonstrating the impact of immigrant family values on children's educational aspirations and achievements. In the process, they have revealed the inadequacy of one of the "radical revisionists" main contentions, namely, that public schooling was an unwelcome "imposition" on the immigrant poor (Smith, 1969; Barton, 1975; Briggs, 1978).

To my mind, though, the singlemost revealing body of historical research to indicate the importance of families as educators is that on ante-bellum slavery. Probing imaginatively into various kinds of documentary evidence left by slaves themselves, scholars such as John Blassingame, Eugene Genovese, Herbert Gutman, and Thomas Webber have taught us how to look at repressive institutions from the clientele's point of view--"from the bottom up"--and have thereby demonstrated how slave families remained vital educational institutions for the transmission of African culture and strategies of survival. Allied to other equally vital institutions indigenous to the quarter community, the slave family inculcated knowledge and values essential to the maintenance of individual integrity, mediated confusing and painful experiences generated outside and within the quarter community, and served as a cultural buffer, spiritual resource, and reservoir of unqualified affection. That scholars have now discovered the potency of familial education under conditions of slavery, where they had previously assumed that slave families did not even exist, ought to serve as impressive evidence that historians are unlikely to make sense of children's past educational experiences unless they pay heed to how and what children were taught at home (Blassingame, 1972; Genovese, 1974; Gutman, 1976; Webber, 1978).

While the role of the family as educator remains largely outside the mainstream of educational history, the Pulitzer Prize-winning historian, Lawrence Cremin, has been elaborating his ideas on precisely this subject for two decades (Cremin, 1970, 1976, 1977b, 1980). Four components of Cremin's approach are most relevant here.

First is a latitudinarian definition of education which has undergone a number of refinements in the past several years, and which in its latest form reads: education is "the deliberate, systematic, and sustained effort to transmit, evoke, or acquire knowledge, values, attitudes, skills, or sensibilities, as well as any learning that results from the effort, direct or indirect, intended or unintended: (Cremin, 1980, p. ix). Second is an institutional elaboration of that definition, what Cremin calls an "educational configuration." Designed to establish linkages among the entire range of educative agencies in operation at different time periods, the concept is fluid and easily accommodates changes over time. It endeavors to include pervasive, nationwide patterns of institutional development, as well as regional and local variations. It seeks to explain shifting relationships among individual institutions comprising any single configuration (home, school, and church, for instance), as well as to explain interactions among holistic configurations (between the several reinforcing educational institutions run by the Quakers in mid-nineteenth century Philadelphia, and the institutions run by the non-

Quaker majority, for example). As Cremin writes on this latter point, "Configurations of education also interact, as configurations, with the society of which they are part" (Cremin, 1977b, p. 142). Finally the concept attempts to account for both consonance and dissonance within and between educational configurations: as, for instance, when families teach one attitude toward money and peers teach another; or when, as in many small towns along the nineteenth century frontier, family, church, school, and workplace taught similar orientations to life without encountering conflicting messages from competing educative agencies.

Complementing the concept of educational configuration is that of "educational biography," through which Cremin seeks to accomplish two things. First, at the level of the individual, to show what it was like to grow up under the influence of different educational configurations: and, second, to view the learner as an active agent in his own education rather than, as in much educational writing, a passive participant (Lagemann, 1979). The final component of Cremin's approach is the case study which, like the educational biography, tries to bring the concept of educational configuration to life by describing it as a series of concrete community experiences. In *American Education: The National Experience*, Cremin analyzes the evolution of educational configurations in New York City; Lowell, Massachusetts; Macoupin County, Illinois; and Sumter County, South Carolina. Each of these communities was chosen because it embodied characteristic educational configurations unique to the region and time period. By examining the life histories of select individuals who came of age in these communities, Cremin demonstrates vividly how educational configurations shape the boundaries of collective educational experience, on the one hand, and, on the other, how individuals utilize learning opportunities with varying degrees of energy and imagination and, thereby, express their own personalities, needs, and purpose.

As should be apparent, each component of Cremin's approach calls attention to the central role of families as educators. But equally important, each also reveals the inadequacy of viewing familial education in isolation from other educative agencies. No more than schools should families become isolated foci of historical or educational inquiry. Rather, Cremin believes, it is the linkages within and between educational configurations, and the varied ways in which different people in different places at different times interact with those configurations, that promise to reveal the sources and consequences of American educational experience–past, present, and future.

Cremin's history obviously opens numerous opportunities to enrich our understanding of the family in the overall educational process. Only by viewing families as active, potent educative agencies throughout their children's development, and by seeing them as part of larger educational configurations, can historians begin to contribute directly to comprehending change and continuity in the role of the family as educator today.

Parent Education Programs: Some Persistent Problems

Against this backdrop, my rather skeptical attitude toward parent education programs will surprise no one. Much of the widespread interest in parent education stems from a dubious assumption that today's family, unlike those of previous generations, is desperately uncertain about how to rear children and much in need of expert advice in defining and implementing educational goals. And much literature on parent education assumes that families are self-contained social and educational agents wholly free to direct their children's educational development, rather than institutions thoroughly enmeshed in complex educational configurations over which they exercise little independent control. As commonly understood, parent education--and note that I am not limiting my remarks to current governmental programs but am referring to all large-scale efforts, whatever the sponsorship or clientele, to upgrade the child-rearing practices of parents--strikes me as a wholly inadequate organizing principle for comprehending or remedying the problems which "parents as educators" face today.

Having said this, I repeat that I am not dogmatically opposed to all parent education programs and that I even helped the PTA design one, with the emphasis on building up parents' confidence and capacities. Clearly I feel that some parent education programs are better than others! Similarly, I realize that children require intelligent, committed, consistent, loving care for optimal development, and that parents today--as throughout this century--are actively seeking guidance and assistance in rearing their young and making family life meaningful. Nonetheless, I believe it is essential that proponents of parent education, whatever their particular clientele or instructional method, begin to understand the tendencies toward superficiality that in the past have undermined their efforts to help parents perform more effectively. In this final section I attempt to isolate several of those historical tendencies, particularly the tendency to see parent education as a solution for deeply-rooted social problems; to exaggerate the power of parents alone to control their children's destinies; to delimit women's potential social contribution to the domestic sphere without placing corresponding constraints on men; and to be naively subservient to the latest findings of psychological science. This overview will surely not do justice to the subject, but it should shed some light on the difficulty of planning intellectually defensible parent education programs.

From the founding of the American colonies, a variety of private and governmental bodies have engaged in what can loosely be termed parent education. In seventeenth-century Massachusetts, for example, individuals called tithingmen were appointed to investigate the family situations of children whose parents were suspected of providing inadequately for their religious and secular education. If the parents were found guilty of neglect and, after being forewarned to educate their offspring, failed to do so, the children could be taken away and placed in other families for proper instruction. Nothing short of a child's soul was at stake.

A formal literature to aid parents in child rearing dates back to the ancient Greeks at least. But for now we need to go back only as far as the mid-19th century, when "advice to parents" books and periodicals first appeared in abundance. Addressed to mothers, this literature conveyed one principal message: self-sacrifice. Woman's earthly duty was to sacrifice every personal desire to the needs of her children and the wants of her husband. This domestic message formed a major component of what Barbara Walter has termed the "cult of true womanhood," which defined the boundaries of acceptable female behavior for most of the 19th century by centering the purpose of her existence in home, husband, and children (Welter, 1966).

While the "domesticity literature" was obviously a form of parent education and reached a wide middle-class audience, it was only toward the end of the century that parent education began to take organized form, first with the creation in New York of the Society for the Study of Child Nature in 1888, and then with the founding in Washington, D.C. of the National Congress of Mothers in 1897. Within two decades the Mothers' Congress claimed nearly two hundred thousand members and, by the late 1920s (by which time it had changed its name to the one by which we know it today, the National Congress of Parent and Teachers or PTA), membership had skyrocketed to well over a million. Hence its ideas on parent education merit special consideration.

In accordance with the "cult of true womanhood," participants at PTA meetings assumed it was woman's divine, biologically-determined function to serve their husbands as "helpmeets" and their children as moral guardians. To aid in this latter task, members held regular "child study" meetings to improve their parenting skills. Their knowledge base was comprised equally of classic educational and moral philosophy (Locke, Rousseau), and more recent scientific writings in medicine and psychology (William James, G. Stanley Hall). An overwhelmingly middle-class organization, the PTA stressed the need to disseminate the latest scientific information on children, along with proper bourgeois values, to the poor. It therefore encouraged members to venture into urban slums and form mothers' groups among impoverished women, in part to convey valuable tips on child rearing, but also to reinforce maternal instincts which, it was thought, poverty tended to erode under the stress of daily life. Finally, the PTA urged members to extend their private family values and concerns into the political arena in order to improve environmental conditions for children. As the PTA saw it, political action and political education were integral to parent education. Any definition of parent education which did not include political action would have been considered narrow and self-serving. In sum, the PTA viewed parent education as both a vehicle for disseminating advice on child rearing and as a lever for changing society by organizing mothers in common cause.

The PTA espoused a view of women and of sex roles that most people today would find unduly constraining: for example, the PTA held mothers directly and fully accountable for their children's destinies. At the same time, however, the PTA's approach to parent education went well beyond traditional definitions of sex roles and significantly extended the sphere of women's legitimate social and political participation. The PTA believed that collective political participation by mothers was essential to the well-being of all children, and urged upon women a role of citizen-activist that seems today boldly unconventional, adventure-some, and certainly not sanctioned by the "cult of true womanhood."

A similar tension was evident in the PTA's approach to the nascent sciences of child development. On the one hand, the PTA considered it essential to convey in popular form to mothers--all mothers, well-to-do and poor alike--the results of recent research in child psychology, pediatric medicine, and nutrition. On the other hand, the PTA's program in parent education was neither dependent on, nor subservient to, the mandates of science. As befits its grassroots origins, the PTA continued to hold traditional, religiously-based precepts in equally high regard. In part, this was because the sciences of child development were not very well-grounded empirically in the years prior to World War I, but this, of course, is more easily recognized in retrospect. While the PTA did not question the practical value of new scientific research on child develop-ment, it continued to place greater trust in mothers maternal instincts and moral sensibilities.

We thus see in early 20th century parent education, as embodied in the work of the PTA, an intriguing balance of perspectives between private domestic responsibility and public political activity, and a reliance on religion and maternal instinct, versus a reliance on science and formal instruction. While there is little reason for nostalgia here, it is important to recognize the existence of this balance and these tensions in the theory and practice of parent education in the pre-World War I era. These patterns disappeared shortly after the war. In the 1920s and 1930s parent education progressed to levels of scientific sophistication undreamed of in late nineteenth century "child study." Yet, in the process of refinement, parent education came to be defined more narrowly, self-servingly, and apolitically as a collection of scienti-fically-derived nurture techniques to be applied solely to one's own children.

The professional field of child development came of age in the 1920s, symbolized best by the founding of several "laboratories" for the scientific study of normal children at such universities as Iowa, Minneso-

ta, Yale, Columbia, Berkeley, and Toronto, and at a number of indepen-
dently operated and funded centers such as the Merrill-Palmer School.
These laboratories served as launching grounds for most leading child
development scholars, many of whom commanded large popular as well
as professional audiences through books, journal articles, and popular
magazine pieces--the Spocks, Brazletons, Whites, and Bronfenbrenners of
their day. Research at these laboratories was funded in a variety of
ways but especially via grants supplied by the Laura Spelman Rockefeller
Memorial Fund, administered by the dynamic Lawrence Frank, which
disbursed several million dollars for basic research, supported numerous
scholars and graduate students, and kept the laboratories alive during the
Depression when they would otherwise have folded.

Unlike most of their counterparts today, but in the tradition of
agricultural research stations, the child development laboratories considered popularization and dissemination of science central to their mis-
sions. For some this was the "price" they had to pay for receiving state
and foundation funding. If we may judge from the energy expended and
the enthusiasm conveyed, however, many researchers genuinely delighted
in contributing to a popular social movement with the potential for
radically transforming how Americans reared their children. This was
especially the case at the state universities. Child psychologists such as
Bird Baldwin at Iowa, John Anderson at Minnesota, and Harold Jones at
Berkeley organized, led, and attempted to evaluate (with considerably
less success) large-scale projects in parent education with the express
intent of communicating the latest scientific findings to mothers.
Concern for dissemination was equally great at private centers such as
the Institute for Euthenics at Vassar and the Merrill-Palmer School,
whose original name--the Merrill-Palmer Motherhood and Homemaking
School--embodied its concern with parental and preparental education in
addition to basic research.

While university scholars played a prominent role in post-World
War One parent education, the key to transforming parent education into
a mass movement was the enthusiastic sponsorship of diverse lay
women's organizations. Most of these groups genuinely revered university scholars as the ultimate authorities on child rearing. The urged
mothers to abandon the myth of maternal instinct and follow instead--at
pain of doing their children irreparable harm--the dictates of science in
all aspects of child rearing, from toilet training to sibling rivalry to sex
instruction.

No organization was numerically more important than the PTA, but
more influential in providing leadership and adding intellectual respect-
ability to the parent education movement was the Child Study Association of America (successor to the Society for the Study of Child Nature).
Under the guidance of such remarkably devoted women as Sidonie
Gruenberg, Josette Frank, Cecile Pilpel, Marion Miller, and Anna Wolf,
the CSAA sponsored the first university course in parent education,

organized dozens of conferences to determine the most effective means to disseminate scientific research, published books and pamphlets on all aspects of child rearing (as well as a sophisticated monthly journal), pioneered in the use of radio as a tool of parent education, and initiated the National Council of Parent Education to coordinate the many lay and professional groups in the field. In addition to the CSAA, other powerful women's organizations invested heavily in parent education, notably the American Home Economics Association and the American Association of University Women. Finally, several new journals and magazines address-ed to children's education and parents' problems appeared in the 1920s. The most popular was *Parents' Magazine*, about which it must suffice now to make only two points. First, the linkage between *Parents' Magazine* and child psychologists could not have been clearer, for the magazine was published with the conspicuous imprimatur of the research laboratories at Minnesota, Yale, Iowa, and Columbia. Second, the magazine was the only major periodical whose circulation and advertis-ing revenues moved continuously upward during the Depression, certainly impressive testimony to its popularity. Under the guidance provided by these several parent educational organizations and magazines, hundreds of thousands of women--mainly middle-class-met regularly to discuss in small groups the latest scientific findings on child development, hoping thereby to find answers to specific problems and also, no doubt, solace and confidence in a shared maternal identity.

It is impossible now to do justice to the varieties of psychological advice disseminate under the aegis of the parent education movement, but a quick synopsis can highlight the major trends (I shall beg the more difficult question regarding influence on parental behavior). The 1920s saw the repudiation of both nonscientific childrearing texts (Locke, Rousseau) and publications of late nineteenth century "child-study" (especially Hall), and the triumph of diverse behavioristic and mental health psychologies. While the child's emotional development received considerable attention, the emphasis was nonetheless generally on habit formation, particularly in the preschool years. If parents did not establish proper behavior patterns very early, there was little hope that later reeducation would make them worthy, contented, and successful citizens.

Experts offered parents lengthy lists of "do's" and "don'ts," all purportedly derived from the scientific study of children. My favorite list was that compiled in an article by the juvenile court judge and parent educator, Miriam Van Waters, on "Nineteen Ways of Being a Bad Parent" (later included, appropriately enough, in her book *Parents on Probation*; Van Waters, 1927). But positive as well as negative rules were also commonly presented to parents, sanctioned by the age-old maxim that "prevention is better than cure." Parents were enjoined not to let undisciplined affection divert the application of prescribed child-rearing techniques; indeed, parents were often portrayed as impediments to healthy growth. What most endangered optimal child development, according to much expert advice, were outmoded customs and inconsistencies based on parents' natural tendency to sentimentalize children and trust to a non-existent maternal instinct. The only way mothers could overcome these dangerous tendencies was to become students of science. Motherhood was a full-time, no-nonsense occupation, a "profession" requiring as careful study and as much time as any in which men excelled. The main outside, "public" activities for which mothers could legitimately spare time were those connected to children's immediate growth needs, such as the discriminating selection of toys, music teachers, clothes, movies, friends, and so forth. Only such devotion, study, and meticulous application of approved child-rearing knowledge would save children later emotional and behavioral problems--"maladjustments," in new 1920s scientific jargon.

In sum, psychological science was widely disseminated to mothers in the 1920s, and emphasized the extraordinary control parents exercised over their children's futures. The intellectual concerns of mothers were directed almost entirely within the family circle; the stress was on their ability to execute scientific mandates. When children failed to mature properly, it was assumed to be the mothers' fault and, moreover, science could pinpoint the precise cause.

The nursery school (as contrasted with the day care center) embodied the new ideal of mothers' subservience to experts in child psychology. The main objective of the early nursery schools was to provide mothers with object lessons in scientific child nurture. Spokespersons stressed the plasticity of early childhood and, in line with findings from the child development laboratories, the irreversibility of traits instilled then. Indulgence of bad habits in such areas as eating, sleeping, socializing, and displays of anger or fear would result inevitably in serious "maladjustments." One way to spare children the harm of parental indulgence was to remove them from exclusive control of their mothers for a few hours each weekday, for the dual purpose of instilling correct habits in the children and, equally central, teaching their mothers how to do so at home. The nursery school was not designed to offer mothers free time to pursue careers. Instead, the nursery school reinforced the larger message of the parent education movement that motherhood was a full-time, precarious profession manageable only under direction by experts. Mothers were expected to be active observers of the up-to-date professional training their children received. In effect, both mothers and their children were sent to nursery school.

This brief sketch of parent education in the post-World War One period only begins to outline its contours, texture, style, and appeal, but several parallels between past and present can be suggested. As in the 1920s, a tremendous outpouring of professional and popular literature urges parents to apply the most "modern" methods of child rearing, at the risk of doing permanent injury to their children (Clark-Stewart, 1979). As in the 1920s, there is lopsided stress on the preschool years and the irreversibility of patterns established then. As in the 1920s, parent educators often assume that parental behavior is the singlemost important determinant of a child's happiness and success. Finally, as in the 1920s, parent education programs and literature focus almost exclusively on mothers, even while (in both periods) denying the existence of maternal instinct. The prime intent remains to teach mothers to perform traditional, private, female role functions more efficiently, and to reinforce the belief that motherhood is as professionally demanding, socially useful, and personally fulfilling as any occupation outside the home.

There are, to be sure, notable differences as well. The switch in emphasis from the affective to the cognitive realm in child development; the major role which the federal government now plays in sponsoring research and dissemination; and the attempts to use parent training programs as potential equalizers of educational opportunity for poor, minority children, have few counterparts in the past. But these changes do not, in my judgment, subtract substantially from equally impressive continuities in approach, design, expectations, and underlying assumptions. Contrary to the impression often given by its modern-day supporters, parent education has a long history in this country. Pondering that history may help us to avoid reinventing the past and proposing simplistic solutions to the complex problems of families as educators (Bronfenbrenner, 1978; Grubb and Lazerson, 1982).

FOOTNOTES

This essay is a revised version of a discussion paper prepared originally for the National Institute of Education Conference on Parents as Educators, held on 19-21 November 1978, in Washington, D.C. I wish to thank Ablex Publishing Corporation for permission to reprint several paragraphs from my lengthy historical overview of parent education in Ron Haskins and Diane Adams, eds., *Parent Education and Public Policy* (Norwood, N.J.: Ablex Publishing Corporation, 1983).

Staff Historian, The Rand Corporation, Santa Monica, California

REFERENCES

Bailyn, B. (1960). *Education in the Forming of American Society.* Chapel Hill: University of North Carolina Press.

Bane, M. J. (1976). *Here to Stay.* New York: Basic Books, 1976.

Barton, J. (1975). *Peasants and Strangers.* Cambridge: Harvard University Press.

Blassingame, J. (1972). *The Slave Community.* New York: Oxford University Press.

Briggs, J. (1978). *An Italian Passage.* New Haven: Yale University Press.

STRENGTHS OF THE HOME AND FAMILY AS LEARNING

ENVIRONMENTS

Norma Bobbitt(1) and Beatrice Paolucci(2)

Department of Family and Child Ecology
Michigan State University
East Lansing, Michigan 48824

Primary Environments for Learning

Where did you learn the alphabet? Who taught you to count? Who taught you how, what, when and where to eat? Where did you learn how to show respect for others? How did you learn about your career choices?

Chances are that when you saw the word "learning", you immediately thought of a school setting. If so, your response is typical. Most people perceive that learning occurs only within a school building. However, if you thought about the pattern of your answers to the questions, you recognized most of the answers identified some family member. Learning does occur within the family and in the home. Also, learning occurs in schools and in community settings. Actually, there are three primary learning environments--the home, the school, and the community--which may be identified as types of educational systems: the informal, the formal, and non-formal. This chapter will focus on the informal learning environment of the home. Learning for this context is defined as the acquisition of knowledge, skills, attitudes, and beliefs which more or less enable effective participation by individuals in their society.

The Home and Family as Informal Learning Environments

An informal learning environment or informal educational system consists of one's near environment as defined in terms of familial boundaries, i.e., the learning that is associated with activities which occur within the home or family situation. Inputs into this system consist of information and resources of family members, friends, and other sources that perform a role or function in the home. For reference

47

purposes, the term "Home as a Learning Center" is used when the focus is on the resources of the home as tools, equipment, facilities and space in the home. "Family as Educator" is used when the focus is on interactions between and among family members.

Most of what each of us learns had its beginnings in the home. In the home, we first developed feelings and learned to talk, to walk, and to make sense out of our everyday surroundings. The persons who cared for and about us, our family members and others living in the home, were our first teachers. Informal learning is not limited to children, as all family members and/or individuals living within the home have an opportunity to learn as each assumes the dual role of student and teacher. Not only does the family teach us directly, but also indirectly by approving or disapproving what we learn elsewhere. This approval or disapproval shapes our learning, thus helping us acquire particular values, attitudes, and skills.

For most persons, the home and family environment is the primary and pervasive setting for learning basic life tasks. Within the family a variety of encounters occur daily that stimulates a continuous need for learning. The normal interactions of one family member with another provide occasions for modeling, reinforcement, and support or rejection for particular kinds of behavior. The home setting provides a natural, realistic, and familiar place available for learning throughout the life span. In the home, learning can be pursued within the context and pattern of everyday life at the time it is needed. Frequently, the home setting provides opportunities for capitalizing on the teachable moments. For example, one can learn how to prepare food, resolve a conflict, or operate media equipment as the situations arise. The home offers a natural setting for "trying out' new learning. The home is convenient and accessible day and night. Learning in the home need not be tied to rigid schedules or limited time periods, so learning can be adjusted to the needs and interests of the individuals or groups of individuals within the family. In many ways, the home and family provide the most crucial setting for learning since it is in this setting that learning begins and learning continues throughout life. Also, the home and family provide the setting for the learning of the basic codes necessary for survival and provide the foundation for future learning.

Changes in American society, such as shifts in occupational and family roles of men and women, increases in geographical distances between extended family units, greater numbers of middle-aged and older people, and the demand to maximize human potential throughout life, call attention to the special functions the home and family members can assume in re-educating and re-socializing its members. The family can and does take responsibility for socialization and education of its members within the home environment. There is a resurgence today for both reemphasizing the educative role of the family and assisting the home in functioning as an effective learning center.

Impact of Home and Family on Learning Across the Life Cycle

Throughout life, the home and family environments have a major impact on the informal learning of individuals within the home and family setting. The family serves as the primary educator and the home serves as the primary learning environment, particularly for infants and young children. Later, the home and family serve as the major gatekeeper as well as the linker of family members with the larger environments of community, school, work and leisure. Through interactions of family members with the larger environments, new information is brought into the family system. Experiences in the home shape the learning of those values, attitudes and skills essential to living in the family and functioning effectively in the worlds of work, leisure, and arts, politics and civic affairs. Children and adults reshape their thinking as a result of learning and therefore learn to function in new ways. Thus, the family system is continuously changing, developing and learning. The linkages between the family system and larger environment are reciprocal processes in which both the family system and the system within the larger environment are modified. The competency of family members in developing and managing these linkages between and among societal systems is an increasingly important task in a world of rapid change and complexity.

The form, that is, the age and sex makeup of the family group, varies across the life cycle and from culture to culture. This changing mix of ages and sexes provides for diversity of role models. In its broadest sense, the family can be defined as a group of intimately interacting person who share some common values, goals and resources, who are committed to one another over time, and who carry out some transactions with the environment outside the family as corporate unit. In most industrialized societies, the family form is nuclear. However, family forms are undergoing change. Some of these changes in form occur as one progresses through the life cycle. Single parents with families are on the increase, as are childless families. There is also an increasing number of single persons living alone but maintaining ties with kin, and communal or cooperative groupings of person both young and old. Variations in family forms make possible a wide variation in ways of daily living, demanding different resources and behaviors and providing different learnings. In all stages of the family life cycle, people learn from each other: parents from children, children from parents, brothers and sisters from each other and from the various and assorted relatives and friends who are linked to the family. The family shapes many of the basic patterns of living for individuals (i.e., eating and language patterns). Learning in the family, carried on through everyday interactions among family members, accounts for a great share of any person's reservoir of knowledge. The family mediates learnings which have originated elsewhere by putting a stamp of approval or disapproval on behaviors brought into the home from outside, corrects language, and reinforces moral behavior. Through the everyday give and take in the family and the continuous honing of our actions by family members, ideas and values are formed and developed, new skills are learned and perfected, and actions are tried out and adopted or discarded.

Regardless of the form or function of the family at a given point in time and space, there seems to be a pattern of sequential development that is more or less predictable for humankind. The concept of individual and family development and the learning of particular tasks during a particular phase of the life span (developmental task) is central to understanding the learning needs and interests of family members. The idea of developmental task encompasses understanding how cultural expectations, physical maturation, and the values and aspirations of individuals and family groups change over time in response to both physiological, psychological, and environmental demands. This concept of predictable changes and their accompanying tasks can be acknow- ledged and can be useful to educators, for it allows them to assist families in identifying those times and conditions which are most conducive to learning. It allows family members and educators to more accurately anticipate the teachable moment!

As families form, grow, and develop, they pass through some predictable changes, each of which affects each family member as well as the family unit. Some of these changes are easily observable, for they are concrete events, i.e., weddings, births, deaths, divorces, illnesses, moves, new jobs, graduations. Other changes are more subtle and less obvious, for they occur *within* each family member; these are the perceptions one has of self in relation to others and in one's own self- concept. Both family events and individual family member perceptions shape the stage in the family cycle. To cogently identify learning possibilities in the home and family setting it is important to keep in mind the essentiality of understanding both the inner physiological and psychological needs of each family member as well as the outward social demands of the family events of marriage, birth, divorce, remarriage, retirement, and death.

Considerably more attention should be given to helping families prepare for entering into normal developmental stages. It is clear that the content of what can be learned at home can be readily recognized by both participants and educators. What is less clear for family members to recognize is the need for future learnings and the "best" ways to learn. Since the nature of family life relies primarily on modeling and has an immediate "felt need" emphasis, it is important that educators help families understand and predict learning needs as well as acquire skill and competence in the learning process. Families require help in identifying when there is a need for new learnings, in setting realistic learning goals, in assessing the credibility of information, in knowing when and where to seek competent help or advice, and in assessing the worth of their learning. Also, families will need assistance with decisions about resources since much of the effectiveness of home based learning is dependent upon the resources available to the family for learning as well as the utilization of these resources. Families use their own human resources--time, skills, and understandings--to assist others with their learning. One of the basic purposes of the family is to help family members develop human capital, i.e., their abilities to become productive members of the society through improving their capacity to lead a satisfying life and to earn a living.

To better understand the role of the home as a learning center and the family as educators across the life cycle, Bobbitt and Paolucci (1975) studied the home learning pursuits of 108 blue-collar families from three life cycle stages. They found that these families had undertaken 1343 self or family planned learning activities during the previous year. These learning activities were classified into 12 different categories such as getting along with people, routine household skills, preparation for the future, maintaining/decorating the home, feeding the family, using money wisely, enjoyment and recreation, care of children and adults, learning values, learning about jobs, health and understanding world affairs. The most frequently mentioned categories of learning were in the areas of feeding the family, leisure, hobby and recreational pursuits, and learning about values, i.e., teaching children values, clarifying and understanding values. When asked what *should* be learned at home, the three categories most frequently mentioned were learning values (moral, spiritual, aesthetic, social values), getting along with people inside the family, and caring for children. While family learning projects were carried out during all times of the year, the summer months of June, July, and August were the most often used. Families said that evenings and weekends were the most popular times for learning projects. Generally, families used many types of mass media for their learning projects--about 18 sources per family. Magazines, television, books, and newspapers were most frequently used.

Families in all stages of the life cycle depended on other persons (i.e., friends, and other family members and relatives) as sources of assistance in varying situations. They turned to these sources of help because they trusted their advice and they were conveniently accessible. Sometimes families needed outside help with their learning projects. Individual family members differed in the source of help most frequently contacted for help in learning: male adults used the libraries and friends; children turned to other children and the extended family; female adults sought information from parents and friends. These contacts were made because each was perceived as a trusted expert, as having knowledge of the learning, or because the contact was convenient or free. In order to determine which information contact to make, they tended to rely most frequently on their own past experience, friends, and professionals.

What were families willing to teach children in the future in order to help them become good family members and good workers? The answer that was consistently given was values. Examples were helping children to learn right from wrong, spiritual values, obedience, respect and responsibility. In order to become good workers, they were also willing to help children learn to get along with people outside the family, care for children, develop routine household skills, and carry out a variety of job-related activities such as applying for a job or practicing job skills at home. Clarkson (1975) conducted a group interview with 15 families which included a mother, father and at least one teenage child. Learning activities, in which a parent and a teenager both participated, included household care and management, leisure and recreation, development and care of family members, development of values, and preparation for career. Most learning activities that were carried out involved at least one other family member, but total family learning pursuits were less common.

Although there is considerable recognition by the families of these learning needs, there is some evidence to indicate that families tend to wait until a problem emerges--almost to the point of crisis--before learning pursuits are undertaken. Given the evidence available on the predictability of family tasks, family life educators could engage in greater efforts to assist families in avoiding crises, and in preventing problems by preparing family members in advance for tasks that are likely to emerge.

The Influence of Home and Family in Shaping and Learning of Children

The pervasive influence of the family upon its children is widely acknowledged in the literature. Parents are the first educators of their children and certainly one of the most important groups of educators. Parents are the lifelong educators of their offspring. Family members are the lifelong teachers of each other.

Children develop self-awareness through interactions with the people and objects in their environment during the early years. Parents who understand child development can foster interactions and reinforce the child, therefore enhancing the child's learning within the home and family. Children not only are influenced by their family environment, they also affect that environment. The home and its members are never the same after the arrival of children. Children are an important stimulus to their caretakers. As the family members respond to the biological needs of the children, a social situation evolves and children become socialized into the family and in turn re-socialize other family members. Every interaction between family members is embedded in a matrix of implicit understandings created from past interactions.

The socialization process begins at birth, as noted by experts such as Lerner and Hultsh (1983), Schiamberg and Smith (1982), White and

Watts (1973), Braga and Braga (1975), and Brazeleton (1974). The child quickly learns whether or not his/her cry or babble brings a response. The quality of interaction with parents and caretakers during the early months has an impact later on ability to function socially and intellec- tually. The ten to eighteen month age range is a most critical stage in the child's learning. During this stage, the development of language, locomobility, and understanding of self and other occurs. As children approach three years of age, they become more interested in group activities. The attitudes and behaviors of other children and adults affect feelings about one's self. In group activities, one learns to share, to take turns and to play with others. Daily living tasks are also learned, such as setting the table, feeding pets, cleaning, and picking up toys. By four years of age, chidlren are learning to handle their emotions in productive ways and find reasonable solutions to their feelings. As children approach the kindergarten age, they are beginning to form a conscience to help them judge their actions. Parents, through learning that is home based, can facilitate the child's learning.

Play provides a significant function in maximizing the role of home as a learning center and family as educator. Most play is learned by watching others play. Babies watch their parents and others in the home play and learn most readily from participating in the play. Even though the child learns a great deal from observing, they learn more by doing. Through play, the child discovers who they are, how their body and mind works and how they feel about themselves and others. The importance of play in the development of individuals has been documented by researchers such as Lerner and Hultsch (1983), Schiamberg and Smith (1982), Sutton-Smith (1974), Evans (1974), and Wolfgang (1974).

Researchers, such as Bell (1973, Lamhie, et. al. (1974), and Laosa and Sigel (1982), have documented that the home setting provides diverse opportunities to create a process for learning and to provide stimulation for developing the cognitive powers, especially for children. Everyday experiences in the home provide practice in developing intellectual skills. The basic intellectual power of children can be increased by providing a nurturing environment for learning. This places a great responsibility on the parents and significant others in the home to provide a nurturing environment within the home for learning. Also it is essential to recognize that the opportunity for early childhood intellec- tual development comes only once in a lifetime and that this significant period occurs before the child enters school.

Concern about the quantity and quality of learning in the home and family environment has been expressed during the past decade because the amount of interaction and learning between American parents and their children has decreased. Urbanization, child labor laws, commuting, the abolishment of the apprenticeship system, centralized schools, the power of television for keeping children entertainingly occupied--all these manifestations of progress seemingly have decreased the opportunity for interaction among and between other family members and children, hence decreasing the potential for modeling experiences which enhance learning.

The family can provide the support for enhancing the cognitive learning of its young members. Of equal importance is the vital role of the family at this developmental point in the formation of attitudes and values. The foundations for humanness are built in the home and family environment as one learns to test a set of attitudes and values, to develop skills of decision-making and communication, to achieve identity and self-direction and to develop the ability to love and trust. Society has much to gain if attention is focused on the vital importance of the role of family members and significant others in influencing as well as recognizing the home setting as a vital center for learning.

Families are aware of their role in meeting the learning needs of preschool age children. A study by Coolican (1973) found that 59 percent of home based learning activities of mothers of preschool children were in the area of developing family and personal competence. Within that category, 80 percent of the learning projects were related to home and family competence (i.e., child development, family relations and family planning, consumer education, sewing, nutrition, food preparation, and family finance). An analysis of these learning projects showed that the major emphasis was on the practical rather than the academic, on the applied rather than the theoretical, and on skills rather than knowledge. Results of Coolican's study (1973) indicated that mothers of young children seemed to prefer learning in the home as an integral part of their daily lives rather than as a separate and isolated activity. The home can provide an environment supportive of opportunities for learning.

H. B. Bell (1973) investigated the use of family resources in relation to selected family characteristics when the family's first child was in first grade. She viewed the child's education as a mutually-shared goal between family and school. Parental estimates of frequency and extent of time use were collected to describe parental inputs to school-related activities. Also mothers were asked about family money use for items related to children's education. About three-fourths of the parents bought reference materials for children's use at home. Almost all parents in the study used time to discuss the school day with their children, to assist children with school work, and to read to children. Bell's data gives evidence that parental commitment of resources (i.e., frequency and extent of time use) to school-related activities was greater in activities carried out at home than at school and that the home and family environment functioned as co-educator with schools. The family, however, rarely realized the extent to which they facilitated the child's educational development.

In addition to time inputs of family members, the family makes investments in materials and equipment that can facilitate learning. Of major importance is learning which occurs as a result of mass media, particularly television. Today, televisions are found in the majority of homes. Television can be an effective transmitter of information, thus enlarging one's knowledge base. Television particularly impacts on children's lives, both because children are impressionable and because children spend large segments of their week watching television. Thirty hours per week is a typical week of television watching for four year old children as noted by Moody, 1980, from a report by Nielsen Company. Television may be used as an assist in broadening children's experiences. Opportunities may be provided which enable family members to assist children in making a distinction between what is real and what is make-believe. Also, television programs may provide opportunities to view a variety of positive approaches to problem solving as opposed to negative approaches. Opportunities to view diverse role models in terms of sex and age may come from diverse television programs. Family members may wish to enhance role model learning by discussing various role models presented in programs. Television may expand children's cultural experiences beyond those that would normally be available by viewing on television the best of the concerts, ballets, and museums. Television also provides an opportunity to develop the cognitive skills of math, science, and language arts, with special programs geared to developing these skills.

Some homes are more effective as learning centers than others. The level and style of thinking in the home is a major factor in think out loud about alternatives, and correctly label objects and materials becomes a productive learning center for the family members. Participation as a family in activities such as watching television, reading to each other, and listening to music provides opportunities for the development of each family member. A number of researchers (Cahoon, et al., 1979; Radin, 1959; Levenstein, 1970; Karnes, et al., 1970; Schaefer, 1972) who have recognized the importance of the family as educator of pre-school children have designed home-based early intervention programs to increase the parents' effectiveness in develop-ing their children's intellect. These early intervention programs general-ly did not involve parents from all socioeconomic groups. Instead, the strategy of the programs was to counteract the effects of poverty on human development--the mother-child interaction. Effects of these home-based learning interventions included gains in IQ for subjects in the experimental groups. These gains were maintained three to four years after termination of the programs.

The evidence indicates that the family ecosystem (family members in home environments) is the most effective system for fostering and sustaining the development of the child. The evidence indicates further that the involvement of the child's family as an active participant is critical to the success of any educational program. Without such family involvement, any effects of intervention, at least in the cognitive sphere, appear to erode once the program ends. In contrast, the involvement of parents as partners in the enterprise provides an on-going system which can reinforce the effects of the program while it is in operation and help to sustain learning gains after the program ends.

Too often home-based learning has been identified only with learning needs that are directly related to activities which are related to the functioning of the household. The home is also an ideal laboratory for learning market as well as non-market skills. Learning to care for children and to prepare food, for instance, can serve one in good stead in jobs related to food service or child care. Most important, however, is the role of family in teaching attitudes and values that are directly related to job success; i.e., punctuality, honesty, positive human rela-tionships, decision-making. Goldhammer and Taylor (1972) recognized the interrelatedness of family and career roles and noted the centrality of careers in shaping family life and of family life in shaping careers. One of four models of career education they proposed is a home-based model. The purposes of the home-based model for career education include: development of educational delivery systems into the home, provision of new career education programs for adults, and the enhance-ment of the quality of the home as a learning center.

Although modern technology has made information about family life more readily accessible to families, some researchers (Bobbitt-Paolucci, 1975; Clarkson, 1975; Coolican, 1973; T. H. Bell, 1973) indicate that families turn inward for help in learning relative to the family; i.e., to near kin and neighbors rather than experts. This has some advantages; however, it could lead to the perpetuation of inaccurate information and myths to new generations. A major task facing family life educators concerned with home-base learning is that of finding appropriate and effective ways to intervene in family learning while noncommittally respecting a family's privacy and self-reliance. Mass media shows the greatest promise for meeting his challenge if families have developed the competencies for evaluating media information. Perhaps in the future, each family will have available to it learning resources via mass media for their particular use. A home mass media center with a computer terminal at the family's fingertips could serve the family both as a source and processor of information. An infinite amount of information from many sources would then be available for efficient family decision-making. The home education center could link the family to formal education centers as well as particular research and information centers. Through it, all family members could more easily become lifelong learners and more effective decision-makers.

The home and family have been and continue to be a major place to learn. The dream of family life educators is to enhance the potential of the home as a learning center. Each of us has much to gain if vigorous attention is paid to the vital significance of family as primary educator and a concerted effort is made to develop the home as a learning center.

Interrelationships Between the Learning Environments of the Home and the School

Many individuals involved in the formal education system, i.e., schools, recognize the essentiality of the interrelationship of the informal education system with the formal education system, i.e, the importance of the linkage between the home and the school for students. Recognition alone is not sufficient to maximize the potential of the interrelationship of the home and school. Purposeful efforts are needed to enhance these relationships.

Sometimes, the connotation of the phrase "home as a learning center" is interpreted to mean that the home is replacing the school as the learning center. This misinterpretation is unfortunate because the intent is to provide a means for acknowledging the importance of the home and family in providing the foundation for the social, emotional, mental, and the physical development of the home products--the children and youth--which the school will receive for further shaping. Children enter school with different genetic endowments and different sets of experiences which shape their overall development. Therefore, the readiness level of each class of students will vary. The quality of the foundation influences the level at which the schools may begin their programs as well as the nature and the diversity of programs that the school needs to offer. The scope and sequence of the school program will also be influenced by the quality of the home products--the individuals who became the students in the school. The home and family not only significantly shape the quality of the entry level product the school receives but continues to shape these students throughout their school years. When students are malnourished and/or hungry, little interest is generated for school activities. Prolonged malnutrition will ultimately impact the child's development physically, mentally, emotionally and socially. If appropriate socialization skills have not been developed, the child may have difficulty in interacting with other students and teachers. The home and family provide the locus for learning manners, proper behavior, and a basic value system. The child's self concept, self esteem and identity, which are integral to emotional stability, are molded within the home and family. The pattern of a child's education and perhaps his limits of accomplishment are established, but not fixed, by school age, T. H. Bell (1973). Children primarily learn their language from their family. Language is the key tool used for acquiring knowledge and will impact the child's progress in school.

Educators such as T. H. Bell (1973), Bronfenbrenner (1974), Leichter (1974), and O. W. Cahoon, et al. in general agree that the more active the parents are in the educational process, the greater the effect of the school program for the student, regardless of whether the program is traditional, compensatory or non-compensatory. Also, educators have noted that the support of education and schools within the home is an important factor in a child's success in school. Therefore, educators have developed activities and programs to help parents become more actively involved in their children's education in order to develop a greater appreciation by the parents and children for education.

The home as a learning center is precious and its nature should be protected. Efforts should be made to limit the degree to which the home is encouraged to assume a formal education role. If an undue share of the school's programs are imposed to the home, there will be less time for performing the important functions of home and family in the teaching-learning process. Additionally, if the nature of learning in the home is shifted from informal to formal, many of the kinds of learnings which presently occur in the home will not occur or will be reshaped. Frequently reference is made to reduced time available within the home and family due to societal changes, such as increased employment of mothers, multiple wage earners within the family, more community demands on time, etc. This reduction in time is often used as a reason for limiting the demands by schools on family time. Admittedly, time is an important consideration in assessing impact on families. However, a more important consideration should be the impact on changing the normal learning process in the home. Learning in the home and by the family is primarily incidental, non-structured, and often implicit. These forms of learning are appropriate for the major purposes of learning in the home and family which are socialization, acculturation, and development.

Schools are critical centers for learning since they are essential to the preparation of individuals for becoming effective citizens and fully functioning members of society. The school as a learning environment evolved because of major unmet needs of children, families, and individuals. The schools have been most effective in accomodating these unmet needs. Schools have helped to create individuals that have developed a remarkably progressive society. Although the approaches to learning may differ in the school from those used in the home, probably each is most effective for their differing purposes.

The diversity that exists in the characteristics of the home and the school as learning centers probably provides the greatest strength to both. Diversity in each provides the clarity of differences between the two. Diversity accentuates the common and unique elements of both. Diversity enables the existence of more than one type of educational system. Diversity ultimately enriches the individual and society.

FOOTNOTES

1. Norma Bobbitt is Professor and Associate Dean, Department of Family and Child Ecology, College of Human Ecology, Michigan State University, East Lansing, Michigan.

2. Beatrice Paolucci, now deceased, was professor, Department of Family and Child Ecology, College of Human Ecology, Michigan State University, East Lansing, Michigan.

REFERENCES

Bell, H. B. (1973). *Family resources used in school-related activities.* Doctoral dissertation, Michigan State University.

Bell, T. H. (1973). *Your child's intellect. - A guide to home-based preschool education.* Olympus Publishing Company.

Bobbitt, N. (1974). *Final report and proceedings of national conference on career education for middle and junior high school,* (47-60). Boston, Olympus Research Corporation.

Bobbitt, N., & Paolucci, B. (1975). Home as a Learning Center. *Final report for U.S. Office of Education* (Contract No. 300748735). East Lansing, Michigan: Michigan State University, College of Human Ecology.

Braga, J., & Braga, L. (1975). *Learning and growing: A guide to child development.* Englewood Cliffs, New Jersey: Prentice-Hall.

Brazelton, T. B. (1974). *Toddlers and parents.* New York; Delacorte Press/Seymour Lawrence.

Bronfenbrenner, U. B. (1974). *A report on longitudinal evaluations of preschool programs: Is early intervention effective?* U.S. Department of Health, Education, and Welfare. Washington, D.C.: U.S. Government Printing Office, Vol. 2.

Cahoon, O. W., Price, A. H., & Scoresby, A. L. (1979). *Parents and the achieving child.* Brigham Young University Press.

Clarkson, S. S. (1975). *Home-centered learning activities of families with teenage children.* Unpublished master's thesis, Michigan State University, East Lansing, Michigan.

Coolican, P. M. (1973). *The learning style of mothers of young children.* Unpublished doctoral dissertation, Syracuse University, Syracuse, New York.

Evans, M. W. (1974). Play is life itself. *Theory Into Practice.* 14:4, 267-272.

Goldhammer, K., & Taylor, R. E. (1972). *Career education: Perspective and promise.* Columbus: Charles E. Merrill Publishing Co.

Gordon, I. J. (1972). What do we know about parents as teachers? *Theory Into Practice, 11*(3).

Green, K. (1979). The family as education. *Families as educators: Challenges and opportunities, 3,* Proceedings Series of the Family Study Center, Division of Home Economics, Oklahoma State University.

Karnes, M. B., Teska, J. A., Hodgins, A. S., & Bodger, E. D. (1970). Educational intervention at home by mothers of disadvantaged infants. *Child Development, 41,* 925-935.

Lambie, D. Z., Bond, J. T., & Weikart, D. P. (1974). Home teaching with mothers and infants. *High/Scope Educational Research Foundation Monograph*, No. 21, Ypsilanti, MI.

Laosa, L. M., & Sigel, I. E. (1982). Families as Learning Environments for Children. Plenum Press.

Leichter, H. J. (1974). *The family as educator*, Teachers College Press, Columbia University.

Lerner, R. M., & Hultsch, D. E. (1983). *Human development*. McGraw Hill, Inc.

Levenstein, P. (1970). Cognitive growth in pre-schoolers through verbal interaction with mothers. *American Journal of Orthopsychiatry, 40*, 426-432.

Moody, K. (1980). *Growing Up on Television.* New York: Times Books

Radin, N. (1959). The impact of a kindergarten home counseling program. *Exceptional Children, 36*, 251-256.

Schaefer, E. S. (1972). Parents as educators: Evidence from cross-sectional, longitudinal and intervention research. *Young Children, 27*, 227-239.

Schiamberg, L. B., & Smith, K. V. (1982). *Human Development.* Macmillan Publishing Co., Inc.

Simpson, E. J. (1973). The home as a career education center. *Exceptional Children, 38*, 626-630.

Sutton-Smith, B. & Sutton-Smith, S. (1974). *How to play with your children.* New York: Hawthorn Books.

White, B. L., & Watts, J. C. (1973). *Experience and environment: Major influences on the development of the young child*, Vol. 1, Englewood Cliffs, New Jersey: Prentice Hall, Inc.

Wolfgang, C. H. (1974). From play to work. *Theory Into Practice, 13*, 279-286.

LIMITS AND POSSIBILITIES OF FAMILY AND SCHOOL AS EDUCATORS

Robert J. Griffore(1) & Margaret Bubolz(2)

Michigan State University
East Lansing, MI 48824

Questions are increasingly being raised about the limits and possibilities of family and school in the development of the child and in the service of society. Issues related to the nature and purpose of education and who shall control education are being raised at various points on an ideological spectrum, ranging from tighter programmatic controls at state and federal levels, to virtually complete control by parents over the education of their children (McGraw, 1978) and disestablishment of state schools (Gardner, 1975).

This chapter will review the historical roles of family and school in education, and their discontinuities as well as complementary and mutually reinforcing functions. Critical contemporary issues related to the roles of schools, and current family and societal trends influencing education will be discussed, followed by a delineation of issues related to design of parent education programs.

Public schools have come under more and more criticism and are charged with failure to carry out their basic job of education in the academic disciplines (A Nation at Risk, 1983). Likewise, families are cited for failing to prepare their children for school learning, for falling down in their responsibility for helping children acquire the psychic stamina and self discipline needed for learning (Etzioni, 1984) and success in school. Pleas are made to return to basics, to raise standards, to rid the schools of such nonessentials as personal and social development courses and similar frills. In 1984 a Constitutional amendment was defeated in the U.S. Congress which would have allowed prayers in public schools, presumably as a means to counteract immorality in society. At the same time, it is proposed that moral education is solely in the province of the family and church (Ryan and Thompson, 1975).

61

The rise in Home Schools is a symptom of the underlying conflict. Ten thousand to 20,000 American families (Holt, 1983) have chosen to teach their children at home. Motives include feeling that it is their responsibility and duty, that they can do a better job of helping children develop skills, interests and academic competencies, or the desire to train children in the moral, political, religious and other values and beliefs of the family. It is estimated that the number of children learning at home ranges from 10,000 to 100,000 (Palmer, 1984). Home schools have their proponents (Holt, 1981; Moore and Moore, 1981, 1982) as well as vigorous critics (Postelthwait, 1983). At the same time that some families are taking their children out of public schools others are advocating the provision of formal education at younger and younger ages, and there are movements to bring preschool education more extensively into the public schools. Extending education downward is seen by some as beneficial to young children and families, as a means of providing publicly supported day care, and also as a means to keep teachers employed and school buildings in use. Within the debates, some voices see the family and school as potential partners, cooperators and collaborators in the development and education of children (Bell, 1975; Lightfoot, 1978; Fantini, 1980; Sinclair and Ghory, 1980). They see family and school as having distinct but interrelated roles which can be mutually helpful to each other, with the child as the main beneficiary. Others, such as Holt (1983) see education at home as a way that children can avoid some of the undesirable and damaging conditions found in the schools such as the often snobbish, conformist, violent, competitive social life.

Historical Perspective on Family as Educator

The division of labor between school and family in the development of children has frequently been defined as that of school being education and that of family socialization. In discussing the latter function Goode (1964) concludes:

> (The) family is the fundamental *instrumental* foundation of the larger social structure, in that all other institutions depend on its contributions. The role behavior that is learned in the family becomes the model or prototype for the role behavior required in other segments of society. The content of the socialization process is the cultural traditions of the society; by passing them on the next generation the family acts as a conduit or transmission belt by which the culture is kept alive. (pp. 4-5).

This emphasis on the role-learning that goes on in the family, while certainly of much significance, has tended until recently to minimize the more inclusive education that goes in families, as well as the socialization that occurs in school and other societal settings. Getzels (1975) pointed out that the conceptual dichotomy of the child's existence into socialization and education resulted in failure to consider the continuities and overlap between these processes, as well as the discontinuities created by the conceptual void. Another consequence of this division was the lack of attention to the historical importance of family as educator. Bailyn's *Education in the Forming of American Society* (1960) pointed out that historians of education had addressed inappropriate questions when they asked, "When did the public schools begin?" instead of "How did colonial Americans educate their children?" The result was a distorted emphasis on schooling and on New England schooling in particular. To gain a true picture of the real educators of colonial America the family, church and print shop and other places of work such as the farm must be included. Cremin (1980) asserts that understanding their role in education in the early years of the country will also reveal the true significance of the 19th century public school movement.

The recent growth in historiography of the family has contributed valuable information on the relationships between family and other educational institutions over the course of American history. Cremin (1979) concludes after an analysis of several works on the family and community in colonial New England that the family was the central institution in explaining the educative basis and power of the community in the early years of our country. The family was a productive institution and the basis of community life. Families operated a farm or family business in which most of the essential resources of food, housing, clothing and other needed supplies and equipment were produced, created or transformed. In this process children worked with their parents and acquired the skills and knowledge for their tasks and roles in life. In colonial America family and church were closely related and the church was the source of much knowledge, values, skills and sensibilities considered necessary for life. One of the earliest educational ordinances enacted by the colonial legislature of Massachusetts was a law passed in 1642 requiring all parents and masters to see that their charges were taught reading, the capital laws, the religious catechism and apprenticeship in a trade. It is important to note that this law did not establish public schools but it exerted the power of the state to require certain kinds of education and placed responsibility for this on the family. It is also significant that children often were apprenticed to other families in the interests of education.

In 1647 Massachusetts passed a law requiring towns of 50 or more families to appoint a teacher of reading and writing and making it possible for tax funds to be used for that purpose. This law also required towns of 100 or more families to provide a teacher of Latin grammar to prepare boys to enter college to study for positions in church and state. Other states followed the lead of Massachusetts and helped formulate the New England conception of public education. Thus, the seeds for state control over education with parental compliance required and the right to use public funds for education, issues currently being debated, were established early in our country's history. Gender differentiation in professions and education was also very evident.

In the southern colonies education was assumed to be a function of the church and family. Legal authority was exerted over children who had no parents or whose parents could not afford to care for them. Apprenticeships and education in literacy and religion were required for these children. For slave children the family and the clandestine black church were the most influential educational institutions.

It can be concluded that the family and church were the dominant educators for the majority of children in the first century of America. Where schools existed they were extensions of the family, rather than substitutes for it (Cremin, 1979). The majority of children did not attend any formal school and a child was lucky if she had as much as two or three years of elementary schooling.

This pattern continued into the 18th century, but several developments stimulated the growth of more and different types of schools. The rise of nonconformist religious groups and resistance to control by the established church led to authorization of schools by various religious groups and other private bodies. Endowed schools, denominational schools and private venture schools for practical education arose in this century. New types of secondary schools arose to provide instruction in a wider range of studies to meet the needs of youth going into trade and commerce. These reflected growing industrialization and urbanization and the realization that the family could not provide the training for the new vocations and professions required for the expanding work of the society. Schools also began to include education in the arts, humanities and sciences.

Education in the family, however, continued to be dominant. For girls, especially those whose future roles were primarily limited to motherhood, homemaking and family life, essential skills and knowledge in home production, child care and household management were primarily learned in the family. America was still a predominantly agrarian society and children learned to be farmers by working with their parents.

In the years between the Revolution and the Civil War America developed educational policies devoted to the new national ideals of democracy, equality, and freedom and turned away from the private systems of education based on economic, class, national, and religious distinctions toward a system of public education free, universal, and open to all. In the first half of the 19th century elementary schools expanded beyond the traditional reading, spelling, writing, and arithmetic to education for citizenship, jobs, and individual development, areas heretofore within the province of family and workplace. Public high schools increased and broadened their curriculum to include college preparatory courses as well as terminal education for those not going to college.

During this period when schooling became a more dominant part of the lives of most children, there was an awakening in some quarters of the significance of the family in education. The parent education move- ment and identification of home economics as a field of study with the aim of improvement of home and family life both had their beginnings in the first half of the 19th century. Their inception primarily took the form of books and periodicals addressed to young women as prospective mothers and homemakers and to parents as guardians of the welfare of future generations. Kuhn (1947) has presented an illuminating portrait of what was considered to be the educational role of mothers through an analysis of the works of New England writers from 1830 to 1860. These publications were part of a reform movement aimed at improvement of society in which the family was singularly important in the domestic education of its members. Kuhn asserts that philosophical, religious, scientific, and social concepts of the period contributed to recognition of children as unique individuals and of the importance of mothers as mold- ers of the mental and moral character and physical health of children. A quotation from Sarah Josepha Hale, editor of the *Ladies' Magazine* and later of *Godey's Ladies Book*, illustrates the aims of the reform litera- ture of the period:

> If God designed woman as preserver of infancy, the teacher of childhood, the inspirer or helper of man's moral nature in its efforts to reach after spiritual things; if examples of women are to be found in every age and nation who, without any spe- cial preparation have won their way to eminence in all pursuits tending to advance moral goodness and religious faith, then the policy as well as justice of providing liberally for feminine education must be apparent to Christian men. (Hale, 1870, viii)

This statement intended to tell the world, especially men, that women were important to society and deserved to be educated, and to encourage women to be worthy of their high purpose. In the literature reviewed by Kuhn mothers are seen as religious and moral guides, mentors in intellec- tual cultivation, guardians of the "temple of the immortal soul," i.e., the physical body, and as "gentle rulers" of the home who would balance and counteract the turmoil and crudities of the business world where men held sway.

Similar views were expressed by Harriet Martineau, a popular English writer of the period who visited America in the 1840's. In her book, aptly titled, *Household Education* (1883) published originally in 1848 she states that "Every home is a school for old and young togeth- er..." and proceeds to a remarkably prescient series of chapters on the development of character, intellect, health, imagination, personal and

family habits, emphasizing childhood but not neglecting life-long education.

It must be noted that these publications do not tell us how parents
actually educated their children--they expressed ideals held by writers
and reformers of the period. Nevertheless, they do provide some indication of the assumed significance of the family as educator during a
period when public schools were becoming more and more widely established, and taking on more of the educational functions formerly carried
by home and church.

In the later 19th century and early 20th century public school education broadened considerably in the areas of vocational education. Such
subjects as agriculture, mechanic, and industrial arts, and home economics became regular parts of the curriculum. The Land Grant colleges
established by legislation in the 1860's "to promote the liberal and practical education of the industrial classes in the several pursuits and professions of life" were a major stimulus to expansion of college education,
research, the training of teachers for teaching practical subjects in the
public schools, and for bringing education to farmers and rural families
through what became the Cooperative Extension Service. The growth of
these new fields of study, such as home economics represents a process
of rationalization and formalization of knowledge and skills, heretofore
largely acquired by experience, trial-and-error and observation in the
family into bodies of "subject-matter" which could be explicitly taught.
These subjects, as well as others, consisted of specialized and technical
knowledge which parents were presumed not to possess and were thus
unqualified to teach. Vocational education in wider fields, such as business, also expanded; employment in business and industry was growing
and children could not learn these vocational skills in the family.

This period also saw the great waves of European migration and
schools were seen as places where all people must become "Americaniz-
ed", acquiring the language and values of U.S. citizenship in order to
have equal opportunity for mobility and success. Cremin (1979) points
out that studies of immigrant communities reveal the significance of
family-community linkages in education and their bearing on social mobility. The immigrant groups formed voluntary associations centered
around the family. They were New World versions of popular education
they had known in the Old World, such as fraternal groups, mutual benefit societies, libraries, music, sports, and drama clubs. These groups
served to sustain the language and culture of the ethnic subcommunity
and to mediate between the immigrant family and the dominant American culture.

The 20th century has seen further expansion of school curriculums
into areas presumably taught by families--health and physical education,
driver education, family life and parent education, sex education, and
values education. The latter areas have aroused much controversy in

many communities, with opponents asserting that these areas are best or most appropriately taught by family or church. Proponents argue that parents are not prepared to teach these areas, just as they are unprepared or disinclined to teach many other subjects because of lack of knowledge, interest, ability or time.

Schools also now provide additional services which families previously provided--school lunches as well as breakfast, psychological and emotional counseling, career guidance, health services, and recreational and social activities on a larger scale. As a result of this expansion of functions schools have been called to serve in loco parentis transferring parental authority to the schools, while at the same time affirming a parental element within the educational process (Fantini, 1980).

At the same time, families have become increasingly excluded from educational decision making, often feared by administrators and teachers or seen as problems (Stevens, 1966). Interactions between school personnel and parents are more institutionalized, often merely ritualized encounters at parent-teacher conferences, visiting days, or PTA meetings, or occurring only when some problem arises concerning a child (Lightfoot, 1978). A recent study of elementary teachers, principals and teacher educators found that while participants had favorable attitudes toward parents helping their children with school work, they did not favor parent involvement in curriculum, instruction and administrative decision making (Williams and Stallman, 1982).

The review of the family as educator might at first glance seem to indicate that the family has moved from being the central educational institution to a peripheral role with the school occupying center stage. This perception was the underlying basis for the distinction referred to earlier of family as socializer and school as educator. This view is now seen to be erroneous and greatly over simplified. In the 1970's there was a growing realization of the importance of the family in the educational process. The volumes edited by Leichter, *The Family as Educator* (1975) and *Families and Comminities as Educators* (1979) provided a necessary and influential corrective to the prevailing distinctions between family and school. Articles on such subjects as the recent historiography of the family, economic aspects of families as educators, early intervention, and parent education all pointed out the critical role of families in particular kinds of learning. In the 1975 volume Margaret Mead used the concept of education to include not only conscious teaching but also the processes of socialization and enculturation. She pointed out the especially important role of grandparents in a society such as ours where change is so rapid that children must teach their parents and where grandparents can make the past real and help bridge the generation gap. Paolucci, Bubolz and Rainey (1976) emphasized the family's contribution to human resource development through the nonformal education that takes place in on-going everyday activities of families, as well as the role of the family in preparing its members to participate in school and other societal systems. The Home and School Institute in Washington, D.C. is an example of an organization formed specifically to foster the family's role in education and cooperation between home and school (Rich and Jones, 1977).

In sum, at this juncture in history the family is seen as continuing to play a highly significant role in the education of children, and other institutions are viewed as assisting the family in its educational functions. In the next section an analysis and discussion of relationships between current educational roles of family and school is presented.

Family and School: Discontinuities and Complementary and Mutually Reinforcing Roles

Family and school must be viewed as an interrelated ecosystem, each having unique goals as well as some common goals for children and society.   The family and school constitute distinct but overlapping spheres which influence each other. There are discontinuities between them as well as conflicting goals, but they can be mutually reinforcing and complementary. Some discontinuities and conflicts are inevitable and can be beneficial, but they can also be hurtful.

Discontinuities between family and school emerge from differences in their structural properties and cultural purposes and functions. (Lightfoot, 1978). The family has principal responsibility for nurturance, development, and well-being of its children, not only in the early years, but over time until they assume independence and responsibility for themselves. Primary socialization occurs in the family and is part of the child all through life. Learning in the family begins at birth and includes learning basic codes necessary for future learning and survival--sensory learning, acquisition of a self and gender identity, language, control of body processes, use of physical and motor resources, and restraint of impulses required for life in a given social group or culture (Paolucci, et al., 1976). The family is singularly important in affective learning. The responsibilities of the school have typically been more narrowly circumscribed, traditionally beginning later in the child's life and are limited in time. The function of the school is to help the child learn certain things which society deems essential or useful for all children in order to function in and contribute to the society.

Relationships within the family are functionally diffuse and all encompassing, while those of the school are more functionally specific and directed to certain elements of the child's personality and development. Parent-child and teacher-child relationships are qualitatively different and maintained for different reasons. Parent-child relationships are intimate and primary, children can demand attention to all needs from their parents. Conversely, relationships with teachers are more secondary in nature and teachers need not feel they must meet all of a child's needs. Within the family, expectations of parents are particular for each of *their* children, while in school, expectations must be more universal, for *all* of the children in the school or classroom. Parents and children are emotionally engaged with each other usually throughout their lifetimes. Teachers and students can become emotionally disengaged, can withdraw from each other, and after a specified time the relationship usually ends (Lightfoot 1978).

The function of the school is transitional, to contribute to the future status of the child. In school the child is judged on differential performance to help him prepare for life in the larger society. The child usually has no role other than student and his or her role is preparatory for the "real" world outside of school. While the family's role is also transitional, within the family the present realities of the child's total life must be attended to; the child can have a place and role in the family not dependent on comparison with others or on some future status.

The preceding is admittedly a broad sociological analysis based on a structural-functional perspective with the family and school presented as performing ideal-typical roles and functions. It is realized that the boundaries between family and school are often indistinct and overlapping and the functions cannot be neatly demarcated. Some children do not have physical and emotional needs met and schools have stepped in to meet them. Some parents and children do not have intimate relationships and children seek emotional satisfaction from teachers and peers. Nevertheless, distinctions can be discerned and such an analysis is useful for examining areas of differentiation, discontinuity, and cooperation. Potential negative consequences can occur when neither system is meeting critical needs of the child; positive outcomes can also be identified when functions are complementary and mutually supportive.

As a result of the lesser emotional involvement and secondary relationship between the child and the teacher, children can move beyond their egocentric, self-centered needs to seeing their place in the group. They also become aware that others have needs and rights. Their conception of themselves as persons in relation to a progressively larger group of others is developed. In school, children encounter personalities and value systems other than those at home, thus broadening their range of experiences, relationships and expectations for the future. They learn competition, compromise and cooperation, behaviors considered essential for social order and cohesion. In other words, schools help children to become more fully socialized and able to take their place in society.

It is argued (Musgrove, 1966) that schools which are merely extensions of the family and which do not provide some conflict and discontinuity with the customs and values of the family stunt the child's social range and blunt awareness and social sympathies and can limit aspirations and potential for growth. Schools, by exposing children to values, knowledge, and role models that are different from those at home help children discover their special talents and individuality, thereby serving as agencies for social change. On the other hand, schools can perpetuate the social structure by transmitting the values of society and duplicating the status and role distinctions in society by such means as tracking on the basis of academic testing, differential counseling, and authoritarian student-teacher relationships.

Discontinuity may produce other negative results. Values and strengths of the family culture can be unknown, ignored, or undermined in school and may conflict with values and practices in the school, creating problems for the child. For example, if a school stresses competition and ignores social cooperation and sharing which may characterize the values of the home or cultural group the child may be confused over which values are best. Efforts in recent years by Blacks, Mexican Americans and other minority groups to have their culture, values, customs, foods, and family structures acknowledged and incorporated in the school environment illustrate concern that their culture not be demeaned or lost.

Discontinuities between the realities of family life the child experiences at home and the family models presented in school can also create problems for children. More than one-fifth of all children in the U.S. under 18 today are being raised by a single parent. Others are being raised as step-children in blended families with allegiance to two sets of parents. Over half of mothers of school age children work outside the home. Given these developments the traditional elementary school textbook family model of Dick and Jane and their natural parents with an at-home mother and working father is woefully limited. While such an overt model is probably less often presented today, notes to "parents", suggestions about what fathers do, etc., may give more subtle messages about the "right" kind of family. Such messages can create guilt, anxiety and shame in children if their family does not match the ideal presented.

Family Factors Influencing Learning and Education

The prior discussion has emphasized the structural differentiation and related but distinctive functions of the family and school which are both functional and dysfunctional for children and society. The roles of the family and school in education considered in a narrower sense of instruction in the areas of reading, writing, mathematics and other academic subjects have generally been more demarcated, with the school charged with the major responsibility. However, recognition of the critical role of the family in fostering this kind of education, and in helping the child succeed in school learning is increasing.

One of the most critical ways in which families influence learning is through their responsibility for the nutritional and other health requirements of family members. Children who are hungry and malnourished perform less well in all life situations and exhibit behaviors that interfere with learning, such as listlessness, unresponsiveness to stimulation, inability to pay attention and concentrate, lack of curiosity and reduced motorsensory development. Some data suggest that early severe nutritional deficiencies may result in permanent impairment of normal maturation of the brain and subsequent impaired cognitive functioning (Stoch, Smythe, Moodie and Bradshaw, 1982). Frequent illnesses also impede the child's progression and achievement in school.

During the 1960s the United States strengthened its efforts to equalize the educational opportunities for children, regardless of income, cultural or ethnic background or geographical location. An important conclusion derived from evaluation of such efforts as Head Start and other short-term preventative and remedial programs was directed at the joint role of families and schools in learning. Comprehensive evaluations of academic achievement of children during these years emphasized the role of families and communities as explaining more of the variation in school achievement than the characteristics of schools themselves (Coleman, 1966; Jencks, 1972). Schooling seemed to be effective if children had the necessary skills and physical-emotional strength for learning and the motivation to learn but was not effective for children who lacked these attributes.

Considerable research has been directed to examining the relationship between education, income and other socio-economic variables and educational outcomes. Decline in intelligence test scores of children has been found to be correlated with increasing size of family and decreasing socio-economic status (Douglas, 1964, Elder, 1962, Sears, 1970). A nationwide longitudinal study of 5000 American families found education of parents to be importantly related to educational attainment of children as well as to characteristics of children which influence their educational attainment. Father's education was highly related to son's education and achievement motivation. Mother's education was strongly related to cognitive skills of sons. (Duncan, 1974).

Relationships between family size and educational attainment have also been found. At given costs and incomes more highly educated parents desire higher educational attainment for their children and have fewer children. In Duncan's study cited above, the negative impact of family size on daughters' educational attainment was twice as great as it was on sons' education attainment. This reflects the greater social value given to preparing sons for occupational and work roles requiring education. In studying the allocation of women's time to market and non-market activities Leibowitz (1972) found that better educated women spent more time in child care than less educated women, hence increasing the child's possibilities for development and educational success. Men from higher social classes with more education have also been found to spend more time with their children than men from lower social classes (Szalai, 1972).

In a review of 100 studies, White (1976) found that, in general, correlations of +.30 to +.50 obtained between SES and school achievement. It has usually been concluded that as socioeconomic level increases, the investment of families in education and human capital building of children also increases. Relationships between structural and socio-economic variables do not, however, tell us specifically what it is about families that influences the educational attainments of their children. Let us turn to research related to these factors.

Studies of Head Start children (Ware and Garber, 1972) identified the following factors to be related to school achievement: (1) materials for learning in the home; (2) parents' awareness of the child's development; (3) rewards for intellectual attainment; (4) expectations parents have for children's schooling; and (5) activities focusing on pre-reading skills. Hess (1969) confirmed these findings and found the mother's teaching behavior, experiences she provides and model she sets were important influences on the child's educational achievement.

Educational motivation is influenced by expectations in the home, by the atmosphere of the interpersonal relations in the family environment, and by feelings the child has about herself. The child acquires her first concept of herself in the family by the way she is treated by others. She can be regarded as a person of worth and competence with some degree of control over her own life, or conversely as being worthless, incompetent and subject to the will and whim or others or fate. She comes to regard herself as others regard her. A strong sense of self worth has been found to be a critical factor in a child's ability to succeed in school. Trust is the basis for self worth, willingness to rely on one's expectations, and to trust others. The early nurturance and love provided to the child in the family are the basis for the sense of trust. Trust in oneself and others is essential for a child to be able to relate to teachers and peers and engage in new experience and new learning. It is the foundation for moral behavior and cooperative human relationships (Boulding, 1973).

The immediate setting of the family ecosystem influences children in other ways that leave an indelible mark on them and their attitudes, values, educational and behavioral potential. The interchanges the family makes with other societal sub-systems such as the church, work and market place, other families and the neighborhood, and the boundaries they establish around their private world influence the child's experiences and the type and extent of information coming into the home environment. The positions of parents in other settings influence their behaviors and attitudes in relation to their children. Kohn's classic studies (1979) emphasized the interactions of occupational and parental roles. Kohn suggests that parental values tend to be extensions of the modes of behavior functional for parents in their positions in the occupational structure and are reflected in styles and circumstances of parental behavior. White collar occupations require the individual to deal with ideas, symbols and interpersonal relations; such parents stress reasons underlying behavior in their interactions and disciplinary techni ques with their children. Blue collar workers, however are required to standardize their work, have much supervision and exercise compliance. Their interactions with children reflect similar compliance to rules and expectations which children bring to their relationships with teachers. Thus, through the requirements of their occupational and domestic roles parents tend to develop views of what is expected and appropriate be havior. These are then transmitted to children and influence their orien tations and expectations and affect their educational aspirations and achievements.

During the last decade research approaches have given more atten tion to the socio-psychological and behavioral processes thought to be conducive to learning. Iverson and Walberg (1980) conducted a quantita tive synthesis of 18 studies of the family environments of over 5000 children in eight countries. They found that parent stimulation of the child in the family showed a consistently stronger relationship with intel ligence, motivation and achievement than did measures of socioeconomic status. The home environmental variables, when combined, correlated from +.70 to +.80 with measures of school achievement involving read ing, vocabulary and problem solving. Bloom (1980) has concluded that the most important parental factors influencing children's learning are: contributions of parents to language development; encouragement of children to learn well; aspirations of parents for their children; provision for assistance in learning when the child needs it most; and ways in which time and space are organized. The relationships between these factors are highest with school achievement involving reading, vocabu lary and problem solving and lowest with spelling and arithmetic compu tation. The home appears to have the greatest influence on language development and general ability and motivation to learn, and the least influence on specific skills primarily taught in school. Sinclair and Ghory (1980) conclude that the above family variables are changeable, in con trast to cultural background, socioeconomic status as measured by pa rental education, income or occupation, and family size which are relati vely inalterable. It is possible, then, to enhance family learning environ ments and behaviors to assist the child with school learning.

In the next section we turn to a review of the historical role of the school as educator and a discussion of contemporary issues related to the functions of the public school.

Historical and Social Roles of Schools

Over the years, the roles played by public schools in society have been grounded in basic philosophical views. A traditional view might provide answers along the lines of those asserted by Ebel (1972). That is, schools are not designed to care for the emotionally disturbed, socially disadvantaged and learning disabled, and they are not designed to keep youth out of trouble and off the streets. Schools also are not responsible for building students' self-concept, reducing test anxiety, or boosting achievement motivation. Nor is it the business of schools to coordinate student's recreation and hobbies. Schools especially are not arenas for social research and remediation, such that every ill of society may be solved through an innovative school-based intervention. Rather, schools are for learning, with the emphasis on intellectual processes, rather than on affective or social discovery.

A more humanistic view of the roles and functions of schools has been presented by Rogers (1963). He has proposed that in schools, students should learn to be "free". Quite in contrast to the traditionalist view, Rogers (1963) proposed that only if we do not trust students must we prescribe what they should learn. Schools, according to the humanistic view, should be places where students can learn to express feelings. Learning must involve the whole person, including feelings. Teachers should not plan lessons or give lectures. They should instead present students with the materials needed for learning and the opportunities to use them. It is assumed that if a climate of opportunity is created, students will take advantage of these opportunities.

In general, an existential position has some similarities to a humanistic position. Freedom and responsibility to choose are fundamental in an existential framework. Students are inescapably free to choose, and indeed are condemned to be free. Thus, students do not need to learn to be free as Rogers (1963) proposed. An existential view of why schools exist might suggest that schools should be a place where students create themselves in the same way that an artist creates a portrait or a composer creates a symphony.

While common sense and rationality would suggest that schools cannot be all things for all students, schools have been expected to play diverse roles and to assume functions once reserved for other institutions. But if the school as an institution cannot be all things, what are the limits of the school as educator?

A very brief and selective history of public education shall provide some examples of the ways in which schools have accepted responsibility, with varying degrees of commitment and enthusiasm, for new roles and functions in increasing magnitude.

The growth of the public school curriculum has generally paralleled the expansion of society's need for more formal educational experiences and commensurately fewer nonformal experiences. To the extent it is believed or legislated that a particular educative experience or opportunity is desirable for all individuals, less tightly regulated organizations, such as the family, cannot be relied upon for the provision of those experiences.

As discussed in a prior section, the transfer of educational authority from the family to school gathered momentum in the 19th century. This occurred at the same time other institutions were assuming other roles and functions previously assumed by the family. Rothman (1972) has observed that institutional action was considered necessary partly because of the disorder and lack of effectiveness of the family in carrying out some of its roles and functions.

Public education may be viewed as a total institution in the sense that it has accomplished whatever it has accomplished by physically removing children and adolescents from society for scheduled periods of time and by very strictly structuring their experiences. In the early public schools, the authority of the schoolmaster was absolutely unquestioned and exceeded the authority of the parent. This was deemed necessary and desirable in order that the school should successfully counteract the deleterious influences of the family and instill in pupils characteristics which would benefit society (Rothman, 1972). Among these characteristics were ambition, initiative and productivity. Few characteristics could be more important to a developing economy than a positive attitude toward work, and it was generally accepted that all children could benefit from acquiring this attitude, regardless of their social class background.

In essence, the public school provided not only an environment in which students could be managed and in which their experiences could be controlled; it also provided a means of shaping the foundations of the developing industrial society in the present and in the future.

The notion that schools have developed largely as institutions of social control has been asserted very emphatically by Bowles and Gintis (1975). Specifically, they argue that schooling has provided a means of preparing a ready supply of workers to carry on the stratified capitalistic system. Schools may be viewed as sorting machines in which the needs of some students are served while the needs of others are not. Historically those whose needs have not been served include minorities, the poor and pupils who are disadvantaged by such conditions as learning disabilities. As Bowles and Gintis (1975) observe, educational development has been brought about by class conflict, and specifically by the demands of workers that the schools should also serve them. However, the schools have consistently maintained their capitalist production orientation by sorting students either formally or informally into groups which either shall be taught or shall not be taught. In terms of formal structure, techniques of tracking and ability grouping have reliably sorted students into segregated groups, and they ordinarily remain in these groups. Sorting becomes a self-fulfilling prophecy which makes it very difficult for most students to rise above their life circumstances and group characteristics.

While the goals of public education in the 19th century and early 20th century were achieved with varying degrees of success with individual pupils and groups of pupils, an underlying goal of the schools was to create uniformity in society. Particularly in the early 20th century with the influx of immigrants, schools assumed the responsibility of Americanizing both children and adults from diverse national origins. The "melting pot" was a particularly meaningful term as it applied to the public schools. However, the schools' role in creating uniformity posed a fundamental threat to immigrant families. Indeed, to become assimilated through the public school required children and adults to renounce their unique cultural heritage and mode of family interaction. The school and the family are in conflict to the extent they do not share values, language and heritage.

Public schools have also been called upon to perform major social change functions, and school desegregation is an example of such a function. School desegregation is a uniquely American phenomenon that has ecological foundations and associations in virtually every social organization and institution. The schools have been deeply involved in the issue since the U.S. Supreme Court ruled in 1954 that separate but equal school facilities are illegal. For several years, programs of school desegregation were designed strictly as remedies for separate school facilities. However, even if unitary systems were created in school districts additional programs have been needed to reduce discrepancies between the achievement of minority pupils and white pupils.

Some of the factors that contribute to discrepancies between minority and white achievement patterns may indeed be inherent in the schools, including the means by which desegregation is accomplished in a district. However, other variables lie in the province of the family and other extra-school institutions. Indeed one need only review the research on the relationship between school desegregation and achievement to see that beyond the mere occurrence of school desegregation, many factors must be considered in explaining its outcomes. The extreme lack of agreement (St. John, 1975; Weinberg, 1977) about the most basic conclusion concerning school desegregation reflects diverse methodologies, poor conceptualization of the basic research task, bias in the research process, or some combination of all these factors. In any case, school desegregation has been one of the most comprehensive and large scale social engineering experiments ever conceived and attempted. As Bronfenbrenner (1976) observes, when you wish to understand something, it is best to change it and note the results. While school desegregation has provided a transforming experiment in the schools, it has not necessarily enhanced our agreement and understanding about what schools are for.

School desegregation serves not only as an example of the ways in which schools may be mobilized in the service of social goals. It also illustrates another trend in American public education, which has been described by Arthur Wise (1979). Wise contends that the recent history of American public schools illustrates an increasingly bureaucratic operating framework. His thesis is that at the foundation of recent educational change is a tendency to rationalize and standardize the ways in which schools operate. Standardization comes about through centralized control from federal and state governments. While federal control has been visible in regard to nondiscriminatory access to the schools, educational policy makers have recently turned their attention to making schools more efficient in regard to learning outcomes as well. It is not clear, however, that legislation can ensure the specific kinds of interventions that would produce schools that are uniformly efficient for all students. However, to the extent standarization occurs at the federal and state levels, local control is likely to be diminished, and this involves a loss of family input through the local schools. Indeed, Wise (1979) observes that the rationalization of the schools and associated centralized control pose a challenge for individual and local influence on the schools, and for the freedom of students and teachers in schools.

Moral Reasoning

Since the early years of the 20th century, the functions of the public schools have clearly proliferated, and at various times have emphasized uniformity, and individualization, comprehensive educational and socialization objectives, or a narrow basic skills approach. At times, affective education and socialization have been accepted as important functions of the schools. For example, moral and values education recently has been enthusiastically embraced by the schools. Whereas earlier generations of educationists might have considered values and moral education to be a frill, in the 1970s these areas advanced to the forefront of the educational enterprise. Some rather diverse approaches have gained keen interest including the cognitive-developmental approach associated with Lawrence Kohlberg. Kohlberg (1975) has proposed that the individual passes through a developmental sequence of stages of moral reasoning.

Until recently programs designed on the basis of Kohlberg's cognitive and developmental theory consisted largely of ways in which students might be assisted in the acquisition of role-taking skills and in acquiring more advanced cognitive structure that would allow more advanced moral reasoning to occur. Kohlberg (1975) has pointed out that discussion of moral dilemmas may be an effective means of accelerating students' attainment of more mature moral reasoning. Perhaps most fundamentally, if students are to advance in their moral reasoning, the school must be a just environment.

Achievement Motivation

The schools have also been involved in the development of programs designed to improve students' achievement motivation. These programs have varied in complexity and theoretical basis, as is the case in regard to moral and values education. In one rather straightforward type of method for enhancing achievement motivation, students are taught to think, talk and act like individuals who have a high need to achieve. In general, the effects of this intensive modeling approach are unclear. Even in those cases where achievement behavior is augmented, one must question whether achievement motivation has been modified in students. Indeed, as McClelland (1972) observes, perhaps the positive effects of such programs are largely a function of students' acquisition of academic skills and teachers' acquisition of classroom management skills.

Health Education

In addition to recent emphases on moral reasoning and achievement motivation, the schools have also been involved in health and nutrition education. Not only are courses in health and nutrition education becoming a more common part of school curriculum; some states are requesting certification for health educators. Brief courses at the secondary level in some districts provide students with choices in regard to courses in this area which they wish to take (Kine, Schlaadt & Fritsch, 1977).

Health instruction often places the emphasis on mental health, drug use, human sexuality, health careers, safety, disease control and prevention, nutrition, and family life, in an ecological context. It would appear that health and nutrition education has attracted substantial support from state and federal sources. Many states have invested heavily in health education programs from kindergarten through twelfth grade. At the federal level, Congress has made appropriations for health teacher preparation and drug education (Kine, Schlaadt & Fritsch, 1977).

Career Education

Another area of particular emphasis in school curricula since the early 1970's has been career and vocational education. Unlike the emphasis in earlier generations, the thrust is now toward total career development from elementary school to retirement (Sievert, 1975). Vocational industrial-technical education at the secondary level includes exploration and preparation. Students may explore occupation preferences and opportunities in terms of their values and aspirations. They may also prepare themselves for specific occupations once they have explored various occupational options.

If there is any doubt about the magnitude of support in the schools for career education, such doubt may be diminished by the fact that career education is now part of regular classroom activities in 9,000 of the nation's 16,000 school districts (Kaercher, 1981). Career education extends beyond vocational-technical education by teaching skills that all students need for employment. It is also a sequential process in which skills learned at the elementary level form the basis for higher-level skills to be learned at the secondary level.

Support for career education comes from the Chamber of Commerce, AFL/CIO, the National Education Association, and state and federal sources. At the federal level, for example, in 1980 the U.S. Office of Career Education placed $15 million in grants to provide incentives to career education program development (Kaercher, 1981).

The federal government has also been interested in entrepreneurship awareness among students at the secondary level. In 1979, for example, the U.S. Department of Education, Office of Vocational and Adult Education, funded the Entrepreneurship Components Project at the American Institutes for Research in Palo Alto, California. In general, the program teaches generic entrepreneurship skills and some applications in a series of instructional modules relating to small business development (McFarlane, 1982).

Modern delivery systems are being developed in the area of career education as well. One system which is now being developed is the Tel-a-Career-Information System (TACI). This system will deliver information on careers to secondary schools for students and counselors via telephone (Tauber, 1982).

Computer Instruction

Still another area of recent curriculum development in the schools is high technology education. In general, high technology may be understood to involve the microprocessor, and thus the influence of videotapes, videodiscs, TV offerings, calculators, and computers (Shane, 1982). The computer is perhaps the most potentially influential instructional device in American education in the last century. Schools are already offering courses ranging from computer literacy to modeling and simulation in mathematics and science (Melred, 1982). They are also being used to teach geometry, to conjugate Spanish verbs and to provide students with vocational advice (Sturdevant, 1982). More than 90,000 microcomputers are now in use in schools, and it is estimated that by 1985, over 300,000 will be in use. Moreover, by 1990, it is projected that one out of every four pupils will have access to a computer (Carro, 1982).

In the next section contemporary family and other societal trends which influence the roles of family and school in education of children are discussed.

Contemporary Family Trends

During the past two decades the state of the family became a subject of considerable discussion, commentary and controversy. Sociological studies and journalistic statements abounded, many suggesting

that the traditional nuclear family was a vanishing species. Some an-
alysts suggested that the new emerging forms were more flexible in a-
dapting to the complex conditions and disruptive changes characteristic
of the modern electronic age. Others viewed change negatively and
longed for a return to a distant past when families were believed to be
strong, and happy, characteristics said to be missing in today's families.
Family life of the past may not have really been happier, but we see it
from the perspective of childhood and since we idealize childhood we
identify and idealize the family of the past along with childhood.

Since the family is an integral unit of society, interrelated with all
other units, as other institutions, patterns and values change, the family
also changes. Likewise, when there are changes in the family there are
impacts on other units of society, such as the school. While it is difficult
to specifically determine the reciprocal impact of changes in social institutions, a review of contemporary family trends can identify critical
areas for intersection and potential discontinuity and cooperation betwe-
en family and school.

Family Forms and Dissolution

The traditional family form of father-wage earner and mother-
homemaker and dependent children accounts for fewer and fewer family
types--an estimated 7% in the early 1980s (U.S. Bureau of the census,
1983). However, the nuclear family of parents or single parent with or
without children continues to be the dominant family structure, in contrast to an extended family type. The difference is that the nuclear
family today appears in diverse forms with many variations and permuta-
tions.

One of the most rapidly increasing family forms is the single parent family, usually headed by a woman. The number of female headed
families that included their own children under 18 increased by 81% from
1970 to 1979. In 1979 there were 5.3 million such families (Current
Population Reports, 1980), one-fourth of all family units. In 1983 more
than twenty percent of all children under 18 were being raised by a
single parent. The rise in births to unmarried mothers accounts for some
of the rise in single parent families, but the high divorce rate of the past
two decades accounts for most of the increase (Cherlin, 1981).

Of all trends in American family life in recent years the rising rate
of divorce has received the most attention. While the divorce rate has
been rising for at least a century the rise in the 1960's and 1970's was
much steeper and more sustained than past increases (Cherlin, 1981). Of
couples who married in 1970, by 1977, only seven years later, one-fourth
were already divorced, and if present rates continue it is estimated that
48% of these couples will eventually divorce. The rate of divorce has
slowed down in the past few years, but barring an unforseen downturn in

the near future, the lifetime proportion of persons ever divorced is likely to be exceptionally high. At present 50% of divorces occur within the first seven years of marriage and the majority involve children. Bumpass and Rindfuss (1979) estimate that overall, by the age of 16, one-third of all white children and three-fifths of all black children born between 1970 and 1973 will experience family disruption because of divorce.

Most people who get divorced remarry--about five out of six men and three out of four women. When either partner in a remarriage has children the structure of the new family, the so-called blended family, can be very complex, involving children from one or both previous marriages as well as from the new one. In 1978, 10 million children lived in a household with one natural parent and one stepparent, amounting to one of every eight children in a two-parent family (Glick, 1979). Visits to noncustodial parents and the increase in joint custody arrangements result in children being members of two families, perhaps with stepparents and step- or half-siblings in one or both.

Employment; Income

One of the most persistent long term trends of American and other industrialized societies is the increase in married women's employment outside the home. In the last few decades the greatest increases have occurred among younger married women with school age and preschool children. Between 1950 and 1980 the percentage of employed married women with children age 6-17 increased from 25% to 66% while the percentage of those with children under six went from 11% to 43% (U.S. Bureau of Labor Statistics, 1979).

While more women have entered occupational and professional fields formerly considered men's work, the majority of women are still employed in female-identified jobs and earn less than men. Traditional attitudes towards women's roles are still widespread and women continue to be more heavily involved than men in family, child rearing, and household work roles, regardless of whether or not they work away from home. Nevertheless, for economic, aspirational and attitudinal reasons the rate of women's labor force participation is expected to remain high.

The labor force participation of younger married women has risen sharply and they are more likely to divorce than older women. While there has been an increase in fathers obtaining custody, in most cases mothers are awarded custody of young children. We can expect, therefore, that not only will the at-home mother be the exception rather than the rule for the majority of American children, more and more of these working mothers will also be single parents.

Another important factor affecting families has been the state of the American economy during the past several years. The recessions of the late 1970's and early 1980's and associated high unemployment have created serious hardships for many American families. The Michigan Panel Study of Income Dynamics (Moen, 1979, 1983) revealed that one in six (17%) of families with children had a breadwinner who was unemployed in 1975. Forty percent of the families of the unemployed suffered financial blows in the 1975 recession. In an analysis of the support received by families Moen (1983) found that the majority of families of the unemployed who suffered economic hardship received no government support. Black families and those headed by women were more likely to be without unemployment compensation. Families with more than one wage earner were much more likely to avoid economic hardship.

Delayed Marriage and Births; Smaller Families

Almost every American adult eventually marries, but more and more are marrying at a later age, a return to an earlier American pattern. In 1960 around 30% of women age 20-24 had never married, while in 1980 this figure was around 50% (Cherlin, 1981). In contrast to the 1950s when getting married on graduation day or shortly after was an aim of many college women, college graduates today are delaying marriage until their middle or late 20's. Desires for a career, for economic, psychological and social independence and for wider experiences are reasons for this phenomenon.

Many women are also having their first child later with the result that one of the fastest growing birth rates is that for women in their late twenties and early thirties. Subsequent children are spaced farther apart and fewer children are being born. These are also reversals of the 1950s when birth rates rose sharply. Women born in 1950 will have an estimated 1.9 children in contrast to the 1933 birth cohort whose fertility rate was 3.2 (Cherlin, 1981).

Black and White Differences

The previous discussion has treated family trends for the population as a whole, without describing changes within ethnic, religious, geographic or social class groupings. For most groups trends have been parallel, with some exceptions. A number of black and white family patterns have varied noticeably. Blacks used to marry earlier than whites, now they marry later. Blacks have higher rates of out-of wedlock births, although their rates have declined recently while the rates for white teenagers have risen. Lower percentages of black women have a husband present in the household. In 1979 less than half of black women age 25-44 had a husband present, compared to three-fourths of white women in the same age group. In 1979 forty-one percent of black families were maintained by women, compared to 12% of white families (Cherlin, 1981). Extended kin networks have been an important part of the family structure among low income blacks, providing a stable functioning environment (Stack, 1974).

Consequences for Children's Education

What are the potential consequences of these trends in American family structure for the roles of family and school in the education of children? Unfortunately there are no simple, clear-cut answers to this question. These trends are interrelated and feed back on each other, and the influence of such intervening variables as family life styles, family and societal values, and social welfare policies and programs preclude drawing definitive conclusions and implications. Neither do we have much research yet on such patterns as growing up in a blended family or in two nuclear families resulting from divorce and joint custody.

We are beginning to have more longitudinal research on the effects of divorce on adults and children which point to some implications for education. Earlier research had found that children function better in a single parent family than in a two parent famiy with great conflict. Hetherington, Cox and Cox, (1979) confirmed this finding but their studies also found that spouses and children both experience much emotional distress after separation. Hetherington and her colleagues (1978) found that adults and children in separated families, in contrast to intact families, had a more chaotic lifestyle, were more likely to eat pickup meals at irregular times, had erratic bedtimes and children were more likely to be late for school. Within two years life had stabilized for most families. Wallerstein and Kelly (1980) studied 131 children from 60 separated families over a five year period. At first, almost all children were profoundly upset; five years later one-third were doing well psychologically, one-third were in the middle range of mental health, but one-third were still intensely unhappy and dissatisfied. Both of these studies had limits and it is difficult to draw generalizable conclusions, but it does appear that separation and divorce are traumatic for most children, and while the majority return to normal development, some experience longer term problems. Both studies indicate that children do better if they have a continuing relationship with both parents, and if the custodial parent establishes an orderly and supportive household routine. The emotional instability, tension and lack of regularity in children's lives especially in the first year following parental separation affect the child's behavior in school and make it difficult for parents to provide the support and help a child needs with school work.

Single parents who are heads of families are also faced with many stressors which may make it difficult to help their children. Weiss (1975) identified three common sources of strain in single parent families: responsibility, task, and emotional overload. Single parents are faced with all of the decisions, must cope with parenting and household work and often with paid work as well. They have no other adult with whom to share frustrations, loneliness, anxieties and emotional demands of children. Two or three decades ago there was considerable concern over the absence of a male figure in single parent families. Fatherless families were thought to have problems in child discipline and in establishing appropriate sex role identification. The research has not supported such an indictment and it has been concluded that the simple fact of father absence or the number of parents were less important than the ability of the remaining parent to function and manage effectively (Herzog and Sudia, 1973). What does seem to be the more critical factor in the absence of a male is the lack of a male income (Cherlin, 1981). Espenshade (1979) after reviewing the evidence on economic consequences of divorce concluded that women were generally left worse off than their husbands. Children are involved in more than half of all divorces and most often live with their mothers. However, a 1975 survey revealed that less than half of separated or divorced mothers were awarded support payments and half of them received them irregularly (Cherlin, 1981). During the 1975 recession two-thirds of female headed single parent families with the youngest child under six had a poverty level income (Moen, 1983).

Families formed by remarriage after divorce or widowhood also face problems. Cherlin (1978) has pointed out that the lack of generally accepted ways of dealing with problems is especially noticeable following divorce. These problems include how to relate to step-parents and the array of step-kin that come with remarriage, resolving sexual tensions between step-relatives, defining financial obligations and matters of discipline. While several studies have found little difference in the adjustment of children living with two natural parents as contrasted with those living with a step-parent, where differences have been found children in step-parent homes were less well adjusted. Kalter (1977) found that girls aged twelve and over with step-fathers had significantly higher incidences of aggression toward parents and peers, sexual activity, drug involvement and school-related problems than girls living with a natural father and mother. Cherlin suggests that the lack of guidelines and societal supports for families formed by remarriage require families to solve difficult problems by themselves often engendering conflict and confusion.

Studies related to the employment of family members have ranged over the past few decades from study of the effects on families of unemployment of men during the Great depression, to the effects of women's employment on children and spouses, to problems of dual career families, and back again to unemployment. Probably no work related area stimulated more research activity, public concern and controversy in the 1960s than the employment of mothers of preschool and school age children. The conclusion reached in most of the research was that mothers' employment per se as a single variable had little effect on the family. Attitudes of mothers and fathers toward the wife's work, whether work was satisfying and voluntary, flexibility of work schedules and the adequacy of alternative child care arrangements and support for other family responsibilities were found to be more significant than simply the fact of working outside the home (Moore and Sawhill, 1978). Positive effects of mothers' employment have also been found, such as

an increased sense of responsibility in children, higher achievement motivation, and higher academic performance. In addition, since most
women work for economic reasons their earnings supplement the family
income. Research on families in which both husbands and wives have
careers has consistently shown that work and task overload and the lack
of adequate child care are among the major stresses encountered
(Skinner, 1980).

Earlier research on unemployment (Angell, 1936; Komarovsky,
1940) emphasized male unemployment and the potential loss to the man's
status and change in interpersonal relationships, while recent research
reflects the economic problems of the 1970s and 1980s and has concentrated on economic loss and hardship and the resulting deprivations for
families and children. Families cope by cutting down on what is
considered less essential: educational pursuits, books, toys, recreational
opportunities, vacations and preventive medical and dental care (Moen,
1983). Children's lives are affected by these mechanisms as well as in
other ways. Family goals may be lowered and there can be increased
ambiguity and anxiety concerning the future as well as perceived or real
loss of control over happenings and outcomes. Family discord and
breakup, more punitive actions toward children and spouse and child
abuse frequently accompany financial misfortune. Elder's longitudinal
study of children who were growing up during the years of the Great
Depression (Elder, 1974, 1983) pointed out some of the emotional and
social problems and difficulties in school which these children faced,
many of which continued into adulthood. His work also revealed some of
the beneficial outcomes of economic hardship such as greater responsibilities on the part of children, more involvement in family work and
strengthening of nurturant family ties. If economic conditions for a
significant portion of the population continue to decline as they have in
recent years, the lives of millions of children will continue to be
influenced. Conflicts over educational and social policies and the roles
and relationships between family and school can be expected. The
extent to which public schools should expand their nutritional, health,
remedial, counseling and other family support services will be vigorously
debated.

The long term effects of the postponement of the birth of the first
child, particularly among better educated women, and of smaller family
size on education has not been studied to any extent. Many first time
mothers have high personal and professional aspirations and present
special challenges for educational institutions such as demands for high
quality early childhood programs. When the number of children is small
there may be extraordinary demands placed upon these children in both
school and family. Another implication of a small family is that its
members have few people with whom to interact on a basis. Small
families may have more intense emotional interactions which can result
in greater stress and tensions than when there are more people to share
frustrations, dissipate aggressive and hostile tendencies as well as to

share loving feelings. On the other hand, fewer children can mean that more emotional, economic and other resources as well as time and energy are available to each child to assist them in learning. Greater interaction with adults may also facilitate language and intellectual development.

The previous discussion of trends in family life has emphasized the stressors and resource constraints faced by families. Many parents have limited income, time, physical and emotional energy and some lack the necessary skills identified as critical to building the competences and strengths of children essential to their success in school. Instability, conflict, lack of regularity and clearly defined expectations for behavior and relationships in the family contribute further to potential problems. These constraints and stressors may call for increased support services to be provided by other social institutions such as the school. On the other hand, many families are stable, have adequate income and other resources and give their children a great deal of encouragement and support. In many homes children are furnished a wide array of materials and equipment ranging from educational toys and books to personal computers. Higher education, broader experience and greater maturity on the part of young persons marrying and becoming parents later, as well as fewer children to share parental time, affection and resources, can result in more enriching family environments. Parental expectations can also mean demands upon schools for higher quality education and a wider range of educational opportunities.

The Report of the National Commission on Excellence in Education (1983) recommends increased homework and urges parents to carry their share of the responsibility for children's education, including monitoring their child's study, nurturing confidence and creativity and to be an active participant in the work of the schools and a model for their children. Nowhere does the report acknowledge the changes in family life which affect the family's capacity to carry out these responsibilities and which influence the roles and functions of the school. The wide range of family forms and the disparity in resources is not recognized. The report fails to acknowledge the interrelatedness of all components of the social system and to realize that one part of the system cannot be changed or improved without consideration of the whole.

Other Societal Trends

In considering change it is well to note some of the other societal trends influencing families and schools. We are increasingly aware of the growing differences and conflicts in religious and moral beliefs and values underlying several current issues about the roles of family and school. These conflicts are manifested in debates over the teaching of the theory of evolution vis-a-vis creationism; over prayers and Bible reading in public schools; over depiction of the traditional roles of men and women in educational materials; over sex education, moral development education and affective education; and the rights of parents to not educate their children in the public schools. McGraw (1978) charges that the position of neutrality on religion in the public schools is in reality a religion of secular humanism and a violation of the First Amendment. Citing Gardner (1975) she maintains that education entails belief formation and that schools are religious institutions. Schools cannot be the value-free institutions for which educators strive; therefore schools should be free from state control. She argues further that education is the primary responsibility of the family and it should be free to educate its children on the basis of family values and beliefs. Hazard (1981) asserts that court decisions have tended to recognize parents' rights to educate their children at home or in some other setting, but also to reinforce the right of the state to regulate, at least in part, the nature and quality of nonpublic instruction. The current rise in home-schools and the reported 12 percent increase in enrollment in private schools (Hawkins, 1982) are manifestations of underlying conflicts over control and content of education.

As pointed out in a previous section, changes in technology, notably the electronic computer and its widespread use in all occupational and professional arenas as well as in the home present further pressures on the family and school. Families are urged to not let their preschool children fall behind by failing to have a computer to assist them in learning. Schools are being asked to provide computers for all students so that the widening economic gap between families will not add further to inequalities in educational opportunities. The computer is one example of the high technology which characterizes our society and which is creating dilemmas about the role of the family and school in vocational and career education. Whose job is it to prepare students for jobs and occupations of the future, the shape and outlines of which are but dimly seen at present? Where do business and industry fit in the picture? Some argue that schools cannot provide the vocational and technical education needed; it is too expensive and likely to be outdated by the time the student finishes the training. Families do not have the knowledge and resources either to give vocational training as they did in years past. Naisbitt (1982) has drawn attention to the significance of not only "high tech" but also of "high touch" in the lives of all of us today and tomorrow. The impersonality of work with machines and technology engenders along with it the need for more intensive human relationships and greater emotional and social skills. Whose job is it to provide affective education?

In the discussion of family trends several references were made to changes in women's roles. Increased employment, later marriage and child bearing, and the increase in female headed families all have a bearing on family functioning. As women's roles change, the roles of mothers and teachers also change. Lightfoot (1978) has pointed out that mothers and teachers have been at the center of the socialization process. Mothers have generally been highly involved in the care and nurturance of young children, and elementary school teachers have been more likely to be women. Both have been given a demeaning and negative caste in this society, in spite of the lip service given to espousing children as our most valuable resource. Lightfoot suggests that mothers and teachers have sometimes been in subtle competition and have been somewhat ambivalent about relinquishing control over children to each other. She avers that as women are freed from some of the narrow, traditional definitions and roles that have constricted them, mothers and teachers can become better collaborators and grow to feel greater mutual respect for each other's sphere of work. They can clarify the boundaries of their own tasks and involvements in the best interests of the child. As women's roles change, men's roles have also begun to shift, albeit at a slower pace. But, we are seeing changes. More men are seeking custody of children, are involved in caring for and rearing young children and sharing family and work roles (Pleck, 1979). Just how these gender role changes ultimately will influence the roles of family and school in education is unclear, and speculation about the future in this regard is beyond the scope of the discussion here. These shifts call for serious and intensive study.

What all of the societal and family changes described above illustrate is that children today live in a diversity of family structures and environments, amid a wide array of values, belief systems and role models, and with great variability in the resources available for education. It can be concluded that the need is greater than ever for schools and families and other social institutions to coordinate their educational activities for the greater possible development of children. Parent education is increasingly suggested and promoted as an effective way to enhance the family's role in education and to equalize educational opportunities for all children. Issues in program development in parent education are discussed in the next section.

Issues in Parent Education Program Design

The findings of research on instructional and program design, have thus far been applied in rather selective ways. The rise of public education in the United States caused educationists to ask fundamental questions about the nature of children and the processes of learning (Griffore, 1981). By and large, the interest remained in K-12 education through the early decades of this century. However, in the 1920's interest began to develop in nursery school education (Frost & Kissinger, 1976), and the 1960's saw a clear increase in interest and resources available for compensatory education and early education programs intended to accomplish a broad range of objectives (Hodges & Spicker, 1967; Kamii & DeVries, 1974; Weikart, 1969).

In K-12 and preschool education programs, thorough study and systematic planning have been considered important. This is not conistently true with regard to educational programs for parents. While school-based educational programs have been accorded the benefit of our best program design and research efforts, family-based education has occasionally been poorly conceived, athoeoretical and haphazard. Since the family is no less an educative and socialization setting than the school, high standards for parent education programs are extremely important.

Clarke-Stewart (1978) provides ample basis for questioning the accomplishments of parent programs and even many of the assumptions on which these programs are based. These conclusions are suggestive of the need for the most careful analysis of programs in the future. Specifically what is known about designing instruction in school programs can and should be applied to parent programs. The application of these techniques and principles also allows the most useful evaluations to be conducted. Rather than judging parent programs only on their outcomes, they should be subjected to process analyses as well. To the extent we wish to describe how parent programs work, we need research that helps to explain the functional relationship between programs and their outcomes.

Some Issues of Program Design

A fundamental gauge of the inherent quality of a parent program or any instructional activity may be found in the answer to the question, "What established logical and/or empirical basis is there for predicting that what is intended will in fact be achieved?" This question can be understood more precisely in two parts. First, what is there about the program that should be predicted to change the behavior of parents, and second, what evidence is there that if parents' behaviors change in the intended ways, there will be some measurable positive outcome for children?

These two questions call for evidence of relationships between program content and parent behavior as well as between parent behavior and outcomes for children. Since the nature of the relationships is usually correlational, it is not possible to infer causal direction. However, while the absence of evidence of causal relationships may not permit control, it does allow explanation and prediction. Moreover, correlational data are often accepted as valid evidence in the natural sciences, as for example, a correlation between smoking and lung cancer.

A valid model of teaching and learning in school should be useful in understanding the strengths and weaknesses of parent programs. In such a model, parents are the students and the outcomes are (1) what parents learn, and (2) how this knowledge is applied in their interaction with children.

Such a model would involve the following types of variables:

1. Learning climate

2. Parent-as-teacher characteristics

3. Content variables

4. Process variables

5. Sibling effects

6. Outcome variables

In the context of parent programs, it is not entirely clear how each of the first five of these categories of variables might influence selected outcome variables. However, their potential for influence may be inferred from what is known about how such variables can influence outcomes in formal K-12 educational programs. For example, many teacher variables may be related to student achievement, such as teachers' use of praise, teachers' acceptance of students' ideas, teachers' questioning behavior, and teachers' use of reinforcement (Dunkin & Biddle, 1974).

Another area of contemporary research has explored the relationship between the "climate" of the learning setting and pupil achievement. Climate refers to a number of ambient variables in the classroom, including the expectations teachers hold and communicate for student achievement. In some studies, climate variables account for over 80 percent of achievement variance (Brookover, Beady, Flood, Schweitzer & Wisenbaker, 1979). To the extent parent programs involve contextual learning situations, the notion of climate becomes potentially important and meaningful. If climate is related to pupils' school achievement, it may also be related to parents' acquisition of parenting skills and knowledge.

A principle that has derived from the last generation of educational research is that learner characteristics are clearly associated with achievement. Several of these learner characteristics are motivational, such as anxiety. In general, extreme anxiety tends to have a debilitating effect on learning (Meyers & Martin, 1974).

Another learner characteristic, locus of control, is also related to achievement. Locus of control refers to the perception that the consequences of one's behavior are either under one's own control (internal locus of control) or under the control of forces in the environment (external locus of control). Internal locus of control is usually associated with higher achievement (Phares, 1973).

Perhaps one of the most important learner characteristics is the motive to achieve. While achievement motivation is a complicated phenomenon and one that is no doubt age-related and task-related, a substantial amount of research has found that its relationship to achievement is consistent and moderate (Atkinson, 1974).

Other learner characteristics have been found to relate to achievement, but suffice it to say that these three variables illustrate the potential importance of considering learner characteristics in parent education.

While learner characteristics influence achievement in their own right, so do the numerous interactions between these learner characteristics and various characteristics of the instruction. Cronbach and Snow (1977) have referred to these phenomena as "aptitude by treatment interactions."

Another category of variables, program content variables, must be considered carefully in the design of the program. Often parent programs are assigned for convenience to broad categories such as cognitive, socialization, or language programs, according to the ultimate effects they are intended to have on the child.

In the interest of program design, however it is more useful to describe program content and goals specifically. Outcome specificity facilitates treatment specificity, and programs that have been successful in teaching parents specific behaviors are noteworthy for their treatment specificity (Brockway & Williams, 1976). This applies to a variety of programs, including behavioral programs; those focusing on conflict resolution; expressive; cognitive; or socialization programs. All would seek to bring about changes in ways that are *a priori* defined to be desirable. All would seek to improve upon what already exists or to shape some behavior or ability in ways that are evaluated positively.

One principal dimension of difference between behaviorally-oriented programs and other cognitive, socialization, or expressive programs is that of the degree of defined functional relationship between the treatment and the intented outcomes. Behavioral treatments are designed to provide a clear functional relationship between how parents learn to interact with their children and the desired children's behaviors. When the desired behavior is accomplished, there is little doubt about the antecedents because this functional relationship is planned rather than discovered by statistical analysis.

A major shortcoming of programs whose treatments lack specificity, and which bear little or no clear, planned functional relationship to the desired child behavior, is that it is not clear how changes in children's behavior or abilities are accomplished.

Clarke-Stewart (1978) observes that we must understand what we are doing in parent programs. A major aspect of this is understanding the functional relationships between treatments and outcomes. It means applying a very precise analysis to programs so that specific goals are intended, and the specific ways these goals are most likely to be accomplished are formulated into treatments.

One of the perennial issues in parent programs concerns achieving an optimal balance of knowledge and skill acquisition. Ryle (1949) described this distinction as "knowing how" vs. "knowing that." While the relative programmatic emphasis of these two categories may be partly a matter of subjective judgment, this emphasis heavily influences program outcomes. Parents who enroll in formal child development classes may acquire a great deal of knowledge but few skills. Indeed, some of these parents may even question whether the professor, a child development expert, possesses practical skills. This suspicion is not entirely without reasonable foundation if one considers the sometimes confusing advice offered by child development experts in numerous and widely available popular primers (Clarke-Stewart, 1978; Griffore, 1980).

Parent programs whose designs purposefully involve certain skill and factual content areas based on intended program outcomes are likely to be programs that succeed in accomplishing their objectives. If skills are the desirable outcomes of the program, then the instructional process should be planned for skills, rather than factual knowledge (Gagne, 1977).

Gage (1978) has discussed the importance of distinguishing between skills and knowledge in the framework of teacher education programs, which may be suggestive of desirable dimensions of parent programs as well. He has noted that relatively recently the attention of teacher educators has turned toward microteaching experiences and other modes in which skills that are inherent in the teaching process are practiced. Referring to techniques of skill learning as "teacher training products," he notes that the Program on Teacher Effectiveness at Stanford University has identified more than 800 such products, all of which may be described and evaluated on important skills-related dimensions. Among these dimensions are the subject matter specificity, the target audience, the target outcome, the materials associated with the product, and the nature and extent of the practice provided. Whether teacher training products take the form of films, books, discussions, or self-assessment techniques, they are, in any case, specifically designed to promote the acquisition of applicable skills. Parent programs might benefit from a consideration of some of the same dimensions that are used to evaluate these teacher education products.

Family factors have been given insufficient attention in the design of parent programs. Indeed, parent education programs infrequently consider complex family constraints and influences on parents as they attempt to acquire and use parenting knowledge and skills.

The complexity of this issue is indeed so great as to prohibit an adequate description here. However, as an example, family size, which influences parents' previous knowledge and experience in parenting, undoubtedly may shape their interests in parent programs. Related to the variable family size is the ordinal position of the individual child whose interactions with the parent might stimulate the parent's interest in parent programs. Clearly, parents whose interests at the moment lie particularly in specific interaction issues with the third child in the family may be different from those of the parent of an only child.

The child's interests are also likely to be best served by programs that take this into account. Birth order and family size may well be related to children's intellectual and personality characteristics. Siblings can exercise powerful influences on a child's developing personality, and various types of family constellations may exercise quite a range of effects. Parent education programs would do well to consider and prepare parents for the possible effects of birth order and family size.

In addition, parent programs might be logically extended to involve whole families, so that siblings are included in the efforts of parents which may be directed toward a specific child in the family. The power of this possibility may be seen by once again referring to the educational literature, particularly on peer tutoring and cross-age tutoring. This literature suggests in general that not only might measurable benefits accrue for the tutee, but the tutor may also profit from the experience, both intellectually and emotionally (Allen, Feldman & Devin-Sheehan, 1976).

Variables from all the categories discussed here, whether teacher variables, parent variables, or family variables, have a meaningful place in the planning of a parent program, especially if they are alterable. Attention has recently been given to the important distinction between alterable variables and status variables. In the realm of educational research, status variables include gender, race and socioeconomic status, while alterable variables include the amount of time students devote to a task, and specific cognitive entry characteristics (Bloom, 1980). Programs would do well to encourage parents to focus on variables that are alterable. Programs that present socioeconomic status as an important dimension of parent behavior must also recognize that it is not necessarily an alterable condition. Similarly, a child's age, sex and race certainly are not amenable to alteration by intervention. Effort that is devoted to describing parent-child interaction in terms of these unalterable conditions is non-productive.

While it is appropriate to take parent, family, and other variables into consideration in planning and designing a parent program, it is unreasonable to expect inexperienced parents to take into account this full array of variables as they attempt to apply what they learn in parent programs. To a degree, programs may have failed to consider the numerous and complicated ways in which what they offer may depend on other environmental and individual variables. They may have failed, in other words, to account for the many interaction effects suggested by the variables reviewed here, focusing instead on the main effects and suggesting unrealistically broad applicability of simplistic techniques. Techniques that are purported to be broadly applicable are only acceptable if they are in fact broadly applicable. Indeed, skills presented to parents should consist largely of truly applicable main effects, or skills whose utility does not involve extremely complex interactions with other variables.

Gage (1978) suggests that teachers will not find relationships between variables that involve complex interactions very useful. The most useful scientific basis for teaching is the simple main effect stating that the relationship between two variables, such as a technique and its outcome, does not depend on other variables. While teachers probably can apply relationships that involve one interacting variable, higher-order interactions involving several variables may not be useful as a scientific basis for teaching. Indeed, understanding and taking into account a larger number of variables is an artistic endeavor that is probably aided by long experience.

Similarly, parents may not find complicated interaction effects to be useful bases for their efforts as parents. While experienced parents eventually may develop an intuitive understanding of such complicated interactions, inexperienced parents, who are most likely to enroll in parent programs, may be least able to use them. Therefore, parent programs probably should deal with main effects and simple interactions in most cases.

Limits and Possibilities of Family and School as Educators: Summary and Implications

This chapter has presented a discussion of issues and contemporary societal developments underlying the roles of family and school in education of children. Implicit in the discussion has been the dilemma surrounding this question: are schools primarily to serve societal needs with education as a means to this end, or are they to serve the individual who is then free to contribute whatever he or she can to society while in the process of meeting personal aspirations and goals?

In response to this question the pendulum has swung from one extreme to another. The recent report of the National Commission on Excellence in Education (1983) by its very title, *A Nation at Risk* has clearly endorsed a position of education in service to society. Declines in educational achievement and standards are said to be indicators of educational disarmament and cause for alarm. They reveal that the United States is in danger of being overtaken in commerce, industry, science and technological innovation by competitors throughout the

world. In other periods of time development of individuals has been a
manifest goal of the school, with societal order or change a latent
outcome.

The position taken here is that schools carry out both functions and
to consider one without the other is a futile endeavor. The individual
and society are two sides of the same coin, and one cannot be served
without the other. The family and school, along with other units of
society constitute an inter-related system in which every component
influences each other. Family and school can be seen as distinct but
interrelated spheres with varying degrees and kinds of overlap. It is not
the purpose here to state what the distinctions and overlap should be for
any given school system or family or cultural group. Instead, what
follows is an attempt to develop a paradigm for viewing the relative
positions of family and school on several dimensions of education of
children and youth.

On all major dimensions in the paradigm family and school are both
seen as having responsibilities toward the child and society. In some
areas the role of the family is seen as primary while in others the school
is paramount. The dimensions included--Individual Learnings and Preparation for Social Roles---are intended as broad categories encompassing
major functions of family and school. Obviously they are not mutually
independent categories, but are offered for analytical and heuristic
purposes. Neither are the sub-categories of learning independent since
one type of learning influences another, but it seems useful to separate
them in order to denote differential responsibility.

The position of each specific item on the Family-School continuum
denotes where major responsibility or contribution is assumed to lie. A
central location indicates equally shared responsibility; one toward the
left indicates that the family has more responsibility while one toward
the right that the school carries a major load. Judgement of the relative
location of each item is based on observation, review of historical and
current experiences of family and school in education, a structural-
functional perspective and research findings. Admittedly, the judgment
is based on a value position of universalism, and open to challenge. The
paradigm presents a broad generalized pattern within which there would
be considerable variability. Additional research and theory development
on the contributions of family and school to specific learnings is needed
in order to develop a more accurate paradigm.

Two other important limitations must be stated. The paradigm
does not include other influences on education, notably friends and peers,
church, youth groups such as 4-H Clubs, Scouts, athletic groups, work
places, and the mass media. In some areas such as recreation and leisure
time pursuits, sex education, vocational and career choices and goals
these influences may be more powerful than either family or school. In
addition, the paradigm is limited to education of children and youth and

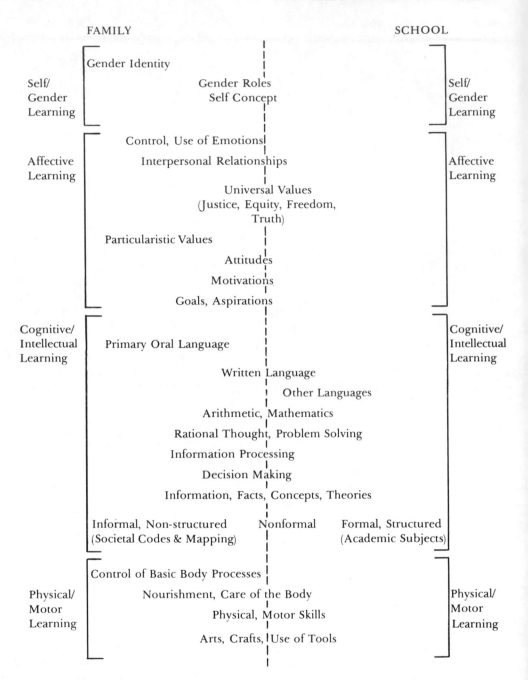

Figure 1. Relative responsibility of family and school in
education for individual learnings.

does not consider lifelong learning which continues after a person leaves her family of orientation and elementary and secondary school. For example, for many work roles specialized education is necessary and a dominant influence. For adult family roles of homemaking and child care the family continues as a significant source of learning throughout life (Bobbitt and Paolucci, 1975).

Figures 1 and 2 indicate that the family and school carry joint responsibility for most major learnings. Very few belong exclusively to either province. The balance is tipped toward the family on gender identity, first language, and control of emotions and bodily processes since these are acquired early in life. The family is seen as very influential in development of self-concept, motives, goals and interpersonal skills, but the school influences these too. Cognitive intellectual learnings are likewise influenced by family patterns and processes, and through education and involvement of parents learning in these areas can be enhanced. The school is seen as having major responsibility for transmitting knowledge of the content of such academic subjects as natural and social sciences, humanities, languages, and mathematics, which depend upon specialized training that most families do not possess. Interest and competence in learning these, however, can be affected by family values, goals and activities. The paradigm recognizes that a great deal of informal learning of community and societal codes and processes (societal mapping) goes on in the family, and that nonformal learning occurs in school, too. The family and school are seen as having joint responsibility for physical motor learning.

Family   School

_____

Family

(Parent, Spouse,
Sibling, etc)

Consumer

Community/Citizenship

Work

Leisure

Friend

_____

Figure 2. Relative responsibility of family and school in
          preparation for major social roles.

Universal values of justice, equity, truth, and freedom with responsibility should undergird public education and are appropriately taught in public schools as well as in the families. Particularistic values of religious or other groups are within the province of the family and groups which they support.

Family and school are seen as sharing responsibilities for preparation for major social roles more or less equally, with the family probably carrying a large share of the learning for future family roles. The underlying principle of universalism applies generally to learnings seen as a unique responsibility of the school, and particularism to those unique to the family.

In sum, both school and family are limited in their educational roles. Neither can do the entire job--the school cannot become a total institution, encompassing all of a child's life and meeting all needs. Similarly, the family, as family, cannot take on the work of the school on a wholesale scale. Family and school perform complementary and interconnected roles. We urge that there be greater awareness on the part of each sphere of the responsibilities, roles, and limitations of each other. If societal trends and conditions present problems which make it difficult for families to provide their essential educational inputs, it will be necessary for schools and other agencies to provide a larger share of the educational supports required. In the same vein, when families understand the resource constraints and other limitations confronting schools they can be better prepared to participate in actions and decision-making which will allow schools to carry out their mandate to provide high quality education for all. More effective and genuine cooperation, coordination and collaboration in the educational process will be to the benefit of children and in the service of society.

FOOTNOTES

1. Robert J. Griffore is Professor and Chairperson, Department of Family and Child Ecology, College of Human Ecology, Michigan State University, East Lansing, Michigan.

2. Margaret Bubolz is Professor, Department of Family and Child Ecology, College of Human Ecology, Michigan State University, East Lansing, Michigan.

REFERENCES

Allen, V. L., Feldman, R. S., & Devin-Sheehan, L. (1976). Research on children tutoring children: A critical review. *Review of Educational Research, 46*, 355-386.

Angell, R. C. (1936). *The family encounters the depression.* New York: Scribners Sons.

Atkinson, J. W. (1974). The mainsprings of achievement-oriented acitivity. In J. W. Atkinson and J. O. Raynor (Eds.) *Motivation and Achievement*, Washington, D.C.: V. H. Winston & Sons.

Bailyn, B. (1960). *Education in the forming of American society.* Chapel Hill: University of North Carolina Press.

Bell, T. H. (1975). Building a stronger America through a more viable home-school partnership. Paper presented at the Annual Convention of the American Association of School Administrators, Dallas.

Bereiter, C., & Englemann, S. (1966). *Teaching Disadvantaged Children in the Preschool.* Englewood Cliffs, NJ: Prentice-Hall.

Bloom, B. S. (1980). New directions in educational research: Alterable variables. In B. S. Bloom (Ed.) *The state of research on selected alterable variables in education.* Chicago: University of Chicago Press.

Bobbitt, N., & Paolucci, B. (1975, October). *Home as a learning center.* Final report of a feasibility study on the home as a learning center, Contract No. 300748735, Department of Health, Education and Welfare, Office of Education, Occupational and Adult Education Branch. East Lansing, MI: Michigan State University, College of Human Ecology, Department of Family Ecology.

Boulding, K. (1973). *The economy of love and fear.* Belmont, CA: Wadsworth Publishing Co.

Bowles, S., & Gintis, H. (1975). The problem with human capital theory: A Marxist critique. *American Economic Review, 65,* 781.

Brockway, B. S., & Williams, W. W. (1976). Training in child management: A prevention-oriented model. In E. J. Mash et al. (Eds.) *Behavior modification approaches to parenting.* New York: Brunner/Mazel.

Brookover, W. B., Beady, C., Flood, P., Schweitzer, & Wisenbaker, J. (1979). *School social systems and student achievement: Schools can make a difference.* New York: Praeger.

Bumpass, L., & Rindfuss, R. (1979). Children's experience of marital disruption. *American Journal of Sociology, 85,* 49-65.

Carro, G. (1982). What's new in education. *Ladies Home Journal, 99,* 101-108.

Cherlin, A. J. (1978). Remarriage as an incomplete institution. *American Journal of Sociology, 84,* 634-650.

Cherlin, A. J. (1981). *Marriage divorce remarriage.* Cambridge: Harvard University Press, 1981.

Clarke-Stewart, A. (1978). Popular primers for parents. *American Psychologist, 33,* 359-369.

Coleman, J. S. (1966). *Equality of educational opportunity.* Washington: U.S. Government Printing Office.

Cremin, L. A. (1975). The family as educator: Some comments on the recent historiography. In H. J. Leichter (Ed.), *The family as educator,* New York: Teachers College Press.

Cremin, L. A. (1979). Family-community linkages in American education. In H. J. Leichter (Ed.), *Families and schools as educators*, New York: Teachers College Press.

Cremin, L. A. (1980). *American education the national experience 1783-1876.* New York: Harper & Row.

Cronbach, L. J., & Snow, R. (1977). *Aptitudes and instructional methods: A handbook for research on interactions.* New York: Irvington.

Douglas, J. S. (1964). *The home and school: A study in ability and attainment in the public school.* London: MacGibbon and Kel.

Duncan, G. (1974). Educational attainment. In J. N. Morgan, K. Dickinson, J. Dickinson, J. Benus and G. Duncan. *Five thousand American families-Patterns of economic progress.* Ann Arbor, MI: University of Michigan, Institute for Social Science Research, Survey Research Center.

Dunkin, M. J. & Biddle, B. J. (1974). *The study of teaching.* New York: Holt, Rinehart and Winston.

Ebel, R. L. (1970). What are schools for? *Phi Delta Kappan, 54,* 3-7.

Elder, G. H. (1962). Family structure: The effects of size and family sex composition and ordinal position on academic motivation and achievement. In *Adolescent achievement and mobility aspiration,* Chapel Hill, North Carolina: Institute for Research and Social Science.

Elder, G. H. (1974). *Children of the great depression.* Chicago: University of Chicago Press.

Elder, G. H. (1983). *Children of depression and war.* Social Change Project, Cornell University, Ithaca, New York. In progress.

Espenshade, T. J. (1979). The economic consequences of divorce. *Journal of Marriage and the Family, 41,* 615-625.

Etzioni, A. (1984, January 9). U. S. needs a moral and social recovery. *U.S. News and World Report, 96,* pp. 59-60.

Fantini, M. (1980). Community participation: Alternative patterns and their consequences on educational achievement. In R. Sinclair, (Ed.), *A two way street home school cooperation in curriculum decision making.* Boston: Institute for Responsive Education.

Frost, J. L., & Kissinger, J. B. (1976). *The young child and the educative process.* New York: Holt, Rinehart and Winston.

Gage, N. L. (1978). *The scientific basis of the art of teaching.* New York: Teachers College Press.

Gagne, R. (1977). *The conditions of learning.* New York: Holt, Rinehart and Winston.

Gardner, J. F. (1975). *The experience of knowledge: Essays on American education.* Garden City, NY: Waldorf Press of Adelphi University.

Getzels, J. W. (1975). Socialization and education: A note on discontinuities. In H. J. Leichter (Ed.), *The family as educator.* NY: Teachers College Press.

Glick, P. C. (1979). Children of divorced parents in demographic perspective. *Journal of Social Issues, 4,* 170-182.

Goode, W. J. (1964). *The family.* Englewood Cliffs, NJ: Prentice-Hall.

Griffore, R. J. (1981). *Child development: An educational perspective.* Springfield, Il: Charles C. Thomas.

Griffore, R. J. (1980). Toward the use of child development research in informed parenting. *Journal of Clinical Child Psychology, 9,* 48-51.

Hale, S. J. (1870). *Womans record or sketches of all distinguished women from the creation to A.D. 1868, arranged in four eras with selections from authoresses of each era* (3rd ed.). New York: Harper & Brothers.

Hawkins, R. B. (1982, November). Educational opportunity, parental choice and community: The case for reforming public education. *Sequoia Advisories.*

Hazard, W. R. (1981). Flight from the public schools. *Compact, 14(4),* 22-23.

Hetherington, E. M., Cox, M., & Cox, R. (1978). The aftermath of divorce. In J. H. Stevens and M. Matthews (Eds.), *Mother-child, father-child relations.* Washington: National Association for the Education of Young Children.

Hetherington, E. M., Cox, M., & Cox, R. (1979). Family interaction and the social, emotional, and cognitive development of children following divorce. In V. Vaughn and T. B. Brazelton, (Eds.). *The family: Setting priorities.* New York: Science and Medicine Publishing Co.

Herzog, E., & Sudia, C. (1973). Children in fatherless families. In B. M. Caldwell and N. H. Riccuti (Eds.), *Review of child development research* (Vol. 3). Chicago: University of Chicago Press.

Hess, R. D. (1969). Parental behavior and children's social achievement: Implications for Head Start. In E. Grotberg (Ed.), *Central issues in research related to disadvantaged children.* Princeton, NJ: Educational Testing Service.

Hodges, W., & Spicker, H. (1967). The effects of preschool experience on culturally deprived children. In Hartrup, W. and Susthing II, N. (Eds.) *The young child: Reviews of research.* Washington, D. C. National Association for the Education of Young Children.

Holt, J. (1981). *Teach your own.* New York: Delacorte.

Holt, J. (1983, December 2). Home schooling lets a child's mind grow. *USA Today,* p. 10A.

Iverson, B. K., & Walberg, H. J. (1980). Home environment and learning, a quantitative synthesis. Paper presented at the annual meeting of the American Educational Research Association, San Francisco, 1979. Cited in R. Sinclair (Ed.), *A two way street home school cooperation in curriculum decision making.* Boston: Institute for Responsive Education.

Jencks, C. (1972). *Inequality: A reassessment of the effects of family and schooling in America.* New York: Basic Books.

Kaercher, D. (1981). Career education: What are our schools teaching kids about work? *Better Homes and Gardens, 59,* 22.

Kalter, N. (1977). Children of divorce in an outpatient population. *American Journal of Orthopsychiatry, 47,* 40-51.

Kamii, C., & DeVries, R. (1974). Piaget for early education. In R. Parker (Ed.), *The preschool in action* (Rev. ed.), Boston: Allyn and Bacon.

Kine, O., Schlaadt, O., & Fritsch, O. (1977). *Health instruction: An action approach*, Englewood Cliffs: Prentice-Hall, Inc.

Kohlberg, L. (1975). The cognitive-developmental approach to moral education. *Phi Delta Kappan, 50,* 670-677.

Kohn, M. L. (1979). The effects of social class on parental values and practices. In D. Reiss and H. Hoffman (Eds.), *The American family: Dying or developing.* New York: Plenum Press.

Komarovsky, M. (1940). *The unemployed man and his family.* New York: Dryden Press.

Kuhn, A. L. (1947). *The mother's role in childhood education: New England concepts 1830-1860.* New Haven: Yale University Press.

Leibowitz, A. (1972). *Women's allocation of time to market and nonmarket activities: Differences by education.* Unpublished doctoral dissertation, Colombia University.

Leichter, H. (Ed.). (1975). *The family as educator.* New York: Teachers College Press.

Leichter, H. (Ed.). (1979). *Families and communities as educators.* New York: Teachers College Press.

Lightfoot, S. L. (1978). *Worlds apart relationships between families and schools.* New York: Basic Books.

Martineau, H. (1883). *Household education.* Boston: Houghton Mifflin.

McClelland, D. C. (1972). What is the effect of achievement motivation training in the schools? *Teachers College Record, 74,* 129-146.

McFarlane, C. (1982). Entrepreneurship awareness for high school students. *Education Digest, 47,* 46-48.

McGraw, O. (1978). *Family choice in education: The new imperative.* Washington, D. C.: Heritage Foundation.

Mead, M. (1975). Grandparents as educators. In H. J. Leichter (Ed.), *The family as educator.* New York: Teachers College Press.

Melred, A. (1982). Information technology for U.S. schools, *Phi Delta Kappan, 63,* 308.

Meyers, J., & Martin, R. (1974). Relationships of state and trait anxiety to concept learning performance. *Journal of Educational Psychology, 66,* 33-39.

Moen, P. (1979). Family impacts of the 1975 recession: Duration of unemployment. *Journal of Marriage and the Family, 41,* 561-572.

Moen, P. (1983). Unemployment, public policy and families: Forecasts for the 1980's. *Journal of Marriage and the Family, 45,* 751-760.

Moore, K. A., & Sawhill, I. V. (1978). Implications of women's employment for home and family life. In A. Stromberg and S. Harkness (Eds.), *Women working.* Palo Alto, CA: Mayfield Press.

Moore, R., & Moore, D. (1981). *Home-Grown Kids.* Waco, Texas: Word Books.

Moore, R., & Moore, D. (1982). *Home-Spun Schools.* Waco, Texas: Word Publishing Co.

Musgrove, F. (1966). *The family, education and society.* London: Routledge and Kegan Paul.

Naisbitt, J. (1982). *Megatrends.* New York: Warner Books.

Naisbitt, J. (1983). *A nation at risk, the imperative for educational reform.* Report of the National Commission on Excellence in Education. Washington, D.C.: U.S. Department of Education.

Palmer, B. (1984, February 2). Teaching kids at home, is it better than the public schools? *U.S.A. Today,* pp. D1-D2.

Paolucci, B., Bubolz, M., & Rainey, M. (1976). *Women, families and nonformal learning programs.* East Lansing, MI: Institute for International Studies in Education.

Phares, E. J. (1973). *Locus of control: A personality determinant of behavior.* Morristown, NJ: General Learning Corporation.

Pleck, J. H. (1979). Men's family work: Three perspectives and some new data. *The Family Coordinator, 28,* 481-488.

Postelthwait, F. N. (1983, December 2). Parents cannot hope to equal the schools. *USA Today,* p. 10A.

Rich, D., & Jones, C. (1977). *A family affair: Education.* Washington, D.C.: The Home and School Institute.

Rogers, C. R. (1963). Learning to be free. *NEA Journal, 52,* 28-30.

Rothman, D. J. (1972). *The discovery of the asylum: Social order and disorder in the New Republic.* Boston: Little, Brown.

Ryan, K., & Thompson, M. (1975). Moral education's muddled mandate: Comments on a survey of Phi Delta Kappans. *Phi Delta Kappan, 56,* 663-666.

Ryle, G. (1949). *The concept of mind.* New York: Barnes and Noble.

St. John, N. H. (1975). *School desegregation: Outcomes for children.* New York: Wiley.

Shane, H. G. (1982). The silicon age and education. *Phi Delta Kappan, 63,* 303-308.

Sievert, N. W. (1975). *Careers education and industrial education.* Boston: Houghton Mifflin Co.

Sinclair, R., & Ghory, W. (1980). Parents and teachers together: Directions for developing equality in learning through environments in families and schools. In R. Sinclair (Ed.), *A two way street home school cooperation in curriculum decision making.* Boston: Institute for Responsive Education.

Skinner, D. A. (1980). Dual-career family stress and coping: A literature review. *Family Relations, 29,* 473-481.

Stack, C. (1974). *All our kin.* New York: Harper and Row.

Stevens, A. (1966). *Techniques for handling problem parents.* Successful School Management Series. Englewood Cliffs, NJ: Prentice-Hall.

Stoch, M. B., Smythe, P. M., Moodie, A. D., & Bradshaw, D. (1982). Psychosocial Outcome and CT Findings after Gross Undernourishment during Infancy: A 20-year Developmental Study. Developmental Medicine in Child Neurology, Vol. 24, pp. 419-436.

Sturdevant, R. (1982). Micro computers and copyright in education. *Phi Delta Kappan, 63,* 316-317.

Szalai, A. (Ed.). (1972). *The use of time in daily activities of urban and suburban populations in twelve countries.* The Hague: Mouton.

Tauber, R. T. (1982). For vocational-industrial education: The Tel-a-Career-Information System. *Phi Delta Kappan, 63,* 355-356.

United States Bureau of the Census. (1980). Current Population Reports, Series P-23, No. 107. *Families maintained by female householders 1970-1979.* Washington, D. C.: U. S. Government Printing Office.

United States Bureau of the Census. (1983). *Statistical Abstract of the United States 1980-1983.* Washington, D. C.: U. S. Government Printing Office.

United States Bureau of Labor Statistics. (1979). *Handbook of Labor Statistics, 1978,* Bulletin 2000. Washington, D.C.: U.S. Government Printing Office.

United States Bureau of Labor Statistics. (1979, October 31). *Multi-earner families increase.* Press Release No. USDL 79-747.

Wallerstein, J. S., & Kelly, J. B. (1980). *Surviving the breakup: How children and parents cope with divorce.* New York: Basic Books.

Ware, W., & Garber, M. (1972). The home environment as a predictor of school achievement. *Theory into Practice, 9,* 190-195.

Weikart, D. P. (1969, March). Comparative study of three preschool curricula. Paper presented at the biennial meeting of the Society for Research in Child Development, Santa Monica, CA.

Weinberg, M. (1977). *Minority students: A research appraisal.* Washington, D. C., National Institute of Education.

Weiss, R. S. (1975). *Marital separation.* New York: Basic Books.

White, K. R. (1976). *The relationship between socioeconomic status and academic achievement.* Unpublished doctoral dissertation, University of Colorado.

Williams, D. L., & Stallman, J. T. (1982, March). A survey of educators regarding parent involvement in education: Implications for teacher training. Austin, Texas: Southwest Educational Development Laboratory.

Wise, A. (1972). *Legislated learning.* Berkeley, CA, University of California Press.

HOME ENVIRONMENT AND SCHOOL LEARNING: SOME QUANTITA-

TIVE MODELS AND RESEARCH SYNTHESIS

Herbert J. Walberg

522 North Euclid Avenue
Oak Park, Illinois 60302

One purpose of this chapter is to present some insights from the Chicago human-capital school of economics that offers justification of psychological research and educational practices focused on the stimulation of students by adults within and outside the ordinary school setting. A second purpose is to summarize and bring up to date the Walberg and Marjoribanks (1976) review "Family Environment and Cognitive Development: Twelve Analytic Models." The earlier review discusses the ability and achievement correlations with family size, socioeconomic status, ethnicity, and other various sociological-status and psychological-behavioral indicators. This chapter stresses the parallel between home and school learning environments and the need for research along with other such causally implicated variables as the quality and quantity of instruction, the social-psychological environments of the class and peer group, and student ability and motivation. The third purpose of the chapter is to summarize and discuss quantitative syntheses of studies relating abilities and educational achievement to socioeconomic status and home environment, including home-based reinforcement, home instruction, and general educational and psychological characteristics of the home.

The Amount and Value of Extramural Time

At the outset, it seems useful to relate research on home environments and learning to the general question of educational effectiveness and to speculate as to why characteristics of the home often account for a larger amount of variance in academic learning measures than do the usual school inputs. Schubert and Walberg (1982) showed that rough, though straightforward, estimates of children's annual time budgets serve as a useful quantitative framework to reveal the immense educative potential of extramural, extracurricular or nonschool activities.

Nominal or potential classroom time consumes only about half the child's potentially educative hours on school days and less than a quarter of all such hours during the year. These hours, for comparison, are equivalent in time to 27 full-time, 40-hour weeks or roughly a half-year's adult work.

Subtracting time attributable to tardiness, absense, leaving early, interruptions and inattentiveness in recent samples of high school classes leaves half this time, on the average, or 540 hours or 13 full-time weeks of intramural hours. Of course, some knowledge presented during these remaining hours the student already knows, and some the student is yet incapable of learning. Perhaps half of the time in school is suitable in difficulty and interest for the typical student. This leaves 270 hours per year or about 6.75 40-hour weeks of effective instruction, which amounts to 35 percent of the intramural hours. This is 12 percent of the potentially educative time on school days, or 6.18 percent of such time during the calendar year. With only 6 percent of the child's potentially educative hours devoted to effective instruction, it may be less than surprising that corporate and military programs can produce such relatively impressive results as teaching near native competence in Vietnamese in 1,300 hours, or about eight months of 40-hour weeks of study, whereas many American school children do not learn to read and write English to meet reasonable standards despite years of study.

It should be emphasized that these estimates are rough and that readers may wish to plug alternative numerical assumptions into the formulation. The estimates, however, give some upper bounds to the effects of curricular activities that schools presently provide and help to explain why their effects seem small, since the range from lowest to highest curricular quality or quantity, or their product, may be slight compared to the range of extracurricular or nonschool figures.

Arguments for the unrecognized value of the student's time and the need for budgeting it productively and wisely may be made on humanistic or economic grounds (Walberg, 1981a). Doubling and even re-doubling productive educational time and its efficiency may go a long way toward raising the fulfillment of human potential through education. Not only is educational productivity often required for later adult accomplishments but also for curricular and extracurricular activities that have consumatory value in their own right. An hour a day of concentrated instruction, effort, and practice may be enough to achieve a degree of comparative excellence (say, the 99th percentile in norms of unselected national samples of comparable age peers) in mathematics, foreign language, chess, ballet, many sports, or comparable pursuits. World-class performance or one's best in such endeavors may require four to ten hours a day over periods of time from one to twenty years (Walberg, 1981a). More explicit pricing and valuing of such goals and more complete factual knowledge of the means to attain them are likely to help educators, parents, and students make more informed decisions concerning time allocation among curricular, extracurricular, and nonschool educative activities.

The Chicago human-capital theory, moreover, should alert educators and psychologists to the dollar value of input of parental time for student development, as well as the immense value in real economic returns to students and society of family and school investments in human abilities (Becker, 1981; Schultz, 1981). Hill and Stafford (1974), for example, demonstrated in a 1965 national sample of about 1,000 households very large differentials in family investments in children as indexed by parental time and its economic value. Mothers of higher socioeconomic status invested 4,100 household hours on each child prior to elementary school; lower status mothers invested only 1,120; and the ratio is 3.7 to 1. Estimated average potential hourly wages in 1965 were respectively $2.08 and $1.52 for higher and lower status mothers. Multiplying wages by hours yields investments or capital embodiments in children of $8,528 and $1,702 respectively, a 5 to 1 ratio, worth $106,324 and $21,220 by 1982 at a 16 percent rate of return, and a difference of $85,104.

Since lower status families are somewhat larger, these figures may overestimate the difference because of scale economics and "public" services within the household. For example, bathing twins may take less than twice the time necessary to bathe a single child, or a story may be read to more than one child at the same time. Hill and Stafford found no evidence of these phenomena in what appears to be the largest and most carefully selected set of data on value of parental time inputs to child development.

The figures may, on the other hand, underestimate the value of investment because of the well-capitalized child's ability to profit more fully from school instruction and other experience. The "fan-spread" of the academically rich getting richer with additional years of schooling may be partly accounted for by under-investment of home inputs before and during the school years (Walberg, 1981a).

Indebtedness to economists whose subject concerns the efficient allocation of scarce resources to competing objectives is acknowledged. Their insistence on more complete and explicit accounting and equations, and desire for estimates of costs and values are most refreshing and stimulating to psychological thought about educational productivity. Newer human capital advocates have begun to show the immense value of parents' and children's time that educators may take too lightly.

Home and School Learning

The quality as well as the quantity of learning time in home and school requires consideration. Developmental and educational psychologists have, of course, increasingly specialized in the last decades, and it is unfortunate that instructional and "home developmental" psychology have grown apart and spawned separate, unconnected theories, constructs, and literatures. There is no a priori reason to think that fundamental learning processes are different in homes and schools or under parents and teachers. Indeed, the great search for complexity in human learning during the past two decades has turned up very little. Those who hypothesized that different educative environments or treatments are more or less suitable for different social classes, ethnic groups, grade levels, subject matters, institutions, and the like have little replicated evidence to show for strongly-held opinions and much empirical effort (Walberg, 1981a, 1981b; Walberg and Haertel, 1980).

A striking convergence of theoretical constructs may be seen in home and classroom research. In the last decade there have been 19 major reviews of research on teaching. When their conclusions with respect to the relations of 35 specific teaching variables to learning outcomes are placed under the first three theoretical categories attributable to Miller and Dollard (1941), they reach a substantial degree of consensus, 88 percent (Walberg, 1981a).

Systematic search and analysis of the primary research studies show that greater implementations of the Dollard-Miller categories-- Cues, Participation, and Reinforcement or Corrective Feedback--in ordinary classroom teaching brings about an approximate one standard-deviation learning advantage to treated groups and places them at the 84th percentile of control-group distributions. These large effects do not vary significantly over characteristics of the studies, namely, student characteristics, study conditions, and methodological rigor of the research. It is encouraging, therefore, that the Hess and Shipman (1965) constructs of maternal teaching behavior are remarkably similar to the Dollard-Miller constructs:

1. Informing: The mother was considered to be informing when she was lecturing or verbally imparting information about the task.

2. Motivating: These are verbal attempts by the mother to elicit the child's interest and cooperation by suggesting to the child that the task would be a rewarding experience or by promising external rewards.

3. Orienting: These are statements to develop a set in the child's mind for the task to follow. ("I'm going to show you how to put these blocks in the right place.")

4. Seeking physical feedback: This refers to verbal attempts by the mother to get the child to sort or group the blocks.

5. Seeking verbal feedback: In this case, the mother asks the child to verbally identify attributes of the blocks or to explain the sorting principles.

6. Positive reinforcement: These are confirming statements that immediately follow correct responses by the child.

7. Negative reinforcement: "No, that's wrong," and similar remarks.

8. Requiring discrimination: These are messages requiring the child to perceive and discriminate the relevant attributes of the blocks.

Although the results of experiments on maternal teaching behavior have not been quantitatively synthesized under these rubrics, the results on classroom teaching suggest that it may be fruitful to do so, if a sufficient number of studies can be found.

A number of syntheses of studies of global or undifferentiated home environment in relation to ability and achievement are summarized below, and a recent review showing large effects of home-reinforcement of school behavior (Barth, 1979) is discussed.

Twelve Analytic Models

Walberg and Marjoribanks (1976) proposed a dozen models for the investigation of the relations of home characteristics to ability and achievement. Subsequent paragraphs discussing these models are numbered correspondingly.

Model 1. Ability as Related to Family Size. The larger the number of children in the family, the lower the mean ability and achievement levels. The sign of the correlation between the two is nearly always negative. No quantitative synthesis of the voluminous research has been carried out to estimate the averge correlation and the possible dependence of the correlation on subjects' characteristics and study conditions. It appears that approximately two-thirds of the correlations are within .10 and .25.

Model 2. Ability as Related to Socioeconomic Status (SES). White (1976) collected 636 correlation coefficients of socioeconomic status (SES) and academic achievement from 100 published and unpublished studies. The mean and standard deviation are .25 and .20 respectively, and the distribution is positively skewed. The correlation declines on average from .25 in the primary grades to .15 in the last year of high school. SES correlates higher with verbal than mathematics achievement (.24 and .19) and the average achievement correlations with parent income, occupation level, and education are respectively .31, .20, and .19. Thus, contrary to great importance given to SES by sociologists, its association is surprisingly weak; and social ascendency through education may be far less constrained by social class than many have claimed.

Model 3. Changing Ability as Related to Family Size and Socioeconomic Status. British and American investigators began extensive longitudinal investigations in the 1930s and found that IQ levels were rising slightly. It was later shown that the mean IQ of draftees rose about one standard deviation between World Wars I and II, and another half standard deviation by 1963.

By the standards of a hypothetical IQ test normed early in the twentieth century, the typical young adult in the United States would now rank very high in measured verbal intelligence. Better nutrition, high quality schooling, and the immigrants' mastery of English probably contributed to this rise. In addition, the reduction of family size accompanying urbanization may have enabled parents to concentrate their energies on fewer children.

Are student academic abilities rising or falling in the present generation, and what are the relative strengths of the underlying causes? These are difficult questions and conflicting evidence abounds. One underlying cause of change in student abilities in this generation may be television viewing. The typical six intramural classroom hours on school days compare unfavorably with the average of seven hours per day in which television is viewed in American households. In a quantitative assessment of published and unpublished evidence through 1980, a steady average decline in school achievement is associated with viewing time of between 10 and 40 hours per week (Williams, Haertel, Haertel, and Walberg, 1981).

Model 4. Increasing Variation in Ability as Related to Family Size and Socioeconomic Status. Two Minnesota and Michigan studies showed bimodal (double-packed) fertility rates across the range of IQ levels. In the larger study of 1,966 individuals (Higgins, Reed, and Reed, 1962), the group with IQ's from 56 to 85 had reproductive rates of 2.42; the group from 86 to 115, 2.21; the group above 116, 2.60. Bajema (1966) found bimodal fertility with respect to the number of years of school completed. Although bimodality of these fertility rates is not sufficient to produce bimodal IQ distributions in the offspring generation, it is likely to increase the standard deviation (SD); that is, to spread the scores farther from the mean, and to make the distribution platykurtic, or flatter than the normal curve. Assortative mating, the tendency for like to mate with like, also increases these tendencies. For example, B. L. Warren (1966) found the correlations of spouses' years of education to be about .60, and the correlation of their socioeconomic statuses (as indexed by father's occupation) to be about .30. Since both these variables are correlated with IQ, assortative mating could also be increasing IQ variation from parent to offspring generations.

An analysis (Walberg, 1974) of data from an American study that reports IQ SD's for parents and their offspring (Higgins, et al., 1962) reveals a significant (p .05) increase from 14.89 to 15.71. Unfortunately, the study started with a special population, children and grandchildren of psychiatric patients. In longitudinal research in Britain, the Scottish Council for Research in Education and Population Investigation Committee (1949) found a significant increase, from 15.48 to 16.10, in the SD of IQ from 1932 to 1947 in a nearly complete sample of population cohorts in Scotland. Emmett (1950) found a slightly higher increase, from 14.21 to 15.00, in a large sample of English districts during the same period.

It is well established in genetic theory and research that assortative mating and bimodal fertility produce greater variation in offspring. Since these mechanisms operate with respect to IQ, years of education, and social class, and since studies of changes in verbal IQ reveal increasing standard deviation, it appears that IQ variation may be increasing, and educators may be confronted with groups of students who have more diverse abilities.

Model 5. Ability as Related to Interaction Between Family Size and Socioeconomic Status. Anastasi (1956) found evidence that the correlation of sibsize and ability is higher in samples of lower SES children than the correlations of these variables for middle and higher SES samples. Although such correlations may be compared, multiple regression analysis indicates the relation of each independent variable to a dependent variable in the context of the other independent variables. For example, the weights of SES, sibsize, and their interaction may be assessed simultaneously.

Other theory and regression analyses support Anastasi's evidence that SES and sibsize interact and, furthermore, show that the inverse of sibsize may provide a better prediction of ability than the simple linear form. Marjoribanks, Walberg, and Bargen (1975) reasoned that, since children share adult resources of intellectual stimulation in the family, the mathematical relationship between sibsize and parental stimulation is not linear but is of a hyperbolic form involving the term, "one divided by the number of children in the family." That is, the amount of parental attention received decreases as the number of children in the family increases, in such a way with each additional child the successive decrements in shared attention become smaller. Therefore, the expected percentages of parental attention given children in one-, two-, three-, four-, and five-child families would be 100, 50, 33, 25, and 20 respectively. Thus, a single child in a family may score higher on mental ability tests because he receives all the available parental stimulation, whereas a child with four siblings may have lower scores because he receives an estimated one-fifth of the available stimulation. Moreover, first borns may tend to be brighter, either because some of them are single children and receive all the available parental attention, or because they receive

100 percent of the parental stimulation until the second child is born, whereas later born children usually have to share the parental attention. The apparent impairment effect of sibsize, however, is conditioned strongly by father's occupation. In an Ontario sample of 185 11-year-old boys, there was no effect of sibsize on ability in professional-managerial homes, but there was an estimated difference of 40 IQ points between single borns and those from six-child families with fathers in unskilled occupations (Marjoribanks, Walberg, and Bargen, 1975).

What may be important in this latter work is the analytic method rather than the findings. A similar analysis of the ability scores of several hundred thousand Dutch males born during World War II failed to support the inverse sibsize relation, but clearly revealed a negative hyperbolic relation of sibsize and ability and an interaction of sibsize and SES (Walberg and Marjoribanks, 1976). A related program of research concerns the "Confluence Model" (Zajonc and Markus, 1976) that represents that a weighted combination of mental ages of the family members indexes the intellectual stimulation of the child. The majority of a dozen studies, however, have failed to support the model. Analysis of other data may show that the form of the functional relations of ability to sibsize varies across SES, time, and nationality.

Model 6. Global Ability as Related to Family Environment. Although socioeconomic status is a convenient construct to measure, it does not yield a comprehensive assessment of the factors in the home that foster ability. Proximate, detailed assessments provide for better predictions of children's ability. For example, an early study of English homes showed that the quality of maternal discipline, even though statistically controlled for SES, predicts ability. Children in intellectually demanding homes where rewards depend on achievement tend to score higher than others on ability tests (Kent and Davis, 1957).

Dave (1963) and Wolf (1964) in Chicago, and Marjoribanks (1972) in Southern Ontario, Canada, have shown that significant variance in verbal ability can be accounted for by sociopsychological assessments of the family environment. From semi-structured interviews with parents, these investigators have rated such factors as parental encouragement of achievement, language, intellectuality, and independence. In the Marjoribanks (1972) study, eight family environment variables were measured: achievement, activeness, intellectuality, independence, English language, second language, and mother and father dominance.

Model 7. Specific Abilities as Related to Family Environment. A canonical analysis of the Canadian data (Walberg and Marjoribanks, 1973) showed that the different patterns of stimulation in the family are related to the differential development of specific abilities. Although the first canonical variate revealed a strong link between general parental stimulation and global ability the second variate showed that the level of father's occupation and parental encouragement of activeness and language are related to higher verbal and reasoning scores but lower number scores. The analysis implies that differential environmental processes may operate selectively to develop certain potential abilities and to leave others relatively undeveloped. Additional research may reveal ways in which parents can develop more specific cognitive abilities in their children.

From a systematic search of educational, psychological, and sociological literature, Iverson and Walberg (1981) summarized 18 studies of 5,831 school-aged students on the correlation of home environment and learning in eight countries over a 19-year period. Correlations (the units of analysis) of intelligence, motivation, and achievement with indices of parental stimulation in the home are considerably higher than those with indices of SES; specifically the medians (and ranges) of 92 simple correlations of home environment and learning are .37 (and .02 to .82) and 62 multiple-regression-weighted composites are .44 (and .23 to .81). Jackknifed regression estimates indicate magnitudes of the correlations do not depend on gender, SES, age, nationality, or learning outcome but that studies using multiple correlations and taking gender and SES into account yield significantly higher correlations.

Model 8. Ability as Related to Ethnicity. Factor analysis (Marjoribanks, 1972) of the eight family environment variables suggests that a more parsimonious description of the family environment might be made by using a few weighted sums of the variables. However, Marjoribanks (1972) showed that different socioeconomic and ethnic groups (Jewish, Southern Italian, Canadian Indian, White Anglo-Saxon Protestant, and French Canadian) are characterized by different patterns of the environment variables, and that the eight variables lead to a richer understanding of group environmental differences. Marjoribanks also showed the extent to which the family environment accounts for ethnic group differences in the cognitive abilities. For spatial ability, all of the group differences were accounted for by the environment, whereas the measures accounted for large proportions of the ethnic group differences in verbal, number, and reasoning ability scores.

Model 9. Ability as Related to Various Sociological-status and Psychological-behavioral Indicators. Investigations of the relationship between sibling variables and cognitive abilities have usually revealed that family size, crowding ratio of the family, and, to a lesser extent, birth order are negatively related to cognitive ability (Walberg and Marjoribanks, 1976). However, when the family environment has been used as an explanatory variable in sibling studies, it has been defined in terms of gross classificatory variables such as socioeconomic status. As a result, research has provided only a general and sometimes contradictory picture of the interrelationships between sibling variables, socioeconomic characteristics, and those social psychological elements of the family that are associated with cognitive performance.

Marjoribanks and Walberg (1975) used multiple regression to examine the relationships of the family environment to father's occupation, father's education, mother's education, sibsize, the inverse of sibsize, crowding ratio of the family, and birth order. The environment was defined in terms of the eight variables discussed earlier. The findings indicated that the most parsimonious account of the variance in the environment scores is obtained by using father's occupation and either of the sibsize variables. Equations using the two terms account for about as much significant variance in the environment scores as equations containing all the measured variables, their quadratic forms (to test for nonlinearity), and their products (to test for interaction). The other sibling variables and socioeconomic status indicators provide no significantly better prediction of the sociopsychological environment of the family beyond that afforded by the two-term equations.

Walberg and Marjoribanks (1976) discuss other relations of background variables and home environment stimulations; and Laosa (1981) presents additional data on the SES-stimulation association. The complexity of the relations uncovered thus far leaves room for division of research labor among anthropologists interested in ethnicity, sociologists interested in SES and family configurations, and social and educational psychologists interested in fundamental learning processes that transcend culture, class, setting, and other variables. The social psychological approach should have the greatest appeal to educators, however, because the variables employed are potentially more alterable, have a consistent, replicable and more substantial correlation with learning, and a more plausible causal basis.

Model 10.   Ability as Related to Previous Ability, Socioeconomic Status, and Family Size. Most of the research on the relationships of the family environment to ability has been restricted by designs that are cross-sectional. Only a small number of studies have employed longitudinal designs and have included measures of prior ability in the research. Walberg and Marjoribanks (1974) used both cross-sectional and longitudinal data that were collected in 1964 and 1968 in an extensive survey of schoolchildren in England (Plowden, 1967) and employed multiple regression models to examine the relationships of socioeconomic status (father's occupation, family income, father's education) and sibling variables (sibsize, birth order) to reading achievement scores (Model 10). Two-term equations containing the 1964 reading scores and father's occupation accounted for as much significant variance in the 1968 achievement scores as complex many-term equations containing all the measured variables, their quadratic forms (to test for nonlinearity), and their products (to test for interactions). The inverse of sibsize explained no additional variance after taking into account prior reading scores and father's occupation. In a series of multivariate studies of physics test scores and intervening classroom environments in the United States and Canada, Walberg (1972) found that about 75 percent (80 percent corrected for criterion errors of measurement) of the post-test variance could be explained by the initial test scores and the learning environment measures.

Model 11. Ability as Related to Previous Ability, and Family, Peer Group, and Classroom Environments. In one of the most comprehensive studies that illustrate Model 11, Keeves (1972) obtained measures of academic achievement from tests given one year apart to 12-year-old children in the Australian Capital Territory, as well as assessments of intervening family, peer group, and classroom environments. The pretest and environmental measures accounted for approximately 74 percent of the post-test achievement in mathematics and for 66 percent in science. The Keeves analysis may have explained less variance than the Walberg study, despite the additional measures of family and peer environments, because of less reliable measures of the environment and achievement variables.

The study by Keeves is one of the first educational studies to use path analysis in research analyzing environmental correlates of cognitive performance. Path analysis is a technique for hypothesizing a network of causal relationships among a set of variables. That is, the analysis proposes for testing that family socioeconomic status and the number of children in the family are superfluous explanatory variables when the comprehensive measures of the family environment are taken into account.

Once a network is constructed, it may be tested using regression analysis. Causality may be inferred from regression under several assumptions:

1. All variables that might affect the dependent variable are either included in the regression equation or are uncorrelated with the variables that are included.

2. Terms are included in the regression equation to handle any curvilinear or interaction effects.

3. The dependent variable has no effect on the independent variable.

These assumptions are rarely met completely, but regression can be useful in experimentally uncontrolled research. Violations of the first assumption mean that a partial and possibly misleading picture of causal relationships is drawn. However, the path-guided regression analysis may provoke research that includes other hypothesized variables in subsequent equations (see below), or that they add no further explanation of the variance, and are thus unparsimonious or are mediated by (share common variance with) independent variables already in the model. The second assumption may be met by including products of the independent variables to account for interactions, and squares or other mathematical forms of the variables to account for curvilinearity. The third assumption requires judgment. Relevant prior events may often be presumed to cause subsequent events rather than vice versa, and common sense can be helpful in provisionally denying reversed causality. It may also be shown that hypothesized variables are not correlated with the independent variables.

A fourth assumption of causal regressions, only now becoming fully appreciated, is that the dependent and independent variables are measured without error. This assumption is highly questionable in educational research. Causal relations may appear weak, not because they are weak, but because both causes and effects are measured unreliably.

Model 12. Ability as Related to the Interaction between Previous Ability and Family Environment. An attempt was made by Walberg and Marjoribanks (1974) to exploit the Plowden (1967) survey of English schoolchildren and the follow-up study (described above). In both surveys, a structured interview schedule had been used to gather information about the family environment and the socioeconomic status of the children in the sample. From the home interviews, indices where constructed that assessed the literacy of the home, parental aspirations for the child, and parental interest in education. A single measure of the intervening family environment was constructed by taking the means of the two assessments of each of the environmental indices. Then a single environment score was developed from an equally weighted composite of the three means. Similarly, an index of family socioeconomic status was obtained by calculating the means of the 1964 and 1968 measures of father's occupation, father's education, and family income, and then computing an equally weighted composite of the three means. The intervening sibsize influence was assessed in the same manner.

The longitudinal analysis showed that large amounts of variance in final reading achievement scores are accounted for by the initial reading scores and the intervening family environment: the major portion of the variance is explained by prior achievement, but the additional variance associated with environment is significant in all cases. In three samples, the product of initial reading and intervening environment adds significantly to the equations, and in four samples, the quadratic form of the initial reading makes a significant contribution. The other products and quadratics were not significant in more than one sample.

The increments in variance associated with the inverse of sibsize and family socioeconomic status are comparatively very small and are significant in only two samples. These very small increments are the apparent direct effects of these variables on final reading achievement that are unmediated by the family environment. The results of this study also suggest that adolescents may benefit as much as younger children from a stimulating family environment.

Intervention Research

Since Burks (1928), reviewers have gravely warned against inferring causality from correlational studies of families and learning and urged that interventions and longitudinal studies are needed. Actually, there is a sizeable number.

Barth (1979) found 24 studies of home-based reinforcement of school motivation, behavior, and learning. His review begins with the sentence: "It has been demonstrated frequently and incontrovertably that classroom behavior can be controlled by teachers who are trained in the use of differential reinforcement and token economies" (p. 436). He might have ended with a statement that the same apparently applies to parents. The studies are rigorously experimental in the Skinnerian tradition. Start-up periods of daily or weekly teacher notes or checklists on classroom behavior and no reinforcements are followed by a period of consumable reinforcers, earned privileges, verbal praise, or response costs geared to the same indicators of classroom performance. Reinforcement is phased in and out; and behavior consistently appears to be controlled. Such programs are impressive in their impacts in normal as well as deliquent children and have remedied a wide variety of problem behaviors and academic deficiencies at small costs to teachers, counselors, and parents.

A quantitative synthesis of studies of other home-intervention programs is now being conducted. These programs are less precisely defined than home-based reinforcement programs, but generally include attempts to include cues, engagement, and corrective feedback in addition to reinforcement. The parent serves a broader role of co-teaching or supplemental instruction rather than only executing the degree of reinforcement to the degree called for on reports by the school teacher. Of the 17 programs located, 16 claim positive results and provide quantitative data on cognitive test scores and other variables. Although sample selectivity and differential drop out rates weaken and possibly vitiate the results of some of the studies, treatment randomization in some studies and covariance and gain scores in quasi-experimentation in others help discount the threats to methodological validity. Although specific assessments are being made for each of several dozen validity threats and of the generality of results across subject categories, conditions, and outcomes, it appears nearly certain that the results are robust. Because of the convergence of research on time, school-teaching effects, home environment, home reinforcement and home-coordinate teaching, there seems little doubt that parents exert a consistent causal influence on academic and other learning that might be greatly expanded if lengthened and made more systematic.

Conclusion

The Nobel-prize-winning Theodore W. Schultz's *Investing in People* shows the large economic returns on society's investment in formal education that has not diminished despite a five-fold rise in hourly earnings since 1900 and a 13-fold increase to $85 billion in the aggregate stock of education embodied in the U.S. labor force. It seems clear, from evidence presented here, that the learning returns on parental investments are also large, but also greatly expandable.

REFERENCES

Anastasi, A. (1956). Intelligence and family size. *Psychological Bulletin, 53,* 187-209.

Bajema, C. J. (1963). Estimation of the direction and intesity of natural selection in relation to human intelligence by means of the intrinsic rate of natural increase. *Eugenics Quarterly, 10,* 175-187.

Bajema, C. J. (1966). Relation of fertility to educational attainment in a Kalamazoo public school population: A follow-up study. *Eugenics Quarterly, 13,* 306-315.

Barth, R. (1979). Home-based reinforcement of school behavior. *Review of Educational Research, 49,* 436-458.

Becker, G. S. (1981). Altruism in the family and selfishness in the workplace. *Economica, 48,* 1-15.

Burks, B. (1928). The relative influence of nature and nurture. In G. M. Whipple (Ed.)., *27th Yearbook of the National Society for the Study of Education.* Bloomington, Illinois: Norton and Norton.

Dave, R. (1963). *The identification and measurement of home environmental process variables related to educational achievement.* Unpublished doctoral dissertation, University of Chicago.

Emmett, W. G. (1950). The trend of intelligence in certain districts in England. *Population Studies, 3,* 324-337.

Hess, R. D., & Shipman, V. C. (1965). Early experience and the socialization of cognitive modes in children. *Child Development, 36,* 869-886.

Hill, R. C., & Stafford, F. (1974). The allocation of time to preschool children. *Journal of Human Resources, 9,* 323-341.

Higgins, J. V., Reed, E. W., & Reed, S. C. (1962). Intelligence and family size: A paradox resolved. *Eugenics Quarterly, 9,* 84-90.

Iverson, B. K., & Walberg, H. J. (1981). Home environment and learning: A quantitative synthesis. *Journal of Experimental Educational, 26,* 33-42.

Keeves, J. P. (1972). *Educational environment and student achievement.* Stockholm: Almquist & Wicksell.

Kent, N., & Davis, D. R. (1957). Discipline in the home and intellectual development. *British Journal of Medical Psychology, 30,* 27-33.

Laosa, L. M. (1981). Maternal behavior: Sociocultural diversity in modes of family interaction. In R. W. Henderson (Ed.)., *Parent-Child Interaction*. New York: Academic Press.

Marjoribanks, K. (1972). Ethnic and environmental influences on mental abilities. *American Journal of Sociology, 78*, 323-337.

Marjoribanks, K., & Walberg, H. J. (1975). Family environment: Sibling constellation and social class correlates. *Journal of Biosocial Science, 7*, 15-25.

Marjoribanks, K., Walberg, H. J., & Bargen, M. (1975). Mental abilities: Sibling constellation and social class correlates. *British Journal of Social a Clinical Psychology, 14*, 109-116.

McLaughlin, B. (1977). Second-language acquisition in children. *Psychological Bulletin, 84*, 435-457.

Miller, N. E., & Dollard, J. (1941). *Social Learning and Imitation*. New Haven, Connencticut: Yale University Press.

Plowden, B. (1967). *Children and Their Primary Schools*. London: H. M. Stationery Office.

Schubert, W. H., & Walberg, H. J. (1982). Discussion of extracurricular activities. In H. J. Walberg (Ed.)., *Improving Educational Standards and Productivity: The Research Basis for Policy*. Berkeley, California: McCutchan.

Schultz, T. W. (1981). *Investing in People*. Berkeley, California: University of California Press.

Scottish Council for Research on Education and Population Investigation Committee. (1949). *The trend of Scottish intelligence*. London: University of London Press.

Walberg, H. J. (1972). Social environment and individual learning: A test of the Bloom model. *Journal of Educational Psychology, 63*, 69-73.

Walberg, H. J. (1974). Optimization reconsidered. In H. J. Walberg (Ed.)., (1974) *Evaluating educational performance: A sourcebook of methods, instruments and examples*. Berkeley, California: McCutchan.

Walberg, H. J., & Marjoribanks, K. (1973). Differential mental abilities and home environment: A canonical analysis. *Develomental Psychology, 9*, 363-368.

Walberg, H. J., & Marjoribanks, (1974). Social environment and cognitive development: Toward a generalized causal analysis. In K. Marjoribansk (Ed.)., *Environments for learning*. London: National Foundation of Educational Research Publications, 259-273.

Walberg, H. J., & Marjoribanks, K. (1976). "Family Environment and Cognitive Development: Twelve analytic models." *Review of Educational Research, 46*, 527-551.

Walberg, II. J., & Haertel, E. H. (1980). Guest Editors, *Rosoaroh Integration Evaluation in Education, 4*, 3-143.

Walberg, H. J. (1981a). A psychological theory of educational productivity. In F. H. Farley & N. Gordon (Eds.)., *Psychology and Education*. Berkeley, California: McCutchan.

Walberg, H. J. (1981b). What makes schooling effective. Washington, D. C. A paper presented at the National Institute of Education Conference on Public and Private Schools.

Warren, B. L. (1966). A multiple variable approach to the assortative mating problem. *Eugenics Quarterly, 13,* 285-290.

White, K. R. (1976). *The relationship between socioeconomic status and academic achievement.* Unpublished dissertation, University

William, P., Haertel, E. H., Haertel, G. D., & Walberg, H. J. (1982). "Television Influence on School Learning: A Quantitative Synthesis," *American Educational Research Journal, V. 19,* 19-50.

Wolf, R. M. (1964). *The identification and measurement of home environmental process variables that are related to intelligence.* Unpublished doctoral dissertation, University of Chicago.

Zajonc, R., & Markus, G. B. (1976). Birth order and intellectual development. *Psychological Review, 82,* 74-88.

MINORITY FAMILY AGENDAS: THE HOME-SCHOOL INTERFACE

AND ALTERNATIVE SCHOOLING MODELS

Lillian Phenice, Estella Martinez and Gale Grant

Michigan State University
East Lansing, Michigan 48823

Educational policies in the United States are moving from a more paternalistic compensatory attitude of earlier years toward a healthier notion of cultural democracy. This latter philosophy supports and emphasizes the concept that the home, community, and school share in the socialization experiences of all children, regardless of their cultural background, and are valuable in their own right. With this movement has emerged a new educational theme, the "new pluralism" or "new ethnicity", which is bringing about curricular reforms in the public schools. This "new ethnicity" has brought about multicultural activities and ethnic heritage programs; however, the future effect of these programs on the school remains uncertain. Whether intense and aggressive assertions of ethnic cultural autonomy and self-determination of ethnic minorities can be absorbed into the present system of public education is difficult to assess at this time (Olneck & Lazerson, 1980). With this awakening and recognition of educational policies that emphasize cultural democracy, a new national consciousness could emerge embodying principles of respect and appreciation of all people who compose the rich ethnic mosaic in the United States.

However, the emergence of this new consciousness is burdened by complex historical happenings and attitudes that have shaped some of the existing educational policies. The cultural exclusionist philosophy (Weinberg, 1977a) has affected our national educational policies for the past century, and these policies have had a determining impact on three very important areas of education that have affected all children. These are: 1) what children ought to learn or experience, 2) how they ought to learn, and 3) how the teachers should participate in the learning processes (Olneck & Lazerson, 1980). Cultural exclusionism in education has resulted in the exclusions of the contributions of minority ethnic groups such as the Black Americans, Native Americans, Mexican-Americans and Asian-Americans from the curriculum of the schools. For the purpose of this chapter an ethnic group consists of those who share a unique social and cultural heritage that is passed on from generation to generation. Status refers to minority groups that have unequal access to power, that are considered in some way unworthy of sharing power equally, and are stigmatized in terms of assumed inferior traits or characteristics (Mindel & Habenstein, 1981).

Cultural exclusionism in education has often led to conditions in which ethnic minorities are completely overlooked or seriously mis-represented when included into children's learning. Most seriously overlooked is the fact of differing cultural styles and priorities in values. For example, many ethnic minority cultures place much higher values on beliefs and behaviors that differ from the competition emphasized by the formal educational system. For the minority child the education system operates by rules much different from those learned at home or in the community, or those strongly emphasized by the cultural milieu of the family. In this atmosphere, learning the nature of competitiveness of other groups, their expectations, and the means to achieve these expectations are not always clear to the child. The child is, therefore, forced to use the competitive skills of his/her own ethnic group. Unfortunately, many of these children find that what skills they possess have little applicability in the larger system--in this case, the educational institution (Blanchard, 1983).

Typically, minority children have been placed in contra-culture learning experiences that exuded with such messages as, "your parent's ways of behaving are not good, and if you want to achieve success you must become like the dominant group." Home and real life experiences of minority children were found to be harmful unless they were like the dominant culture group. For the child, membership in an ethnic minority group was considered to be a depriving experience. These conflicting interpretations of the relationship of ethnicity to education raised complex issues. History of the interface between the minority child's home and the school itself tells the story of the conflict. The emphasis in the home was to shape character according to one's ethnic values and beliefs. The responsibility of the school was to promote collective and individual material progress in order to attain national unity through cultural homogeneity. The mosaic of diversities of ethnic groups and their cultural values and beliefs were to be abandoned and discarded for the American way of life which promised to lead towards upward social mobility and a quality of life.

There was a national idea of the superior way of doing and thinking. These ideas were found entrenched in the textbooks and in the formal education system. Values and characteristics that were assumed inferior were stereotypically portrayed with negative overtones and unsavory traits. According to Olneck and Lazerson (1980), the assumption made was that there was an American identity to which all could or should aspire. Newcomers were expected to abandon practices and traits associated with their groups in the old world. At the same time, there was hesitation as to whether all ethnic groups could fully become "American," for some groups were viewed as being better Americans. Old ideas of superior and inferior people expanded into full blown racist theories in the 19th Century. This Americanization movement tried to submerge the complex relationship between ethnic background and national identity.

The Americanization of the children became a standard mode of practice in the schools. Celebration of national holidays, the salute to the American flag, the one-time removal of foreign languages from the curriculum are a few concrete examples existing today of a national ritualization symbolizing the process of Americanization. The use of U.S. history to establish a link to the past with what is happening in government structures today is another example of rationalizing the existence of an educational dinosaur, cultural exclusionism. Children are being taught a very restricted history of the American people, for recognition is given primarily to historical figures and events which embody the traits and qualities held in esteem by the majority group (Rodriguez, 1983).

Ethnic Minority Responses

Although most educators sought to promote cultural homogeneity and the assimilationist model of American society, a few more moderate spokespersons spoke about the contributions and strengths of the various ethnic minority groups. Along with earlier spurious movements toward acceptance of cultural pluralism as the basis from which to form the basis to build a nation, other political happenings allowed for increasing state involvement in the education of the nation's young people. With the decentralization of the structure and functioning of schools came conflict as the schools received local ethnic and political pressures. Ethnic minority groups that were strong enough could now have some force in the decision making processes of the schools and some of the special needs of the group could now be heard. Groups that were strong and cohesive became dissatisfied and shunned the public schools altogether and established their own alternative schools. Others began to pressure public schools to preserve and to direct its efforts in recognizing the cultural heritage of the various ethnic groups. Most ethnic minorities fell into this category by identifying and supporting the public institutions, in opposition to educational programs that denigrated their group. These minorities insisted that educational achievements should not force the individual to reject his/her familial and group values. Ethnic resistance to denigration and the rights of children to remain identified to their own home and community socialization processes were advocated by educators such as Ramirez and Castenada (1974). These educators suggested that the lack of educational success of minority children is not a result of belonging to certain minority groups nor a result of presumed deficient values learned from parents. They also observed that the problem resided in the prevailing American educational philosophy which denied the right of minority children to be educated in a manner consistent with their own cultural values and beliefs.

Examples of ethnic resistance to denigration were protests against biased textbooks. Many groups forced revisions in materials that denigrated their ethnic status as groups. Blacks pressured school systems to reject textbooks that portrayed them in any negative stereotypical roles. Jews opposed anti-Catholic and anti-Semitic books and teaching materials. More cohesive groups attempted to incorporate their own traditions and languages into the school curriculum. As ethnic minorities, they had to cope with the inferior settings of lower class communities with limited resources to work with. Education for Japanese-American and Chinese-Americans depended on the ebb and flow of discrimination, economic conditions, and international relations with their national country of origin. Mexican-Americans and other Hispanics found themselves legally white but not necessarily "Anglo" and were sometimes segregated on racial grounds depending upon the darkness or lightness of their skin or recognizable surname. Black Americans resorted to improve their opportunities by turning to their own families and communities for strength and support. They also found it necessary to establish elementary schools, training programs and black colleges to enhance their children's opportunities through education (Weinberg, 1977a). American Indians suffered greatly at the hands of the majority and their imposition of the white man's educational agenda. However, despite these impediments all ethnic minority groups have drawn upon their own sources of strengths and limited resources to shape the educational system in which they found themselves and more recently have begun to shape and determine educational policies that affect their children.

The Ethnic Minority and the Legacy of History

American Indians. For the North American Indians, the heritage of the interface between home and school was stained with oppressive degradation of the worst kind. Prior to the 1800's several Indian tribes started their own school system completely financing and managing their own system. For example, the Cherokee tribe developed an extensive school system that taught both English and Cherokee using the alphabet developed by the famed Sequoyah. By the mid 1800's the rate of literacy was estimated to be 90 percent, demonstrating the success of this system of education. Other tribes such as the Creeks, Chickasaws, and Seminoles also maintained school systems. Unfortunately, by the end of the 19th century these schools were closed by Federal order (Shaeffer, 1979).

During the final decades of the 19th century, new educational policies were adopted to alienate the Indians from tribal and group loyalties and to promote assimilation. Tribally run schools were undermined and government sponsored schools, especially boarding schools, were instituted. The Indian child, it was argued, needed to be removed not only from the family but from the reservation as well. To accomplish this, the off-reservation boarding schools were created (Jackson & Galli, 1977). This idea of teaching North American Indians in boarding schools away from reservations was pioneered by Richard Pratt in 1878. Pratt, an army officer, was authorized by the Bureau of Indian Affairs (BIA) to convert an abandoned army barracks at Carlisle, Pennsylvania, into a boarding school for Indians. The Carlisle School was based on the Anglo conformity ideology that the Indian's heritage was not good enough for the American society and had to be replaced by skills and attitudes of the larger society. The best way to do this was to permanently remove the Indian children from their tribal surroundings (Hertzberg, 1971). This model then became the expanded effort of the BIA and represented the most intense effort to employ schooling as a device to transform North American Indian children into so-called model citizens of the United States. North American Indian children in government schools were not permitted to wear long hair, to dress in their tribal costumes, to engage in tribal rituals, or even to speak their native languages (Hertzberg, 1971). Any signs of loyalty to one's ethnic heritage, be it dress, language, or traditions, were viewed as evil and primitive. With military like discipline and corporal punishment the schools promoted resistence and compounded the already existing problems of poorly educated teachers, poor facilities, geographic isolation, and poor living conditions. Government policy for Indians before the 1920's was, thus, explicitly directed at detribalization.

Later as a result of data obtained from the 1920 Bureau of Census and 1928 Brookings Institution findings of not succeeding to Americanize Indians, along with strong advocacy of special interest groups, Federal policy began to shift to stress the strengthening of tribal social structure and culture as a more effective means of promoting assimilation. Even with the cutbacks of funds to promote educational quality in the 1950's, legislation strengthening of tribal structures improved the situation for the North American Indian substantially (A. Josephy, 1971).

As of 1980, American Indians and Alaskan Natives had a population of approximately one million living in all states, but they were most heavily concentrated in the states of Oklahoma, Arizona, California, New Mexico, Alaska, and North Carolina. American Indians, like other minority groups, are becoming urban dwellers. There are approximately 493 recognized Indian tribal groups in the United States with approximately 250 different Indian languages spoken (USDHEW, 1971). This diversity within the population itself creates stresses on the interface between the home and the school.

According to Evelyn Blanchard (1983), Indian children's facility in the English language is among the poorest of any group in the United States, for they consistently score among the bottom of reading measurements. The low financial status and poverty levels of many American Indian families often make it impossible to buy books and educational materials for children. These reading materials are not necessarily stimulating to the Indian children nor to their parents for they are written in English with middle-class themes. Also parents themselves may not speak or understand English any better than the child in order to help read the stories to the child and share in the experience. It is no wonder then that during the mid 1970's, 35 percent of Native American school age children discontinued their participation in schools. We must realize, however, that this is an improvement over the 42 percent rate of the late 1960's (USDHEW, 1975).

Another serious problem that has beset the interface between the Indian home and school is the more recent astonishing and disturbing practice of removing children from their homes and families. A 1976 survey conducted by the Association on American Indian Affairs found that within the American Indian population of approximately one million, there were 47,249 children under the age of 18 not living with their families (AAIA, 1979). These children were in boarding schools, foster and adoptive placements, many of them in non-Indian and non-Native settings. In earlier years there was no concern with the age of the child before considering removal from the family, but today it is believed to be inappropriate to place elementary school children in boarding institutions. Parents as well as the tribe were deliberately denied a voice in the educational programs of their children. The impact on the family and the tribe was considerable. Generations of Indian children were denied the education required to survive in their world of culture and conflict. Most were unable to invest themselves in their new experiences, and the resultant handicaps from these experiences are blamed for the disruptions of Indian family life today (Blanchard, 1983). Also, historical denial of a voice in their children's education has created an atmosphere of distrust and poor communication between American Indian parents and school officials for generations. The reluctance of North American Indian parents to attend school functions and parent-teacher conferences represents an implicit message of mistrust and suspicion of the educational system.

A leading Indian educator, Patricia Locke, president of the National Indian Education Association, has proposed that the values inherent in Western education are an assault on Indian children. Indian children must learn the activities necessary to survive in their world; however these should be taught as skills rather than imposed as values. This allows children to make their choices with Indian values as its basis for exercise (cited in Blanchard, 1983). It also allows Indian children to be highly sensitive to balance and imbalance which is a part of the heritage of Indian culture.

Although many aspects of American Indian education have improved according to Josephy (1971), they are not qualitatively measurable. But how does one measure excellence? And excellence for what? Today some children never enter school, while others drop out. According to the Commission on Civil Rights (1973), American Indian children often find their educational experience hostile and they have no choice but to leave. They feel set apart from the school due to socialization of different priorities in values and behaviors that run contrary to the public schools. American Indian parents, for example, usually socialize their children to be independent and hesitant to embarass their peers, while teachers reward docile acceptance and expect school children to correct one another in the classroom.

Separation of the home from the school may also be reinforced by teachers who do not wish to have parents interfering with their job. Parents often maintain distance from the classroom as well, which further isolates the school from the home. This lack of interaction between the home and the school creates difficulty in addressing the issues faced by the Indian child. Some of the problems that beset this interface between the home and the school are:

1. Underenrollment.
2. Need to adjust to a school with values sometimes dramatically different from those of the home.
3. Need to make curriculum more relevant.
4. Special difficulties faced by children in boarding schools.
5. Unique hardships encountered by reservation born children who later live and attend schools in large cities.
6. Language barrier faced by the many Indian children who have little or no knowledge of English.

(Bureau of Indian Affairs, 1975)

These situations have led to a lack of educational innovations and a failure to provide special concerns targeted to the needs of the American Indian child. According to Josephy (1971), some improvements are being made in some of these areas where programs on Indian children are those developed by Indians themselves.

Asian Americans and Pacific Islanders. During the late 1800's, racial discrimination kept Chinese and Japanese children out of the San Francisco's public schools to protect California's white children from the invasion of Mongolian barbarians. The educational policies of the exclusionists followed by those of the segregationists that were directed at the Asian population had a long term effect on the adaptation of these groups to the public school systems of this country.

The Chinese came to the United States during the days of the 1849 gold rush. Expelled from various trades and occupations as well as many residential areas, the Chinese had little choice but to congregate in Chinatowns and rely on the protective ethnic associations for assistance. A tradition of separate associations formed. Housing codes kept them in the ghetto, and they found themselves segregated both socially and spatially. The traditional associations and the family clan offered them familiarity and the protections they needed. In order to protect and preserve their culture, Chinese temples and schools were built and old world festivals were held with traditional practices.

The Japanese, Koreans, and the Philippinos came to the West Coast at least a generation later. Many came as sojourners to a land of opportunity where they had hoped to seek their fortune and then return home (McLemore, 1980). Consequently, they were willing to work for lower wages than members of other groups and to work longer hours.

Bonacich (1972) argues that, therefore, it was not totally unnatural that Asian-Americans met with discrimination and negative attitudes of a sojourner who is only here temporarily to get as much as one could from the host country and leave. This created an atmosphere of mistrust of the Asian foreigner followed by discrimination.

As discriminations were directed at the Asian population, the position of the Chinese and Japanese association-run language schools was strengthened. These schools were often associated with religious teachings and traditional values and culture. Initially these language schools were highly effective. At the turn of the 20th century, however, the Chinese as well as the Japanese were becoming more involved in the public school system of this country.

The merging of Asian children into the public schools encountered many obstacles. There were many conflicts between the public school authorities and Asian parents due to the segregationist stand. The most important stand by the Asian community was during 1905 and 1907 when the Japanese families resisted a San Francisco school board requirement that Asian children attend segregated schools. In May of 1905, the San Francisco school board called for separate schools for Japanese children. By the following Fall with the build up of anti-Japanese sentiments, all Chinese, Japanese, and Korean children were required to move to the Oriental Public School. Parents decided not to send the children to that school and wrote to the Japanese Consul who in turn relegated the sentiments of the Japanese people of California to the government in Japan. In order to placate the brewing political crisis with Japan, Theodore Roosevelt sent the Secretary of Commerce and Labor, Victor Metcalf, to California to negotiate a settlement with the public school officials and the Japanese parents. This was a case of removing the 93 Japanese students from the 28,000 student population to the Oriental Public School. The outcome of this event neither ended segregation in California nor settled any issues involving the jurisdiction of federal government, state, and/or local autonomy in educational policies (Olneck & Lazerson, 1980).

Also, as a result of segregationist actions in the 1920's Chinese children were expelled from the white schools and the action was then upheld by the local courts. To preserve the purity and intergrity of the white race and prevent amalgamation, separate schools for Chinese were established (Parrillo, 1980). For example, the Mississippi Chinese developed parallel institutions when they were excluded from the white prototypes. Chinese sought redress of grievances through the courts, petitioning for equal rights. They won for their children the right to attend public schools, and they fought to desegrate the schools. By 1950 their status had improved and the schools and churches were opened to them (Parrillo, 1980).

Meanwhile in the Territory of Hawaii, where there was a sizeable Asian community, the public school system authorities tried to attack the Japanese and Chinese supplementary language schools but were unable to intervene due to the support of the U.S. Supreme Court's decision to limit the rights of the public school system to intervene in private language schools. In spite of occasional outbursts of intimidation from the public school sector, the sizeable Chinese and Japanese population residing in the very heart of a cosmopolitan Hawaii made it an impossible task. The Chinese and Japanese ethnic groups mobilized to preserve their private language schools as well as the cultural heritage of their forefathers.

With the advent of easier access to the public school systems, more and more emphasis and commitment were placed on the public sector for the education of their children. The private language schools became less effective in inculcating the language and traditional values of the ethnic groups they represented. Traditionally, Japanese parents have encouraged their children to get an education, and since 1940, the Japanese have had more schooling than any other group in the United States, including white (Kitano, 1969). Kitano suggests that the ability of Japanese-Americans to seize available opportunities derives from Japanese-American families and communities which provide ample growth opportunities, present legitimate alternatives, provide conditions of relative tolerance and treatments, and provide effective socialization and control of its children. According to some social scientists (Schaefer, 1979), there is a substantial congruence between Japanese culture and middle class American subculture which has aided the group in adapting to acculturative changes. The Japanese culture demands high ingroup unity, politeness, respect for authority, duty to community, and high achievement orientation, all traits acceptable to middle-class Americans.

More recent Asian immigrants such as the Koreans are on the average more highly educated than most other nonwhite groups. Today's

Korean-American families are almost totally the result of immigration that began during the Korean War (1950-1953). Many Koreans were well-educated and arrived with professional skills as a result of reflecting the filtering effect of the United States immigration laws enacted in 1965 minimizing nationality, emphasizing work skills and relationship to an American (Schaefer, 1984). Many Koreans face the cultural conflicts common to first generation born in a new country.

Many Vietnamese refugees were members of the middle class migrating for political rather than economic reasons. Many were well-educated with marketable skills, and nearly half spoke English (Schaefer, 1979). At first public opinion opposed the federal government's decision to admit the Vietnamese refugees because of what the people thought would be an economic threat. Although the initial public outcry was hostile, the response changed as time passed. In a relatively short time, offers from church groups flooded in so that by December 1975 all refugees who were in relocation centers had been placed with sponsors (Parillo, 1980). When the last refugee left the last immigration center there were more sponsors than refugees. The Vietnamese were scattered throughout every state including Alaska. The largest concentration was sent to California (27,300), followed by Texas (9,300), Pennsylvania, Florida, and Washington state (Newsweek, 1979). Many look to the United States as their future home and home of their children.

Because Vietnamese refugees were scattered they were usually unable to establish ethnic communities to ease their adjustment. Many accepted jobs well below their occupational positions in Southeast Asia and with this has come a downward social mobility. However, available data show that the Indo-Chinese refugees on the average increase their earnings at a relatively fast rate. Their beliefs that life is essentially predetermined and that the amount of good fortune one receives usually comes from metitorious or self-sacrificing actions act as a social conscience for upward mobility of the group. Therefore, children are conscientiously instructed in the ways of living that results in their desire to please others especially by showing respect to superiors and kindness to inferiors. This is turn impinges on the future destiny of the family and loved ones. This destiny is affected by how one conducts one's life in the present. This results in harmony within all social relationships among Vietnamese as well as other people (Parillo, 1980). In order to maintain "just middle" the Vietnamese try to avoid hurting others by compromising. With this "Middle Path" of Buddha thinking ingrained in the Vietnamese child and parents, the interface between the school and the home may be easier than for most newcomers.

Asian immigrants have come to the United States from Burma, Cambodia, Indonesia, Laos, Malaysia, Pakistan, Thailand, and other countries. There are also Pacific Islanders from Guam, Samoa, Fiji, Tonga, and other parts of Micronesia (Parillo, 1980). Data and specific information about these groups are rather scanty except for Bureau of

Census data. These groups have entered an America that is far less racially hostile towards Asians than it was in the past. Many have come here with marketable job skills along with traditional family cohesiveness. Asian-Americans teach their children that efforts pay off and the route is through education. All these strengths plus their value of patience, industriousness and stoicism will ease their transition and facilitate the meshing of the interface between the home and the school as a newcomer to the United States.

There are an estimated 3,500,000 people of Asian and Pacific Island origin in the United States today comprising 1.5 percent of the population (Bureau of Census, 1981). Most live in the West and highly urbanized areas. This ethnic and racial minority represents a population that is diverse in cultural norms, historic origins, and social and economic status, and indeed sharp differences exist within this group. Presently, 32 percent of the population is under 17 years of age. This data indicate that it is a young population that is growing at a faster rate than the 27 figure for whites.

Black Americans. The exclusion and segregation of black experience in education is succinctly discussed in the book *A Chance to Learn, the History of Race and Education in the United States* by Meyer Weinberg (1977). The poor quality of public schools for blacks in all our history is well documented. In 1933, Carter G. Woodson addressed the issue of blacks and education in "The Mis-Education of the Negro." He points out a vivid paradox in relation to the education of blacks, "the most important thing in the uplift of the Negroes, is almost entirely in the hands of those who enslave them." The extended effect of the miseducation of blacks as recently as a generation ago suggests the tenacity of the infrastructure on which past educational experiences are built. The state of black Americans and education today is but an echo of the insights of a man over fifty years ago. Throughout the black experience in this country the question of education has been a significant part of black Americans' struggle for equal existence.

Throughout the United States, black Americans have emphasized the importance of education. Whatever the approach, doors were closed and blacks received little support from the larger community to improve their institutions or to gain equal access to white institutions. For the majority of black children, public school education meant attending segregated schools (Schaefer, 1979). Legal segregation was reinforced by subtle discrimination such as through the rhetoric of special education for those of limited abilities (Olneck and Lazerson, 1980). Blacks pressured authorities to establish integrated schools or to demand more funds and more black teachers for schools. The National Association for the Advancement of Colored People (NAACP) and other groups filed court cases that had limited success but laid the basis for the 1954 desegregation ruling (Parrillo, 1980). Several court cases challenging the school segregation laws in Delaware, Kansas, South Carolina, and Virginia reached the U.S. Supreme Court in 1954. The justices ruled unanimously that the "separate but equal" doctrine was unconstitutional. The NAACP quickly met the challenge to school districts in 17 states in which school segregation existed. These efforts were met with resistance and mixed success (Commission on Civil Rights, 1974). For many blacks the issue was not integration but improving their facilities and underpaid teachers (Pettigrew, 1964; for a different perspective see Berman 1966, Moore, 1971). At the present time when the nation at large is questioning the effectiveness of the educational system, it will be noteworthy to see if and how the long-standing concerns of this large minority group will be manifested in the reformation of the American educational system.

Today, the black population constitutes the largest ethnic minority group in the country. Fifty-three percent is located in the South, 18 percent in the Northeast region, 20 percent in the North Central region and the smallest proportion in the West with 8.5 percent. Twelve states have a black population of one million or more with New York ranked first followed by California and Texas (U.S. Bureau of the Census, 1980).

The number of black persons attending school increased by approximately one-half million from 7.8 in 1970 to 8.4 in 1981. This gap in school attendance rate between blacks and whites is thought to have been eliminated partially as a result of compulsory attendance laws for persons of elementary and secondary schools (Mathey and Johnson, 1983).

Hispanic-Mexican-American. This is a very difficult group to characterize due to its historical legacy of being reported by federal and state authorities some times as white and at other times in history as a separate ethnic group. Hispanics are often lumped together in the public mind as a single group when in fact they embrace many different people of rich and varied cultures.

Separation by ethnicity of Mexican-Americans was especially true of those states bordering Mexico. Public schools for Mexican-Americans were slowly made available to them on the segregation basis. For example, the opening of the public schools in Corpus Christi was only made available to Mexican-American children 20 years after its opening. Throughout history, however, a small number of Spanish-speaking children who belonged to the middle class in status and were well integrated and assimilated into the mainstream of America were allowed free access to the high schools (Olneck and Lazerson, 1980).

The unequal access heightened with the increased social and economic problems of Mexico and the labor shortages in the United States resulted in immigrations from Mexico. These groups of immigrants were poor, spoke little English, and maintained close ties to their homeland, Mexico. Enrollment and attendance problems flourished with numerous other educational problems besetting the populations of that area of the country. By 1920 a pattern had emerged, separate schooling in greatly inferior facilities for Mexican-American students, deliberate refusal to make educational use of the child's cultural heritage, especially the Spanish language, and a shorter school year (Weinberg, 1977). The use of Spanish in the public schools was forbidden, and even the use of the language in private schools was attacked by school authorities. Educational funds targeted to the schooling of Spanish-speaking children were siphoned off to Anglo schools, leaving the Spanish-speaking schools with poor facilities and poorly paid staff. In the Southwestern parts of the United States, patterns of discrimination, segregation, and financial deprivation dominated the education of Mexican-American children throughtout the second and third quarters of the century as it had the first quarter (Weinberg, 1977).

There have been movements of segregation of Mexican-Americans not under the guise of racism, but under the patronizing attempts that Mexican-Americans can best profit from education if they are put into classes they can most benefit from and that means a separate class. There was also the notion that because of the transient nature of this group of people, it was best to separate them from others where they could learn best and not disturb the more stable students. During the 1920's and the 1930's, parents and communities waged outright protests against inadequate facilities and teachers. Not until World War II were the protests loud and consistent enough to be heard by the government. Some educators believe that matters may have worsened for the Hispanic population as the urban population has grown over the years, and paradoxically the bilingual education program may in fact segregate the children again in the 80's.

Today Hispanics represent 6.4 percent of the population, totaling an estimated 14.6 million people. Mexican-Americans are the most numerous with approximately nine million. Puerto Ricans are second and Cubans third among the Hispanic population. Approximately 55 percent of the Mexican-American population, 73 percent of the Puerto Rican population and 83 percent of the Cuban population reside in metropolitan areas (U.S. Bureau of the Census, 1983). By moderate estimates the Hispanic population will be the largest minority group in less than 25 years. In Los Angeles, 70 percent of all children in Head Start Programs are Hispanics. A recent ethnic survey of the Los Angeles Unified District showed a 44 percent total Hispanic student enrollment, but in grades K through 6 the enrollment is more than 50 percent (Los Angeles Unified School District, 1978). Approximately 41 percent of the Hispanics are under 17 years of age, indicating a quickly growing young ethnic population.

Beyond Ethnicity and School:
The Interface Between Home and School

The relationship between ethnicity and school success is as complicated as the interface between the home and the school. The ethnic experience is varied and affected significantly by specific backgrounds and forms of discrimination. For America's largest minority groups, black Americans and Mexican-Americans, school achievement is rarely translated into economic rewards commensurate with those gained by whites with equivalent schooling (Pinderhughes, 1982). Whereas for Japanese-Americans, school achievement appears to be related to group values and prior acquaintance with public-like schooling. Upon arrival in the United States the Japanese may have been America's most well-educated immigrant group. Over 90 percent of arriving immigrants were literate in Japanese and had at least eight years of schooling which was considerably above the educational attainment of the average American at that time (Kitano, 1980). Distinctive views of education by ethnic groups may explain why certain groups respond differently to schooling. Emphasis on ethnicity and school success, however, should not obscure other processes of differentiation that have little to do with ethnic values and much to do with the discrimination and exclusion in education which characterizes the interface between home and school for ethnic minority families.

In this section an attempt will be made to describe the relationship between the two larger minority families/communities and the educational system. The basic premise of this discussion is that many black and Mexican-American parents are dissatisfied with the present educational system. Due to deep rooted racism embedded in the system, they find little or no value in its present form. Consequently, some parents have turned to alternative schools for educating their children.

The Black Family and the School

After many years of struggling with the inequity of the educational system, many black parents are questioning the feasibility of obtaining equal, quality education for their children via the present education system (Jones, 1975). Despite this realization, "the value placed on education and employment is reflected in the growing proportion of blacks who study beyond the complusory age and the number achieving higher education and employment levels" (Hines & Boyd-Franklin, 1982, p. 98).

James D. McGhee, in *The State of Black America 1983,* discusses the demographics of blacks as related to education and employment. He states that for the first time in history high school educational attainment for blacks has continued to improve. The median years of school completed has risen from 9.9 in 1970 to 12.0 in 1980. "This means that the median educational level for black adults has risen from an eight grade, elementary school to a 12th grade high school level in a period of 20 years" (p.13). Although we can see an improvement in educational attainment for blacks, to date only one-half of black adults have graduated from high school. In 1970, 35 percent of black adults and 58 percent of white adults had graduated compared to 51 percent of black adults and 70 percent of whites in 1980. These figures are based on individuals aged 25 years old and older.

In 1979 the majority of black college students were first-genera-tion college students. The educational backgrounds of the parents of black college students in 1979 and 1980 reveals that, the overwhelming majority (70%) of those parents had never attended college and 45 percent had not graduated from high school. These percentages demon-strate the high achievement orientation of the black family.

Ogbu (1982) suggests that even though black parents stress the importance of educational attainment with their children, they also convey the fallacies of the educational system when they discuss the experiences and frustrations that they and others have had with employ-ment. This further suggests that black children enter school with the hopes of getting a good education which will lead to a good job. However, they carry with them an unconscious mistrust of the society that not only controls the job market but the educational system as well.

Black Parent Involvement

Although there is persuasive evidence that black parents stress the importance of education to their children, the reality is that black parental involvement in the school system is limited. Historically blacks have viewed the educational system as one of the major areas of institutional racism and felt hopeless in a fight against such a giant (Perkins, 1975). This feeling of hopelessness is further accentuated by factors such as parental unemployment, limited access to adequate transportation, but most importantly the parental perception that school administrators discourage involvement in the area of school policy making.

One of the most crucial issues related to the education of blacks is the relationship between the home and the school. The traditional attitude of education being the important factor in the economic advancement of blacks still prevails. Yet, the relationship between the black home and the school is not as positive as it was in the past. This relationship is rapidly changing because the educational system is failing to meet the educational needs of the black child. According to James (1974), the factors that contribute to the present hostile climate between the black community and schools are: 1) The feeling of powerlessness that is prevalant in the urban areas where a significant number of black children are being educated. In these large urban settings parents have little or no opportunity to make decisions about the policies that affect their children. 2) The effect of the desegregation process on the black community. According to Hamilton (1975), one of the underlying assumptions of desegregation and busing was that blacks needed to assimilate with whites in the existing school structures. This helped to foster a breakdown in the communication between the black home and school. "In the past, especially in the south, the school and black home complimented each other in the black community: There was a high level of parental involvement in the school and its activities" (Jones, 1975, p. 13). Prior to desegregation, schools in black communities served a dual function. Along with the church, the school was a social center and the education center of the community. Black teachers and principals were respected leaders in the community. Desegregation changed the positive dyadic relationship that existed between the home and schools. However, the impact of desegregation and busing has not been all negative. In fact, research data indicate various outcomes such as 1) significant reduction of the gap between minority and majority students measured educational outcomes; 2) gap in achievement scores have remained essentially the same; 3) gap actually increased (Brookover, Brady & Warfield, 1981).

There is a growing realization in the black community that the faith black Americans placed in the white dominant education system will never adequately address the needs of the black community. Today blacks are realizing the inherent truth of the words of Carter G. Woodson in his book *The Miseducation of the Negro*. As James (1974) stated, "the established system is a manifestation of white racism and a vehicle for the destruction of the black heritage" (p.61). In reaction to this reality, the black community is becoming more active in the arena of school policy and decision making as it affects its children. The growing phenomenon of "black awareness" contributes to the changing relationship between the home and school (James, 1974).

Black Student-Teacher Relationships

Research on teacher attitude and minority student achievement suggests several factors influence student achievement, including teacher attitude and teacher expectancy or "the Pygmalion effect." Scott (1975) suggests that a teacher's attitude about a child is critical, primarily because outside of the family teachers are often the first adults to communicate attitudes about the worth of a child through verbal and nonverbal behavior. Numerous studies have shown that student self-concept influences student achievement and that achievement is motivated by positive expectation of teachers (Scott, 1975, p. 114). Archibald and Chemers (1975) found that "the openness, flexibility and sensitivity of the teacher's cognitive and perceptual systems can have effects on the satisfaction and adjustment of students" (p. 93). However, these characteristics were not necessarily sufficient. When warmth and openness were combined with an ability to understand and relate to others who were culturally different from themselves, satisfaction increased. In relation to minority students the dimensions of openness and sensitivity are especially crucial.

The "Pygmalion effect" is the act of creating the results that are desired. Rosenthal, after testing this effect in psychological research, attempted to test it in the education arena. His research in 1973 suggests that, in the teaching of minority students, stereotyping is particularly prevalent. This finding suggests that teacher expectancy is influenced by the prejudicial attitudes they have of certain students. Rosenthal and Jacobson (1968) concluded from their research on teacher expectation that when teacher expectations are raised and these expectations are communicated to students, the students achieve at a higher level. This research has not escaped criticism. Weinberg (1977) suggests that the Pygmalion effect research is not conclusive, but it does "seem to favor a hunch" that teacher expectation influences student achievement. Other studies have demonstrated similar effects in interracial settings (Rubovits & Maehr, 1973; Coats, 1972; Epps, 1980).

Multiethnic/Multicultural Education and the Black Child

In his book, *Multiethnic Education Theory and Practice*, James Banks (1981) states,
"Multiethnic and multicultural education are characterized by much conceptual confusion and a wide range of competing ideologies regarding the role educational institutions should play in the ethnic group. Ethnicity, multiethnic education, and multicultural education are often used by educators to convey diverse and often conflicting meaning and policies" (p. 35).

Although there is ambiguity centered around the concepts of multicultural and multiethnic education, the effectiveness of programs designed around these concepts may be beneficial for black children. According to Hollins (1982), the experiences, perceptions, and values of multicultural education are often dominated by the idealized notions of the Anglo American middle-class culture.

Multicultural programs have not been effectively integrated into instructional programs. Recognizing ethnic heroes and holidays, including the contributions of ethnic groups in literature and social studies curriculum content and posting ethnic pictures on classroom walls is not enough. The real issue of multicultural education is two-fold: 1) the recognition by all individuals, regardless of race or status, of the right of different groups to exist and to have access to status and power in American society, and 2) the movement must go beyond classrooms and toward effective changes in the power relationships in the larger social, political, and economic system (Cheng 1979).

Banks (1981) states that America is not the "melting pot" that it has traditionally been thought to be; instead he suggests that American culture consists of a shared universal culture with a subset of ethnic subcultures and communities. From this perspective all Americans participate within the universal American culture and society and within his or her own ethnic subculture. He calls his position "multiethnic ideology". Banks suggests that schools need to adapt this ideology in order to successfully educate children. According to this philosophy, a total systemic school reform is required. Schools must become more consistent with the culturally diverse nature of the human environments around them. Areas suggested for initial school reform include: School policy and politics, the ethnic and racial composition of the school staff, its attitudes and perceptions, the formalized and hidden curriculum, the learning styles and cultural behavioral patterns favored by the school, the teaching strategies and materials, the testing and counseling program, the languages and dialects sanctioned by the school, and the role of the community in the school.

In order to be comprehensive, multicultural education needs to be broad in scope; at the same time educators need to pay special attention to the individual learning styles of the children. Gay (1981) suggests that communication is an important factor in the teacher/pupil relationship in the culturally plural classroom. She suggests that teachers need to be familiar with the communication habits of black Americans. Teachers need to have knowledge and awareness of the following cultural information: 1) the emphasis given to developing verbal dexterity within black socialization processes; 2) the perception and use of words as power devices; 3) the fact that black culture stems from an oral tradition; 4) the significance of style and delivery in communication among black Americans; and 5) the important role of nonverbal nuances, symbolism, and metaphoric language in black communication.

Both Hale (1982) and Hollins (1982) emphasize the importance of culture as it relates to learning style. If we accept the notion that culture determines how one learns and what one learns, then from a dialectical perspective the content of any multicultural education program should be drawn from the cultures represented in the classroom. Specifically, teachers should have instructional programs that teach according to the unique learning (cognitive) style of black children. In her book, *Black Children Their Roots, Culture and Learning Style,* Janice Hale (1982) examines the impact that African-American culture has on the black child's ability to learn in the school setting. Factors such as the degree of open space, freedom of movement, the use of rhythm in speech and verbal interplay between teacher and student, and varying the format of problem-solving tasks may greatly influence how black children learn.

Alternative School Models and the Black Child

During the 1970's, a vast number of alternative schools were developed. These schools were designed to offer a legitimate alternative to conventional school programs. Smith, Gregory, and Pugh (1981) investigated how effective alternative school models were in meeting the needs of students. They developed a SAS (Statement About Schools)

Inventory to assess how well a school satisfied the needs of its students as judged by both the student and teachers. The sample consisted of seven alternative and six comprehensive high schools in four states. The findings indicated that students in alternative schools were more satisfied with the way the school met their needs. The teachers in alternative school settings were more satisfied with the job they were doing than were teachers in conventional schools. This study demonstrates the effectiveness of these alternative school programs.

Robert Barr (1981) says that alternative schools have become firmly implanted in the mainstream of public education in the last decade. He further suggests that these schools are being used to address the most serious problems confronting the education system today. He suggests that the trends for alternative schools for the 1980's are as follows: 1) alternative schools as a strategy for school reform; 2) alternative schools as a means of reducing violence, vandalism and disruption; 3) alternative schools' contribution to the back-to-basics movement.

What are the components of effective alternative school models for black children? Cureton (1978) suggests the following factors: 1) oral involvement, 2) teacher-centered instruction, 3) continuous participation by students and 4) a rejection of the "deficit" and "different" philosophies. Cureton provides a list of four private and ten public schools that are making a difference in the education of black children.

Westside Preparatory School. According to Hollins (1982b), Marva Collins, the founder of the Westside Preparatory School, has demonstrated remarkable accomplishments with successfully educating black children. Hollins suggests that the significant factor in the success that Marva Collins has had is "cultural congruence". She defines cultural congruence as the relationship between the curriculum and the black pupil's cultural experiences outside the school. The cultural experiences include characteristics of behavior and functions observed in family settings, peer group relationship, and religious settings which are incorporated into the curriculum. In her analysis of Ms. Collins' educational program, Hollins discussed each of the components of "cultural congruence" mentioned above. She concluded that the success of Marva Collins' instruction also is due to the interaction of the following factors: good discipline, high motivation, high teacher expectation, positive reinforcement, adequate/quality time on task, well-organized curriculum and genuine concern for children. Marva Collins incorporates relevant aspects of the Black-American culture in her classroom instruction and thus learning is facilitated through congruence between instructional activities and pupils' cultural experiences.

Council of Independent Black Institutions (CIBI). The Council of Independent Black Institutions is comprised of a network of Africentric schools operating in various black neighborhoods across the nation. These schools provide an alternative to the public school system. Lomotey (1981) defines independent black institutions as "institutions void of outside control and influence, Afrikan in color, culture, and conscienceness, and with a structured program aimed at correcting a deficiency - giving concrete alternatives" (p. 15). The goals for the CIBI are as follows:

1.   To develop and implement instructional methodology that will ensure maximum academic achievement for our children.
2.   To create and sustain independent black institutions that provide educational cultural and social development for our communities.
3.   To train and deploy teachers to serve in our black independent institutions.
4.   To establish a network of mutual support and reinforcement of Afrikan values in the education of our families.
5.   To serve as a liaison between CIBI and other national and international institutions dedicated to the liberation of Afrikan people.
6.   To serve as an accrediting agency of Pan-Afrikan Nationalist schools.
7.   To provide direction and inspiration for black people through our example of Nation building.

These Africenter schools are the result of people-building, family-building, community-building, and Nation-building act as self-respect, self-determination and self-reliance.

Black-Family-Community-School Affair

Hamilton (1975) suggests the need for the recognition of education in the black community as not simply a child-oriented affair, but as a family-community-school-oriented affair. Smith (1975) presented a model for parental participation in inner city schools that contains the three components that Hamilton stressed: family, community and school. This model was designed to involve parents and community residents directly in the inner city schools in a manner that is both positive and productive. This organizational model includes four elements: 1) an educational council; 2) a school community task force; 3) grade level parental organization; and 4) a system of room representatives. Smith's proposed model, if implemented, would foster parental/-community involvement in the schools through 1) parental/community participation in decision and policy making, 2) parental involvement in the non-academic areas of the school setting, such as monitoring lunchrooms, halls and recreational areas, and 3) closer parent-teacher interaction as they work as a team to enhance the educational program delivered to students. Although only the highlights of this model are presented here, one can see that it is quite different from the traditional PTA and yearly parent-teacher conference structure predominating the present educational system. Smith contends that a model of this type would help to accomplish the following things:

1. Heighten the degree of visibility between the school staff and community residents.
2. Provide the school with an access to the community, facilitating the development of an understanding of the cultural orientation of the people in the community which should ultimately result in a more relevant educational program for the youngsters.
3. Provide community residents with access to the school, facilitating the development of an understanding of the problems the school faces in its endeavors to educate children with too few adequately prepared teachers in overcrowded, dilapidated facilities.
4. Provide a mechanism facilitating the development of the accountability of the school staff for their activities with youngsters.
5. Force parents and teachers to plan jointly for the educational development of the children.
6. Help facilitate and speed up the transition from central office bureaucratic control to local community political control (p. 25026).

Smith's model is an example of school decentralization. Decentralization, as defined in James (1974), is "a method of distributing authority in such a way as to give parents, citizens and local school officials greater involvement in or control over the educational decisions which affect children" (p. 62). James suggests that decentralization is only one technique for increasing parent participation. "Other strategies . . . include making school facilities available to the community as a center for various social and educational services, and the use of local residents as aides and tutors" (p. 63).

Mexican-American/Hispanic Family and the School

Hispanic cultural values include the importance of family, the Spanish language, authority, respect, dignity, responsibility, and obligation to family members (Nieto & Sinclair, 1980). Cooperation and obedience to elders are also valued in the home.

The importance of the family or "la familia", a concept repeated throughout the literature on Hispanics, refers to the precept that the bonded unit of individuals known as family takes precedence over any one of its members as individuals. Family loyalty is similar to cultural loyalty, but has even greater value because it is made up of persons. Traditional Hispanics are considered more often person oriented as opposed to being goal or object oriented (Alvirez & Bean, 1981).

The Spanish language is more than a means of communication. It is also a mode of transmitting the cultural thought patterns of human behavior to the younger generations. Differences in how much Spanish children speak in the home depends on the origin of the ethnic group and present geographical location (Laosa, 1977). Even within a community there is heterogenity in the home language environments. Laosa's research provides evidence that among Puerto Rican children in New York and Cuban American children in Miami, the majority speak Spanish most frequently in the home. Among Mexican-American children in central Texas, 45 percent speak English most frequently in the home while 30 percent speak a combination of Spanish and English in their family environments and 23 percent speak both Spanish and English with equal frequency without combining the two languages. Carter and Segura (1979) attribute the greater use of English among Mexican-Americans in the Southwest to the long history of schools prohibiting and punishing children for speaking Spanish among themselves at school. Regardless of how much the Spanish language is spoken in the home, it is of significant cultural value.

Hispanics also place importance on authority, and in the home it is delegated primarily in terms of sex and age. Traditionally, males and elders hold the positions of authority in the home (Alvirez & Bean, 1981). This is not to say that the elders and males are the primary decision makers in the family. Several researchers have found that egalitarian conjugal roles are the predominant pattern of decision-making in most Chicano families regardless of socioeconomic status or area of residence (Bacca Zinn 1975; Grebler, Moore & Guzman, 1970; Hawkes & Taylor, 1975; Staples & Mirande, 1980).

Closely related to authority is respect or "respeto." Respect for those family members who are in authority positions is consciously taught to youngsters at an early age. Children are reminded to listen attentively to their elders, to obey them, to help if they need it, and to honor them. Children are also taught and expected to be responsible in various ways at an early age (LeVine & Bartz, 1979). This is reflected in the behavior of older children who often share in the responsibility of caring for younger siblings.

Obligation as a cultural value implies that family members are obligated to one another. In the case of children, for example, siblings have priority over friends in matters of play as well as other concern. These cultural values are important in understanding the conflict and misunderstandings that have occurred between the home and school. Unless these Hispanic values are acknowledged as important by school officials and teachers, there can be little accomplished to bridge the gap that exists at the interface of these two systems.

Mexican-American Families' Educational Aspirations and Perception of the School

The aspirations of Mexican-American parents for their children's educational attainment are not matched by their expectations for occupational attainment. This may be a reflection of the reality that few of the parents can afford to prepare financially for the future education of their children. Therefore, many parents do not systematically plan for their children to be academically prepared for college. In addition, families are uninformed about the number of years and the nature of the schooling required for their children to reach their educational aspirations. Mexican-American/Hispanics often do not realize the all-important difference between education as an abstract reality and schooling and a required institutional procedure (Fratoe, 1981; Parra & Henderson, 1982). It is important to note, however, that a mother's aspirations for her children's educational attainment have been found to have significant importance among Chicanos (Carter & Segura, 1979; Vasquez, 1978).

Mexican-American's perception of school tends to be one of dissatisfaction. Research findings of Parra and Henderson (1982) indicate that Mexican-American parents are dissatisfied with the teaching of academic skills. Parents also feel that by not taking cultural background into consideration, the school shows a lack of responsibility for the social and emotional development of their children.

According to Carter and Segura (1979), Mexican-American children often view their teachers as prejudiced and discriminatory toward their ethnicity. It is readily apparent that the teacher does not understand the Mexican-American child's need to be accepted when research studies report that children's attitudes become more negative as the year progresses. Children's evaluations of teachers and curricula also become increasingly less favorable as they progress through the years of school.

There is also incongruence between Mexican-American parents' perceptions of home-school roles and those of the school system. Mexican-American parents do not perceive their role as teachers of intellectual tasks to their children. Many parents, particularly the poor, generally do not deliberately engage in the intellectual development of their children in the home. They consider teaching children intellectual tasks to be a school function. The teachers and the school are considered the authority on intellectual matters, and the cultural value of respect for authority dictates that the home respect the school. Moreover, due to low educational attainment, many Mexican-American parents lack the skills and experience essential to see to it that the children are prepared intellectually for school entry. These parents believe the school is staffed by highly trained professionals who have the best interests of their children at heart (Carter & Segura, 1979; Parra & Henderson, 1982; Stewart, 1981).

The school, on the other hand, with its middle-class values expects that "basic intellectual abilities and academic motivation are developed in substantial degree in the home before children attend school . . ." (Parra & Henderson, p. 298). Fratoe (1981) interprets the tendency of Mexican-American parents not to participate in school activities as failure to reinforce educational values of the society.

Mexican-American Parent Involvement

Most Mexican-American parents are not actively involved in school activities. Their lack of participation is interpreted by school officials as a lack of concern about their children's education. Hispanic/Mexican-American parents who have participated in school activities often perceive their participation in school activities as demeaning and insignificant (Carter & Segura, 1979; Nieto & Sinclair, 1980). Many schools often do very little in encouraging and involving parents in a meaningful way (Nieto & Sinclair, 1980; Padilla, 1982). Because of a lack of communication between the school and the barrio, the average poor family does not learn the necessary steps to support its children (Carter & Segura, 1979). This finding has significance for Mexican-Americans since the school retains and positively reinforces those children whose values, aspirations, conduct, and home life more closely correspond to those of the majority social class. Mexican-Americans, particularly the poor, lack the skills and experience necessary to participate in the schools to the extent expected by middle class school standards. Furthermore, conflicting perceptions of home and school roles in educating children place most Mexican-American children at a disadvantage in school because the home is the most important source of continuity in encouraging cognitive growth in children. Early childhood education literature suggests that fundamental intellectual abilities and academic motivation are instilled in children before they attend school.

Mexican-American Student-Teacher Relationship

Not only is the home-school interface inconsistent in terms of values transmitted to children, but educational services are inadequate. As reported by Fratoe (1981), the inequality in the distribution of educational resources for Hispanics has been well documented. There are poorer quality and smaller facilities in nonmetro schools with large Hispanic enrollments. The teachers at these schools have less training or advance degrees, and there are fewer special programs offered in the schools. Discontent with schools and confrontations with school authorities in metropolitan areas suggest that educational services in urban areas are equally as poor as those in rural areas (Carter & Segura, 1979).

The incongruent interface results from more than the relationship between the different cultural milieu of the home and school. It is also a product of the minority group's status within the larger American society. Segregation of Hispanics/Mexican-Americans in the schools in an historical fact. It was not until the League of United Latin American Citizens (LULAC) filed a law suit against a Texas school district that such segregation became unlawful. In 1948, the federal court at Austin decided in Delgado versus the Bastrop Independent School District that segregation of Mexican children was contrary to the Fourteenth Amendment and, therefore, unconstitutional. The court, however, allowed segregation in the first grade to continue. The reason given was that children might have language difficulties (Meier & Rivera, 1981).

As a minority group, Hispanics/Mexican-Americans are not only segregated in the school, but they are segregated in occupations as well. For example, Hispanics/Mexican-Americans are disproportionately represented in semi-skilled and unskilled types of employment (Olivas, 1982). It is, therefore, unrealistic to expect most Mexican-American children to value their schooling to the extent of being motivated to stay in school when the reality for them is that academic performance is irrelevant to occupational status.

Although Hispanics approve of education as an abstract goal, attrition rates indicate that school is an unrewarding experience. Aguirre and Cepeda (1981) report that the following core issues are most often cited in the literature as explanations of the educational disparity for Mexican-Americans:

1. Validity and reliability of testing instruments used to measure achievement and performance.
2. Counseling practices that are guided by middle class values.
3. Unequal school facilities and human resources.
4. Segregated school and linguistic differences.

There is definite conflict in home and school values and perceptions held by Mexican-Americans and school officials. Family values of a respect for the parents and a responsibility to obey one's elders make it difficult for these young, inexperienced persons to know exactly what is expected of them. This conflict creates a dichotomy for the child which in turn is not conducive to learning and is damaging to self-esteem. One example of the harm done to the self-esteem of Mexican-Americans is that schools have discouraged, prohibited, and even punished children for speaking their home language at school (Carter & Segura, 1979; Jordan, 1980). The effects of such practices are evident when young children are instructed by their parents not to speak Spanish at school even when they are enrolled in a bilingual education program which encourages the use of Spanish at school (Jackson, 1981).

Bilingual/Bicultural Education and the Mexican-American Child

As a transmitter between the home and school interface, bilingual education can fill the gap in communication between the Mexican-American home and the school. The Bilingual Education Act of 1968, also known as Elementary and Secondary Education Act (ESEA) Title VII, resulted primarily from the determined struggle of Latino groups (Nieto & Sinclair, 1980). Although other linguistic and cultural minorities have bilingual education programs, the Hispanic population is more often identified with the issue of bilingual education.

Concepts fundamental to bilingual education are:

1. Basic concepts of learning are initiated in the child's own language.
2. Language development is in the child's dominant language.
3. Language instruction is provided in the second language.
4. Learning content and concepts are taught in the child's dominant language.
5. Subject matter and concepts are also taught in the second language.
6. The child's positive identity with his cultural heritage is promoted (Meier & Rivera, 1980).

President Reagan's philosophy favoring state and local decision making prompted the Bilingual Education Improvements Act of 1983. This act would amend fundamental concepts of the Bilingual Education Act of 1968. If this legislation is passed, school districts will have the option of using approaches which do not require instruction in the student's dominant language. The local school would again be considered the authority on methods to use in teaching children whose English proficiency is limited with a provision that the method selected be the most desirable for the children to be served (National Clearinghouse for Bilingual Education, 1983). The Reagan Administration proposal of a 32 percent reduction of 1983 and 1984 funding for bilingual education threatened to seriously impair services for bilingual children. The 1985 budget request for bilingual education is based on the administration's proposed legislation to amend and extend the Bilingual Education Act with funding at the 1984 level (National Clearinghouse for Bilingual Education, 1984). As part of the public education system subject to prevailing societal attitudes and values, bilingual education continues to be impacted by volatile funding allocations determined by public policy.

Discontinuities between home and school contribute to the problematic home-school interface for which bilingual education was viewed as a solution, but parental involvement was not mandated in its original legislation. From her examination of the federal regulations governing parental-community participation in bilingual education, Matute-Bianchi (1979) concludes that the requirements were nothing

more than "vaguely worded requests for compliance" (p.
Sinclair (1980) also suggest that parents are uninvolved
decision making and that schools are either unwilling or u
to involve parents meaningfully.

The inclusion of family values in the educational
recognized element for successfully teaching bilingual children.
Mexican-American parents, however, have not been encouraged to
involve themselves in the school so that their values could be understood
first hand and integrated into curricula. Matute-Bianchi (1980) attributes her observations of "apathy and confusion, as well as frustration
and controversy at the local site level" (p. 32) to a lack of federal policy
mandating parent-community involvement in bilingual schooling.

The fundamental concept of bilingual education--to promote children's positive identity with their cultural heritage--implies an alliance
between the school and the home. The family can best provide the
cultural information the school requires in order to meet the educational
needs of bilingual children because the linguistic needs of bilingual
children differ from those of each other as well as from those of other
children. Some Mexican-American children are monolingual speaking
only Spanish; others are bilingual, with either Spanish or English being
their dominant language. In addition to their linguistic needs are their
heterogeneous cultural needs which bilingual education originally promised to meet (Stewart, 1981).

To date the failure of the school to educate bilingual children
continues. Although school failure has been acknowledged for many
years, more than a decade of research has shown that equal educational
opportunities still do not exist for bilingual children. Equal educational
opportunity for Mexican-American as well as other ethnolinguistic
minority group children was a promise of the Bilingual Education Act
(Aguirre & Cepeda, 1981; Padilla, 1982). The educational purpose of
bilingual programs is to help children acquire the intellectual skills
necessary to compete successfully in the American socioeconomic mainstream. If this purpose were accomplished, it could help remove the
social and economic barriers between minority groups and the larger
society. In addition, bilingual education provides opportunities for all
children to learn about and experience cultural pluralism (Padilla, 1982).

Migrant Education

In 1966, Congress amended Title I of the Elementary and Secondary
Act to mandate programs and projects directed specifically at meeting
special educational needs of children of migrant farm workers because
these children were the most educationally deprived children in the nation
(Jordan, 1980). In 1980, reports to Congress stated that the educational
achievement of these children was still extremely low. The disparity
between home and school is one explanation found in the education

.terature for the severe educational deprivation of these children. Most children of migrant farm laborers are Mexican-American. The home language is Spanish. The educational attainment of parents is four to six years of formal schooling, and many do not speak English (Jordan, 1980).

Jordan's report (1980) cites examples of the discrimination migrant children face in the school. It is not unusual, for example, for a teacher to spray perfume on a child because "they all smell so bad" (p. 3). Administrators have also been known to discriminate. One principal appointed students to report children who speak Spanish among themselves so that they could be punished. Such practices are damaging to the self-concept of the child. This type of modeling also encourages the perpetuation of prejudice among the children who witness behaviors such as these. A solution to problems facing migrant children is seen as involving parents meaningfully in the education of their children.

Parent advisory councils (PACS) are mandated as a required element of the Title I ESEA. Nevertheless, meaningful parent involvement in migrant education programs is still almost nonexistent (Jordan, 1980). One explanation Jordan gives for this problem is that parental involvement is not specifically defined by Congress in the mandate. Agencies operating migrant education programs must consult with a PAC or risk loss of funding. It is not clear, however, what the PACS are to do once they are formed or what is meant by appropriate consultation with the PACS (Cortes, 1980).

For migrant parents to get involved in the education of their children they must first be told about the programs and what their participation can mean to their children. The implication is that a great deal of home-school interaction is necessary to explain the details of how parents can participate. Initial parent involvement is the responsibility of the school under this program and must be carried out with awareness and sensitivity to the home background. This is a difficult task given that migrant parents are concerned about not being able to communicate with school personnel, and that their requests or demands may result in reprisals against their children. Since their own school experiences were hostile and unrewarding, many migrant parents believe that they will be treated with contempt by school personnel (Jordan, 1980).

Other constraints, such as federal policy trends, have adversely affected the children of Hispanic migrant farm workers. The extension of the definition of "migrant" to include children of mobile populations other than farm laborers caused a decrease in the funding available to the farm worker group originally intended for migrant education programs. Funds are not only allocated to serve more groups of mobile children, but are being consistently decreased (Cortes, 1980). The Reagan Administration 1984 budget attenuated two migrant education programs, the High School Equivalency Program and College Assistance Migrant

Program. In addition, migrant education funding was reduced nearly 50 percent (U.S. Office of Management and Budget, 1983). President Reagan's 1985 budget proposes a funding estimate at a higher level than the 1984 budget (Executive Office of the President, 1984). Nevertheless, attenuated programs are slated for elimination.

Alternative Schooling Models and the Mexican-American Child

There is very little information on alternative schooling models for Hispanics. The few alternatives that do exist, however, are too few and too small to meet the educational needs of all Hispanic children.

After-School Programs. According to Padilla (1982), the concept of a community organized after-school program has long been known throughout the Southwest as an *escuelita* (little school). The *escuelita* is operated by volunteers from the community who try to provide the language and cultural experiences which the Hispanic child does not receive in school. Financial support for the escuelita is derived from fund-raising events sponsored by the community. Although the primary function of the *escuelita* is to transmit language and culture to children, it has also been known to provide tutorial services. In addition to members of the community, Chicano university students have been actively involved in such alternative educational programs for children.

The "little school of the 400" were preschool classes to teach Spanish-speaking children the 400 most common words of American English in preparation for entering public school. These schools were the result of the growing consciousness of World War II minority group veterans to form organizations for the purpose of launching literacy and educational improvement campaigns (Keller & VanHooft, 1982).

Bilingual Preschools. More recently, bilingual preschools have been established to work with economically disadvantaged bilingual children. Montessori principles and materials were used in designing bilingual/bicultural programs in California and Texas. Jackson (1981) studied the bilingual language components of an experimental bilingual Montessori project to determine whether or not any changes took place in the ability of children to understand and speak both Spanish and English over an academic year. Of the 78 children in the program, 54 were Mexican-American, 15 were Anglo, 8 were Black and 1 was Chinese-American. The children represented a broad range of socioeconomic backgrounds, but most came from traditional Mexican culture environments of a large city and a small town. Others commuted from various neighborhoods to participate in the program. Since some children were monolingual and others were bilingual, both languages were to be used constantly in the preschool.

Jackson found that children responded best when addressed in their dominant language. The heterogenity of language backgrounds in each class motivated the children to learn and use the two languages in meaningful contexts. Many bilingual children were hesitant to use their Spanish home language, and Jackson reports that one child reported that her mother instructed her not to speak Spanish at school. Many Mexican-American children showed either no gain or a decrease in their Spanish language test scores. The group as a whole, however, showed a significant gain in Spanish language test scores. The children learned a significant amount of Spanish and English. It was recommended that the program be modified to develop a separate set of materials for Spanish and English lessons, to emphasize Spanish more, and to recruit more Spanish-dominant or Spanish monolingual children.

Autonomous Schools. The Chicano movement of the 1960's was a catalyst in the development of culturally relevant alternative schooling models. In 1973, there were at least 13 Chicano experimental educational programs in California as well as others throughout the Southwest. The Southwest Network of the Study on Commission on Undergraduate Education and the Education of Teachers (1973) evaluated eight of the California alternative Chicano schools and found the programs were not clearly defined, and many were suffering serious funding difficulties. Community involvement was lacking, as was communication between programs. Many of the schools were relinquishing their autonomy by turning to outside organizations and the Federal government for financial assistance. Very few of these programs have survived.

Presently there are a very few autonomous Hispanic alternative schools. The *Escuela de la Raza Unida* in Blythe, California, is an example of one successful program which has operated for 12 years. It is a community based organization meeting the needs of farm workers' children. The non-profit school offers bilingual/bicultural classes for grades kindergarten through 12. In 1982, the school directors proudly established a bilingual educational radio station which has been successfully operated by high school students in the program.

Another alternative school which was established in the 1960's is the Escuela Tlatelolco in Denver, Colorado. A bilingual/bicultural educational program provides preschool, primary, secondary, and undergraduate students a curriculum that incorporates Chicano culture and history, with emphasis on coordinated study and practical experience in the urban community.

Other types of alternative schooling models offer specific programs to teach skills needed to function in the public schools. For example, the Spanish Education Development (SED) Center, established in 1971 in Washington, D.C., provides a year-round bilingual-multicultural preschool and bilingual-bicultural tutorial program for school age children. The preschool is a comprehensive program of a day care and educational enrichment that strives to provide Hispanic children with the skills necessary to succeed in the public school (Educacion Liberadora, 1982).

The 1848 Treaty of Guadalupe Hidalgo, which ended the Mexican-American War, sought the right of language maintenance for Mexicans who became American citizens when the northwestern territory of Mexico become the southwestern United States (Keller & Van Hofft, 1982). Today, however, central to the problematic interface between the Hispanic home and the public schools is a lack of communication that culminates in a failure to educate Hispanic children, evidenced in school attrition rates of 35 percent (Olivas, 1982). Alternative schooling models or non-traditional means of educating children are viewed as one way to bridge the communication gap between home and school.

Conclusion

There is a growing recognition that individuals need to have positive feelings and ties to their ethnic heritage. With this change in attitude, educational policies have worked towards building tolerance through mutual understanding. The concept of cultural democracy is being symbolically accepted into the educational system. This implies that individuals have the right to maintain a bicultural identity--that is, to retain one's identification with an ethnic group while at the same time learning to adopt mainstream values and lifestyle when necessary.

Multicultural education has become a very popular and acceptable vehicle for meeting this goal. The language, heritage, values, patterns of thinking, and motivation of more than one culture are included in a curriculum. This educational "housecleaning" may be occurring only at a rhetorical level for some areas of the country, however, for some minority children the struggles of the recent years have lessened the gap between minority and white students' academic performance. Reform takes time and must start in the early years of schooling. The home, community, and school have a decisive role in the decision making process on what children ought to learn, how children ought to learn, and how teachers and parents should participate in the learning process.

REFERENCES

Aguirre, E. & Cepeda, R. M. (1981). Hispanics and education in the 1980's. In The National Hispanic Center for Advanced Studies and Policy Analysis, *The State of Hispanic America* (pp. 16-32). Oakland, CA: BABEL, Inc.

Alvirez, D., Bean, F. D., & Williams, D. (1982). The Mexican-American family. In C. H. Mindel, & R. W. Habenstein (Eds.), *Ethnic families in America* (pp. 269-292). New York: Elsevier Science Publishing Company, Inc.

Archibald, R., & Chemers, M. (1975). The relationship of teacher's cognitive style to minority student satisfaction. In *Education, Interventions, Strategies and Blacks* (pp. 85-97). Washington, DC: The Journal of Afro American Issues, A Division of ECCA Publishers.

Association on American Indian Affatirs (1979). *Indian Family Defense*, 11, New York.

Baca Zinn, M. (1975). Political familism: Toward sex role equality in Chicano families. *Aztlan: International Journal of Chicano Studies.*

Banks, J. (1981). *Multiethnic education theory and practice.* Boston: Allyn and Bacon, Inc.

Berman, D. M. (1966). *It is so ordered: The supreme court rules on School segregation.* New York: Norton.

Blanchard, E. L. (1983). The growth and development of American Indian and Andean native children. In G. Powell (Ed.), *The psychosocial development of minority group children,* New York: Brunner/Mazel, Inc.

Bonacich, E. (1972, October). A theory of ethnic antagonism: The split labor market." *American Sociological Review, 37, 547-559.*

Bureau of Census Statistical Abstract (1981). Washington, DC: U.S. Government Printing Office.

Bureau of Indian Affairs (1975). *Federal Indian Policies,* Washington, DC: U.S. Government Printing Office.

Carter, T. P., & Segura, R. D. (1979). *Mexican-Americans in School: A decade of change.* New York: College Entrance Examination Board.

Cheng, C. W. (1979). What is "an equal chance" for minority children? *Journal of Negro Education, 48*(3), 267-287.

Coates, B. (1972). White adult behavior toward black and white children. *Child Development, 43,* 143-154.

Commission on Civil Rights (1973). The southwest Indian report, Washington, DC: U.S. Government Printing Office.

Commission on Civil Rights (1974). *Twenty years after brown: The shadows of the past.* Washington, DC: U.S. Government Printing Office.

Cortes, M., Barcelo, C. J. Jr., & Schroyer, J. (1980, January). The needs of elementary and secondary education: Policy issues paper on migrant education. In *A compendium of policy papers* (pp. 659-674). House Committee on Education and Labor, Congress of the U.S.

Epps, E. (1980). The impact of school desegregation on aspirations, self-concepts and other aspects of personality. In R. L. Jones (Ed.), *Black psychology* (pp. 231-243), New York: Harper & Row, Publishers, Inc.

Executive Office of President (1984). *Budget of U.S. Government FY 1985.* Washington, DC: Superintendent of Documents.

Educacion Liberadora (1982, January). Information and resources center, Latino Institute, Research Division. *2*(5).

Fratoe, F. A. (1981, September). *The education of nonmetro Hispanics.* Rural Development (Research Report No. 31). U.S. Department of Agriculture, Washington, DC.

Gay, G. (1981). Interactions in culturally pluralistic classrooms. In J. Banks (Ed.), *Education in the 80's multiethnic education.* Washington, DC: National Education Association.

Grebler, L., Moore, J. W., & Guzman, R. C. (1970). *The Mexican-American people: The nations second largest minority.* New York: The Free Press.

Hale, J. E. (1982). *Black children their roots, culture and learning style.* Provo, UT: Brigham Young University Press.

Hamilton, C. V. (1975). Education in the black community: An examination of the realities. In M. Walker (Ed.), *A history of education of Afro-Americans in America.* Milburn, New Jersey: R. F. Publishing, Inc.

Hawkes, G. R., & Taylor, M. (1975). Power structure in Mexican and Mexican-American farm labor families. *Journal of Marriage and the Family, 37*(4), 807-811.

Hertzberg, H. W. (1971). *The search for American Indian identity.* Syracuse, New York: Syracuse University Press.

Hill, R. B. (1972). *The strengths of black families.* New York: Emerson Hall Publishers, Inc.

Hines, P. M., & Boyd-Franklin, N. (1982). Black families. In M. McGoldrick, J. Pearce, & J. Giordano (Eds.), *Ethnicity and family therapy* (pp. 84-107). New York: The Guilford Press.

Hollins, E. R. (1982). Beyond multicultural education. *The Negro Educational Review. 33*(3-4), 140-145.

Hollins, E. R. (1982). The Marva Collins story revisited: Implications for regular classroom instruction. *Journal of Teacher Education, 33*(1), 37-40.

Jackson, C., & Galli, M. (1977). *A history of the Bureau of Indian affairs and its activities among Indians.* San Francisco: R & E Research Associates, Inc.

Jackson, S. L. (1981). A bilingual Montessori program for preschool Mexican-American children. In T.H. Escobedo (Ed.) *Education and Chicanos: Issues and Research* (pp. 167-185). Monograph of the UCLA Spanish Speaking Mental Health Research Center (serial no. 8).

James, R. L. (1974). The educational needs of black Americans. In A. Castaneda, R. L. James, & W. Robbins (Eds.), *The educational needs of minority groups* (pp. 45-79). Lincoln, Nebraska: Professional Educators Publications, Inc.

Jones, F. C. (1975). The disjunctive relationship between the Afro-American experience and conventional educational efforts. In L. Gary & A. Favors (Eds.), *Restructuring the educational process: a black perspective* (pp. 12-20). Washington, DC: Howard University.

Jordan, I. (1980, January). Meeting the challenge--serving migrant children. In *A compendium of policy papers* (pp. 675-679). House Committee on Education and Labor, Congress of the U.S.

Josephy, A., Jr. (1971). *Red power,* New York: McGraw-Hill.
Keller, G. D., & VanHooft, K. S. (1982). A chronology of bilingualism and bilingual education in the U.S. In J.A. Fishman, & G. D. Keller, (Eds.), *Bilingual education for Hispanic students in the U.S.* (pp. 3-19) New York: Teachers College, Columbia University.
Kitano, H. L. (1969). *Japanese Americans: The evolution of a subculture.* Englewood Cliffs: Prentice Hall.
Kitano, H. (1980). Japanese. In S. Thernstrom (Ed.), *Harvard Encyclopedia of American Ethnic Groups* (pps. 561-571). Cambridge, Massachusetts: The Belknap Press of Harvard University Press.
Laosa, L. M. (1977). Socialization, education, and continuity: The importance of the sociocultural context. *Young Children, 32*(5), 21-27.
LeVine, E. S., & Bartz, K. E. (1979). Comparative child-rearing attitudes among Chicano, Anglo, and black parents. *Hispanic Journal of Behavioral Sciences. 1*(2), 165-178.
Lomotey, K. (1981). Nation building in the Afrikan community: It's time to build solutions to the education problem. California: Sunshine Printers, CIBI Publication.
Mathey, W. C., & Johnson, R. L. (1983). American black population 1970-1982. *The Crisis. 90*(10), 10-18.
Matute-Bianchi, M. E. (1979, June). *The federal mandate for bilingual education: Some implications for parent and community participation.* Paper presented at the Ethnoperspectives Forum on Bilingual Education, Ypsilanti, Michigan.
McAdoo, H. (1981). Patterns of upward mobility in black families. In H. McAdoo (Ed.), *Black families* (pp. 155-170). Beverly Hills: Sage Publications, Inc.
McGhee, J. D. (1983). The changing demographics in Black America. In J. D. Williams (Eds.), *The state of black America 1983* (pp. 1-44). New York: National Urban League, Inc.
McLemore, S. D. (1980). *Racial and ethnic relations in America.* Boston: Allyn & Bacon, Inc.
Meier, M. S., & Rivera, F. (1981). *Dictionary of Mexican-American history.* Westport, Connecticut: Greenwood Press.
Mindel, C. H. & Habenstein, R. (1981). *Ethnic families in America: Patterns and variations.* New York: Elsevier North Holland, Inc.
Moore, H. (1971). Brown vs Board of Education. In R. Lefcourt (Ed.), *Law against the people: Essays to emystify law, and order and the court.* New York: Vintage.
National Clearinghouse for Bilingual Education (1983, March-April and May-June), *Forum,* VI (2,3).
Nieto, S., & Sinclair, R. (1980, April). *Curriculum decision-making: The Puerto Rican family and the bilingual child.* Paper presented at the annual meeting of the American Educational Research Association, Boston, Massachusetts.

Ogbu, J. U. (1982). Equalization of educational opportunity and racial/ethnic inequality. In P. Altbach, R. Arnove, & G. Kelly (Eds.), *Comparative Education* (pp. 168-190), New York: Macmillan.

Olivas, M. (1982, July). The condition of education for Hispanics. In *La Red/The Net* (Report No. 56). Ann Arbor, MI: The University of Michigan, Institute for Social Research.

Olneck, M., & Lazerson, M. (1980). Education. In S. Thernstrom, A. Orlov, & O. Handlin (Eds.), *Harvard encyclopedia of American ethnic groups* (pp. 303-318). The Belknap Press of Harvard University Press, Cambridge, Massachusetts.

Padilla, A. (1982). Bilingual schools: Gateways to integration or roads to separation. In J. A. Fishman, & G. D. Keller (Eds.), *Bilingual education for Hispanic students in the U.S.* (pp. 48-70). New York: Teachers College, Columbia University.

Parra, E., & Henderson, R. W. (1982). Mexican-American perceptions of parent and teacher roles in child development. In J. A. Fishman, & G. D. Keller (Eds.), *Bilingual education for Hispanic students in the U.S.* (pp. 289-299). New York: Teachers College, Columbia University.

Parrillo, V. (1980). *Strangers to these shores.* Boston: Houghton Mifflin, Co.

Perkins, E. U. (1975). *Home is a dirty street: The social oppression of black children.* Chicago: Third World Press.

Pettigrew, T. F. (1964). *A profile of Negro Americans.* New York: Van Nostrand.

Pinderhughes, E. (1982). Afro-American families and the victim system. In M. McGoldrick, J. Pearce, & J. Giordano (Eds.), *Ethnicity and family therapy* (pp. 108-122). New york: The Guilford Press.

Ramirez, M., & Castaneda, A. (1974). *Cultural democracy, bicognitive development and education.* New York: Academic Press.

Rodriguez, A. M. (1983). *Educational policy and cultural plurality.* New York: Brunner/Mazel, Inc.

Rosenthal, R. (1973). The pygmalion effect lives. *Psychology Today, 7,* 56-63.

Rosenthal, R., & Jacobson, L. (1968). *Pygmalion in the classroom. Teacher expectations and pupil's intellectual development.* New York: Holt, Rinehart & Winston.

Rubovits, P. C., & Maehr, M. L. (1973). Pygmalion black and white. *Journal of Personality and Social Psychology, 25,* 210-218.

Schaefer, R. T. (1979). *Racial and Ethnic Groups.* Boston: Little Brown and Co., Inc.

Scott, G. D. (1975). Teacher attitudes and perception: The impact on achievement of black learners. In L. Gary, & A. Favors (Eds.), *Restructuring the educational process: A black perspective* (pp. 108-123). Washington, DC: Howard University.

Smith, C. H. (1975). Organizational model for parental participation in inner city schools. In *Education, interventions, strategies and blacks*. Washington, DC: The Journal of Afro-American Issues, A Division of ECCA Publishers.

Southwest Network of the Study Commission on Undergraduate Education and the Education of Teachers (1973). Lincoln, NE, Curriculum Development Center, *Chicano Alternative Education*. Hayward, California: Bay View Regal Printing Service.

Staff (1979, July 2). United Nations High Commissioner on Refugees. *Newsweek*.

Staples, R., & Mirande, A. (1980). Racial and cultural variations among American families: A decennial review of the literature on minority families. *Journal of Marriage and the Family, 42*, 887-903.

Stewart, I. S. (1981). The larger question: Bilingual education, family and society. *Childhood Education, 57*(3), 138-143.

U.S. Bureau of the Census Supplementary Reports (1980). *Race of the Population by States 1980*. Washington, DC: U.S. Government Printing Office.

U.S. Department of Commerce, Bureau of the Census (1983). *Conditions of Hispanics in America Today*. Washington, DC: U.S. Government Printing Office.

U.S. Department of Health, Education, and Welfare (1975).

U.S. Office of Management and Budget (1983 June). *1983 Catalog of Federal Domestic Assistance*. Washington, DC: Superintendent of Documents.

Vasquez, M. J. (1978). *Chicana and Anglo university women: Factors related to their performance, persistence and attrition*. Unpublished doctoral dissertation, University of Texas, Austin.

Weinberg, M. (1977a). *A chance to learn: A history of race and education in the U.S.* Cambridge, Massachusetts: Cambridge University Press.

Weinberg, M. (1977b). *Minority students: A research appraisal*. U.S. Department of HEW National Institute of Education, Washington, DC: U.S. Government Printing Office.

Woodson, C. G. (1972). *The mis-education of the Negro*. New York: AMS Press.

COMMUNICATION: KEY TO SCHOOL-HOME RELATIONS(1)

Edward E. Gotts and Richard F. Purnell

Edward Earl Gotts, Ph.D.
Appalachia Educational Laboratory
P.O. Box 1348
Charleston, WV 25325

Richard F. Purnell, Ph.D.
University of Rhode Island
Kingston, RI 02881

The purpose of this chapter is to introduce and define, review the literature and current thinking on, and report the authors' research endeavors and results on the topic of school-home communication. The fundamental premise for being concerned about this topic is that the educational progress and well-being of children are the mutual interest of schools and families. Unfortunately, various forces in our society have been at work for some years to demutualize this important relationship. The study of school-home communications offers a very promising means of realigning the interests of the home and the school, with our children being the primary beneficiaries of greater collaboration between the two.

Concept of Relational Connection Between School and Home

Educators and parents have positive but vague notions about school-home relations (Gallup, 1980). By and large, they readily distinguish relations from attempts to "modify families to serve the school's purposes" (which, e.g., *parent involvement* connotes to some school personnel) and from efforts to "organize families to take over schools" (which, e.g., *parent participation in decision-making* has come to suggest in other circles). It is our interpretation, therefore, that the term *relations* is to be understood in the connectional sense of relatedness, as when parties are mutually or reciprocally interested in a common matter (Goffman, 1967). More will be done with this bi-directional quality later in the chapter.

Despite the ease with which it is understood, *relations* is too broad a term to provide a clear, operational focus for research or for yielding practical recommendations. Consequently, we emphasize the *communication* aspect of school-home relations in our perspective on the topic. *Relations* is the more abstract term and refers to a construct which must be inferred. While *communications* is broad, it is less abstract. An attempted act of communication can be observed; it has concrete empirical referents; it can be recorded, segmented, rated, and so forth (Cherry, 1966; Scheflen, 1978).

Additional support for this emphasis comes from the fact that communications are regarded as the keystone in relations between educators and families by various prominent, close observers of and commentators on the changes that are taking place in American life styles (Combs, 1979; Toffler, 1980; Naisbitt, 1982; Futrell, 1983). Indeed, in his *Megatrends,* Naisbitt (1982) tells us that "...in an information society the game is people interacting with other people... The life channel of the information age is communication" (p. 22).

Nature of Communications Between School and Home

Major elements in the communication process include (a) the communicator or source; (b) the message, of which content is one aspect (c) the channel, medium or interpersonal network; and (d) the receiver or audience (Budd, Thorp, & Donohew, 1967). Equally important are the relations among all elements (Cherry, 1966); the affective dimensions of the message (Gotts, 1967); the sequential structures or recognizable boundaries or "frames" (Scheflen, 1978); extraneous matter or "noise" which masks the message (Collins & Raven, 1969); and the encompassing internal and external contexts wherein the meanings of messages are to be grasped (Greene, 1972). Using communications as the conceptual frame of reference for research into school-home relations offers, as can be seen, a wealth of analytic tools.

Essentially and ideally, then, *school-home communication* takes place when the school transmits a message to the home and that message is received as intended by its sender. Even though we will use this label to include both messages sent by the school to the home and vice versa, for the convenience of discourse, we encourage distinguishing the latter from the former when desirable by rearranging the order of the words to: *home-school communications.* Moreover, although other forms of interactive communications occur and are possible, we call the two major forms of school-home communications: (1) Individual (Type I) and (2) School-wide (Type S). Examples of Type I are messages about the child's academic progress, attendance, and interest, whereas examples of Type S are PTA/PTO announcements, newsletters, notices of conference times, and discipline codes.

Communications per se, nevertheless, has certain shortcomings as a term for describing to practitioners and parents the results of research efforts into school-home relations. This is so because in recent years the notion of mutual or reciprocal relations has been dropping out of its meaning. This debasing of the term is evident in the coinage of such needed current technical refinements as *one-way* versus *two-way* communications.

There are tell-tale signs all around us of the need for schools to re-examine their style of communicating to the home about Type I and Type S matters. They are abundantly signaled in the current landscape of the language used by writers to describe the dominant forms of communication to the home that are widely practiced by many schools in our society (e.g., "one-way," "top-down," or "authoritarian"). Solutions that Naisbitt (1982), Seeley (1981), and other contemporary commentators offer to the dilemma of one-sided efforts dwell on the use of "two-way," "mutually-exchanging," "partnership" styles of communicating by schools. As one well-known investigator on the subject (Lightfoot, 1978) has sharply described the problem, schools and families have become "worlds apart" in their relations and communications. Thus if educational architects are to have a say in bringing about more than just an "exasperating tolerance" between the school and the home, attention must be given to the dynamic and changing interplay between these two significant influences in the development of our children. Ideally, ways must be found to make their emerging relationship a collaborative one that strengthens both.

Assessment of Needs in This Area

In order to assess the educational needs of its seven-state region (i.e., Alabama, Kentucky, Ohio, Pennsylvania, Tennessee, Virginia, West Virginia), the Appalachia Educational Laboratory (AEL) developed a group of needs statements through a modified Delphi process in seven individual state conferences attended by representatives of parents, students, business and community interests, and educators. AEL staff generated additional statements based on literature reviews and results of other regional studies in which they had been engaged. During a validation process, a cross-section of about 100 validators from each state assigned priorities to the needs statements.

This foregoing method of identifying needs was, of course, designed to result in the identification of needs significant to this region and to its several states. Thus, no claim can be made that the needs so identified as priorities are valid for other regions of the country. It is, nevertheless, true that the AEL member states come from multiple regions and reflect great diversity of demography, politics, economics, and so forth. It is, therefore, not unreasonable to expect that needs common to two or more of these states might well be identified in other regions of the county, if similar study methods were employed.

When the AEL-generated statements' ratings were factor analyzed to determine their underlying structure, two of the top three (i.e., largest factors extracted) contained statements pertaining to school-family relations. These are discussed briefly below.

The first of these factors could best be described as dealing with "special needs families" and their particular life circumstances (e.g., families with both parents working outside the home, single parents, lower socio-economic class families, rural families, and those whose teenagers are "out of control"), in relation to which schools could play a constructive or helping role.

A second major factor was identified as dealing with "programmatic approaches for improving school-family relations" (e.g., through inservice training of school personnel; by finding new methods to involve parents of older children and teens in their children's learning; and by improving the basic academic skills of parents themselves through continuing education).

The two foregoing factors suggested three areas of possible emphases for AEL's regionally-oriented longer-term R & D programs: (1) research into the situations confronting families with special needs and into ways that schools might relate effectively to their circumstances; (2) inquiry into programs and practices which might serve to improve school-family relations for all families, with special emphasis on those with older children and teenagers; and (3) study of ways to improve the preparation of school personnel for working with families.

The present chapter looks especially at our work in the second of the preceding areas, using school-home communications as an operational frame of reference. Whereas our research and development activities have been oriented to improving practices in this region, we expect that their implications for practice under other conditions and in other settings will prove to be relatively transparent and transferable. Before proceeding to examine our work, however, it will be helpful to examine selectively the research and practice literatures that have informed our thinking.

Review of Literature

The literature reviewed in this chapter will focus on parent involvement programs which have been implemented in elementary and secondary schools. Thus, while it is acknowledged that much of the impetus for parent involvement with schools has stemmed from the literature reporting preschool program effects which involved parents in a variety of ways, these findings are not reported here. Many researchers feel that changes in home environment can influence cognitive functioning and academic performance as late as the adolescent years (Keeves, 1975; Schaefer, 1971; Walberg & Marjoribanks, 1976). It is through these years that the home and the school share the responsibility of educating children.

This review is organized into five major sections. They include: (1) the literature related to parent/family/home environment variables which significantly influence child achievement and adjustment in school; (2) survey findings which document parental interest in school (3) the results of studies and projects to improve school-home relations; (4) a summary discussion of major problem areas identified in the literature; and (5) a very brief look at additional related literature and topics.

Overview of Literature

Home Environment Factors That Influence Child Achievement and Ability

The literature abounds with assertions that a child's family and home environment are more important to academic achievement than teacher or school related variables (Dobson & Dobson, 1975; Mize, 1977; Nedler & McAfee, 1979; Schaefer, 1971; Walberg & Marjoribanks, 1976). Schaefer concludes from research findings that "schools do not change the child's level of intellectual functioning, they merely educate him at the level of functioning established and maintained by the family and the community" (1971, p. 18). Before reviewing studies that deal specifically with school-home relations, therefore, it is helpful to become briefly familiar with studies relating to the home environment.

Mize (1977) reports findings of independent research studies to the effect that from 50 to 85 percent of the variance in achievement scores, IQ or verbal ability can be attributed to parent/family/home environment variables.

Walberg and Marjoribanks (1976) review the literature on family environment and verbal-educational ability and report studies in which child achievement level was correlated with a variety of variables. They conclude that (better) family environment measures are important to include in educational studies to allow for more precise measures of the educational effects under study. They recommend comprehensive interviews (as opposed to the mere collection of data such as SES, family size, or the number of books and magazines in the home) and going beyond examining effects on child achievement to more global views of child development and adjustment measures as outcome indicators.

A report showing that a complex set of variables, including degree of urbanization, the number of adult-oriented organizations to which the parent belongs, the parent's health, parent educational level, and parent's occupational mobility, was required to predict favorable child outcomes (Gotts, Spriggs, & Snow, 1980, pp. 24-25) lends further support to

Walberg and Marjoribank's findings that simple demographic measures alone cannot account for the variance.

Schaefer (1971) reports that Douglas, in a sample of 5,000 children in England, "found that interest and involvement with the child's education were far more important than the quality of the schools, even after statistically controlling for family socioeconomic status" (p. 19).

Nedler and McAfee (1979) review the findings of the 1966 Coleman Report, which "concluded that differences in school facilities and curricula are not significantly related to school achievement. The most important single factor in achievement is the home background of the child and fellow students" (p. 14). The continuing debate over the Coleman findings reveals that, although these inferences about school effects are much disputed, those about home are not.

Parental interest in reading and the encouragement of reading activities are frequently cited as important in developing positive attitudes toward reading. Dobson and Dobson (1975) report findings by Ware and Garber that parental "press" for reading, and the availability of materials in the home are predictive of school success. From this they have concluded that certain home-centered activities could increase the likelihood of improved school performance.

Kifer (1976) reviews how reading for pleasure among 10 year-olds was positively correlated with parental encouragement of both reading and school achievement. He also reviews the findings of Crandall and Battle which show that parental behaviors were positively correlated with students' willingness to expend effort studying.

In a survey of students in grades 6 through 12, socioeconomic level was found to be positively correlated with aspirations for educational achievement. Greater participation by the student in family decision-making was associated with more positive personality development and better school coping skills (Epstein & McPartland, 1977).

Several studies have indicated that although school performance and home environment variables are not directly causally related, a change in home environment may lead to changes in student outcome. Keeves (1975) used path analysis techniques to study the ways in which the educational environments of the home, the peer group, and the classroom accounted for changes in performance in two subject areas, mathematics and science, over the period of one year. He acknowledges that while some variables in the student's home cannot be changed (e.g., income level, family size, and parent education level) some environmental factors can be influenced and might make a difference, even in adolescent years. From his findings, Keeves concludes that if parental attitudes and interest in schooling could be increased, they might positively affect the achievement level of the student. Additionally, he reports that certain home factors, such as home-school relationships, the use of books and library facilities, and an environment conducive to homework completion, influenced achievement in science but not in mathematics (p. 458).

Walberg and Marjoribanks (1976) reach a similar conclusion that, "adolescents may benefit as much as younger children from a stimulating family environment ... A stimulating family environment for several years is likely to lead to some enhancement of cognitive abilities" (p. 546). Likewise, Schaefer's review of studies leads him to conclude that "with increased intellectual stimulation, higher rates of mental growth and higher IQ's can be achieved" (1971, p. 20).

Mize (1977) cites some research by Hicks which indicates that students whose parents have positive attitudes about school have higher academic achievement, social adjustment, and emotional stability. The study concludes that if parents become involved in school activities, not only will their own attitudes improve, but their children's attitudes and achievements will likewise improve (p. 76).

Mize (1977) also recalls that the effects of change in parent attitudes on adolescent school performance have been demonstrated by Brookover. In that study parents were taught to increase the academic expectations they held for their children. With this change in parental attitude, students' self-perceptions improved, as did their school grades.

Parent Attitudes Toward Schools

Surveys have been done on parent and citizen samples, both locally and nationally, which confirm that parents feel education is important and want to stay informed of their child's progress in school (Etheridge, Collins, & Coats, 1979; Gallup, 1980; Hubbell, 1979; Valentin & Alston, 1978). Parents also want to be more involved in the schools. They prefer volunteer service and improved parent-teacher relationships, rather than involvement in the governance of the school system (Alden, 1979).

Eighty-four percent of the respondents to a recent Gallup poll (1980) favored a plan which would involve parents at the beginning of every semester in reviewing child achievement and planning for a home-school program to assist the child's educational development. Forty-five percent of the sample selected parent training "to help parents become more fully involved in their children's education" as a priority for the federal Department of Education (Gallup, 1980, p. 41).

Ingram (1978) reports, on a study by Carter in which interviews were conducted with a representative sample of voters who received some form of communication from the schools. Those who received communications were more likely to vote and to vote favorably on school-related issues (pp. 20-21). Yet Hubbell (1979) found that two out of three adults surveyed have no contact with the public schools but want to stay informed of such things as student test results, curriculum and teaching methods used in the schools, and the role of the school board especially as it relates to budget decisions. In light of these findings, it is not surprising that Hubbell reports decreasing confidence in public schools, especially among non-parents, and an increasing feeling that the financial support to schools is sufficient.

The evidence suggests that schools must take the initiative in improving community awareness of the educational programs offered, and in involving more citizens in school programs. Ingram (1978) reviews Sloan's findings that suggested "the most frequent way parents learned about the school was through their children, the school newspaper, and parent-teacher conferences. Parents preferred to be informed through (a) the school newspaper, (b) parent-teacher conferences, (c) PTA, (d) being told by their child, and (e) a phone call or note from the teacher" (p. 23).

The mass media are effective vehicles for informing the public about the schools in a community. Ingram (1978) cites independent studies by Grout and Cohn showing that people were influenced by what they heard or read about schools in the mass media. The most effective method of reaching people, however, is through personal contact (Ingram, 1978).

Herman (1972) offers a rich collection of program suggestions to implement long-term communication between the school and community. The goals are to develop mutual understanding and public support for educational programs. Yearly attitude surveys are conducted with all residents in the school district to identify problem areas. Each problem is assigned to an action committee that studies the situation and makes recommendations to the superintendent. The results are widely publicized in newspapers. There are no evaluation data from this program; however, it is clear from the wealth of activities employed that the superintendent places a high priority on community involvement and support.

On a local school level, Criscuolo (1979) suggests methods for keeping parents better informed of children's reading progress. A New Haven, Connecticut public school system writes a newspaper column for parents whose children are having trouble reading in school. The schools provide parent resource rooms where parents can feel comfortable visiting the schools to participate in discussion groups, borrow reading materials and make learning games to use at home. Reading progress letters are sent to parents which provide extra practice stories when students complete a new level of reading. Schools provide parents with homework-type activities that they can do with their children and send home "reading recipes" each week.   There are no evaluation results reported.

Epstein (1983) set out to show teachers parents' reactions and experiences involving school-home relations and to provide parents with insights into their own reactions and those of other districts' parents. Her survey of 1269 parents in 82 first, third, and fifth grade teachers' classrooms in Maryland addressed the question: What are the effects on parents of teacher practices of parent involvement?

Results show that, in general, parents have positive attitudes about their child's school and teacher. Furthermore, Epstein's (1983) abstract states that "many parents receive few or no communications from the school, few are involved at the school, and most believe that the schools could do more to involve parents in learning activities at home that would benefit their child."

A number of positive effects on parents by classroom teachers who use home learning activities more frequently are also noted. However, Epstein (1983) reports finding that routine communications from the school or parent involvement at the school do not have as strong and consistent effects on parents as teachers who frequently use home learning activities.

Review of Home-School Programs

Several classification systems of home-school-community relations have been developed and reported (Filipczak, Lordeman, & Friedman, 1977; Gordon, 1979; Gotts, Spriggs, & Sattes, 1979; Mize, 1977; Nedler & McAfee, 1979). The literature in this review has been organized into a framework which views communication between the home and school on a continuum. This ranges from programs in which the primary focus is on the school through programs which view the home as central. While programs do not fall neatly into specific categories under this approach, the following areas are described: (a) teaching parents to be tutors of their children, (b) home-school communication which encourages more parent contacts, (c) involving parents in counseling programs, (d) coordinated home-based reinforcement programs, (e) parent involvement to strengthen the home environment, and (f) parent involvement in decision- or policy-making roles. Very little mention will be made of programs known as "parent education" or "parent training," which are designed to "help parents become better informed about child rearing and about daily life as it affects child rearing" (Nedler & McAfee, 1979, p. 217). The need and desire for parent education has been substantiated in survey results (Gallup, 1980; Gotts, Coan, & Kenoyer, 1977; McAfee, 1979). However, these are usually instructional as opposed to being partnership programs, and so are not included here.

Training parents as tutors. When parents of low-performing children are trained as tutors, studies have found that these children outperform children of untrained parents (Hofmeister, 1977; McKinney, 1975). Rich, Van Dien, and Mattox (1979) advocate the parent-as-teacher approach because research has shown it to be an effective way of increasing student achievement. They reason that parents are more likely to maintain involvement when they can see that what they are doing makes a difference. Additionally, it is more cost effective to utilize volunteer resources rather than additional school personnel. Involvement in a training program also significantly and positively affects parental attitudes toward the school (McKinney, 1975).

Mize (1977) reports on a program developed by Della-Piana, Stahmann and Allen to assist children, in grades three through six, who were below grade level in reading. Parent involvement in group and individual training sessions accounted for 25 percent of the variance in the reading comprehension scores; the experimental group outperformed the control group in both oral reading accuracy and reading comprehension.

The effect of training parents as tutors may be partially attributable to increased school-parent contacts. Mize (1977) reports a study by Schiff in which students whose parents were trained to offer home lessons through parent-teacher conferences were compared with students whose parents received standard report cards. The experimental group had better school attendance records, better study habits, fewer school behavior problems, and greater gains in reading (p. 76). It is not clear to what extent the teacher contacts alone influenced parents' attitudes and interest in school; however, it is noteworthy that there was a difference between the two groups.

Communication between home and school. The implementation of communication between school personnel and parents has been shown to increase rates of attendance (Duncan, 1969; Parker & McCoy, 1977; Sheats & Dunkleberger, 1979; Shelton & Dobson, 1973), to improve school performance (Bittle, 1975; Duncan, 1969: Shelton & Dobson, 1973), and to increase parent-initiated contacts with the school (Bittle, 1975; Duncan, 1969; Mager, 1980; Parker & McCoy, 1977).

Excessive absenteeism is associated with poor school performance, negative attitudes toward the school, and increased risk of school drop-out. Consequently, schools are interested in improving attendance. When the principal made calls to parents of first and second grade children who had high rates of absenteeism, not only did school attendance improve, but parents also contacted the school to report absence due to illness (Parker & McCoy, 1977). Sheats and Dunkleberger (1979) found that parent contacts could be made by the school secretary as effectively as by the school principal; for both groups absenteeism was reduced by about one-third.

Mager (1980) attempted to identify characteristics which would distinguish elementary teachers with a high frequency of teacher-initiated parent contacts from those who had a low frequency. The high-frequency teachers reported: themselves to be upper-middle class more often; more frequent parent-initiated contacts; a larger variety of reasons for parent contact; seeing themselves as more responsible for contact; and feeling more comfortable that they were meeting parent expectations.   The low-contact group reported a stronger sense of support from parents.   There was no difference between the groups related to the principal's support or encouragement of parent involve-ment activities.   The limitation of self-report data in this study can not be ignored.   However, if the teacher's reports accurately divided the groups into high and low numbers of parent contact, it may be that parent-initiated contacts occur more frequently with teachers who more often contact parents.

Barth (1979) reports the findings of Hickey, Imber and Ruggierro of the effect of a home-based reinforcement program on parent-teacher communication.   They found that during baseline, there were no parent-initiated contacts; however, after implementation of the parent involve-ment program, twenty parent-initiated contacts were made.

Bittle (1975) reports a study in which a first grade teacher recorded academic and non-academic information for playback on a telephone answering device. This was then available for parents to call 24 hours a day.   In a class of 21, the average number of calls was 20.5 per day, indicating that most students' parents were calling to listen to the recording.   By comparison, during a 30-week baseline *prior* to implementing the telephone system, only five parent-initiated contacts had occurred.   Such a system was found to improve academic perform-ance in spelling and to facilitate classroom procedures such as obtain-ing permission slips for special events.   Not only was this system relatively inexpensive, it required a minimum amount of teacher time and resulted in a savings of teacher time in simple classroom bookkeep-ing and preparation activities.   Although there was no personal contact between parents and teacher, Bittle suggests that the message could include prompts to encourage face-to-face contact with the teacher.

Duncan (1969) conducted a study in which school counselors met individually with parents of students entering junior high. These students were compared to students who had entered the previous year. Parents had been invited to attend an orientation session before the school year began, but no individual conferences were held unless specifically requested. At the end of three years in junior high school, a number of impressive findings were reported. For example, (1) the average daily attendance was different at the .001 level of significance, in favor of the group whose parents had individual contact; (2) there were fewer school drop-outs in the parent-contact group (two as opposed to eight in the other group); (3) the mean grade point average of the parent-contact group was higher; (4) parents of the parent-contact group came to school more often than the comparison group; and (5) they came more frequently to see the school counselor concerning curriculum or grades as compared to the other group whose parents contacted the principal instead concerning discipline or grade dissatisfaction. However, because there were no data on grades, attendance, etc., prior to entry into seventh grade, it is possible that differences existed between the groups prior to parent-counselor contacts. Additionally, there was no control for possible differential counselor treatment of the two groups.

When teachers were trained in the Family Involvement Communication System (FICS) to improve communication skills in relating to parents, after which they made home visits, the average daily attendance and the grade point averages of children in the study improved when compared to a control group selected from classrooms of teachers who had received no training (Shelton & Dobson, 1973). It is not clear from the study how significant the special teacher training was, because the control group parents received no home visits. Additionally, teachers may have been biased in the assignment of grades in favor of those children whose families they visited. Nevertheless, the findings do tend to support the notion that increased parent-teacher communication will improve school attendance.

Parent counseling. Myers (1971) found that parent counseling significantly (p less than .05) increased grade point averages of under-achieving children. The study had limitations in the small number of subjects (seven in each of two groups) and in the way in which parents were assigned to the experimental and control groups. Dobson and Dobson (1975) report Wechsler's findings that underachieving boys whose mothers participated in small-group counseling sessions showed improved self-acceptance as long as six months after the counseling program had been completed.

Hayes, Cunningham and Robinson (1977) compared the effectiveness of counseling directly with students to the effectiveness of counseling their parents. Subjects were fifth and sixth grade students who had classroom behavioral problems and who were from four schools in low socioeconomic neighborhoods. There were no differences between the two treatment groups. However, when compared to a control group, the group which had received intervention through parent contact scored more favorably on three scales: the *Junior Index of Motivation,* the *Coopersmith Self-Esteem Scale,* and the *Manifest Anxiety Scale.* It was not clear if tests were given in a pre-post design, since the authors did not report on initial differences between the groups. Thus, the findings are not conclusive, although, they tend to support the notion that counselors can be more effective when working with parents than when working directly with students.

Home-based reinforcement. In an extensive review of the literature related to home-based reinforcement of school behaviors, Barth
(1979) concludes that feedback to parents, more frequent than standard
report cards, can significantly affect and improve school behaviors. The
implementation of home-based reinforcement programs requires very
little time on the part of the teacher, and is effective in a very short
period of time, regardless of the type of training which parents receive.
It is not clear how long such a program can be operated effectively,
although the literature suggests that once a system of regular communication between the home and school is begun, home-school contacts
increase. Fairchild (1976) advocates the use of such a system because it
increases communicaiton between the home and school, involves the
parent in reinforcing behaviors which are conducive to improve school
performance, and presents a united front to the child.

Edlund (1969) reports that a daily checklist system, completed by
the teacher and sent home to the parent, is effective with students from
kindergarten through high school in increasing the number of accurately
completed class assignments and in increasing the amount of time spent
in appropriate social behaviors. Parents required no more than six
training sessions to learn how to apply consistent reinforcement for
check marks indicating desirable behavior. Both parents and teachers
found the program easy to implement and carry out; teachers found that
such a program decreased the amount of time they were spending on
problem behaviors.

Barth (1979) reports on a study conducted by Blackmore during a
summer school session for preadolescents in which school behavior notes
were sent home daily, and good reports were cashed in for privileges and
money. After continuing the use of school notes into the regular school
year, the "subjects were on task 83% of the time, which equalled their
peers, and bettered their baseline performance by 19%" (p. 449).

In a peer-tutoring program to improve the reading performance of
2nd, 3rd, and 4th graders, it was found that peer-tutoring in combination
with home-based reinforcement was more effective than peer tutoring
by itself (Trovato & Bucher, 1980). Children were matched in triads and
randomly assigned to one of three groups: control, peer-tutoring, and
peer-tutoring plus home-based reinforcement. In oral reading, the gains
were 0.19, 0.77, and 1.27 years for each of the three groups, respectively. In comprehension, the gains were -0.13, 0.50, and 1.04, respectively.
The authors conclude that peer-tutoring significantly increases reading
performance. The addition of a home-based reinforcement program
further significantly improves reading.

Lahey et al. (1977) reported that daily report cards sent home to
parents were effective in reducing the amount of disruptive behaviors
during rest periods in two kindergarten classrooms. They concluded that
systematic feedback to parents can be effective with little modification

of teaching style and without extensive training for the parents. The authors caution that with children who have severe behavior problems, parents might need training to avoid the consequences of punitive action for poor reports.

Case studies of the successful use of home letters or home notes, in which the parent contingently reinforces the child for good behavior, are reported by Fairchild (1976); Imber, Imber, and Rothstein (1979); and Jason and Soucy (1977). Barth (1979) reports Thorne's study in which an adolescent's truancy rate decreased from 65% during the 46-day baseline period to 6.6% during the three months of the project. Additional program descriptions using a daily reporting system lack specific data, but report favorable outcomes (Dickerson, Spellman, Larsen & Tyler, 1973; Stitley, 1978).

Parent involvement with primary emphasis on the home. It has already been seen that when parents have greater communication with the schools, receive training as tutors, engage in general information exchange, or participate in specific home-based reinforcement programs, the effect on student performance is positive. In this section of the review, programs which place major emphasis on the role of the parent in influencing child development will be examined.

Mize (1977) evaluated the effects of the implementation of the Systematic Training for Effective Parenting Program (STEP) on a sample of mostly blue collar parents from four elementary schools which were using the Individually Guided Motivation System (IGM) developed in Wisconsin. Parents were asked to contract for bi-weekly meetings with their child, during which time they would discuss the accomplishments of the past few days, and spend time sharing thoughts and ideas. They were also asked to spend time each week with their child on some reading-related activity. Teachers likewise contracted for conferences to be held twice weekly. Mize reports post-test comparisons between the experimental and control groups to be significant beyond the .01 level on each of seven variables. The experimental group parents had more conferences with the teacher, spent more time with their children in reading activities (three hours in two weeks compared to six minutes by the control group), and had more positive attitudes toward education, as assessed by the *Education Attitude Survey.* The children in the experimental group reported self-esteem nearly two standard deviations above that of the control group, as measured by the *Coopersmith Self-Esteem Inventory;* were rated by their teachers and self-rated on two separate attitude measures as more motivated to learn and as having more positive attitudes towards school; and gained 12 months in reading compared to a one-month gain in the control group, as measured by the *Metropolitan Achievement Test for Reading.* Parents, teachers, counselors, and principals evaluated the program favorably on an open-ended questionnaire.

In an unpublished study, Walberg found increases in reading achievement and IQ scores of children in a large urban school where "parents, teachers, and children drew up written contracts of participation and responsibility in the educational and school process" (Lightfoot, 1980, p. 14).

Mize (1977) describes a report in *Newsweek* on Operation Higher Achievement in inner-city Chicago elementary schools, which brought parents and teachers together in monthly workshops to discuss how they could improve the level of educational achievement. Parents were encouraged to read to their children and to provide regular study times at home. Teachers visited homes and parents visited classrooms. The rate of parent participation in the monthly meetings was 70%. The reading achievement scores of the 400 participating children improved by 1.1 years, which was six months higher than for the achievement of children enrolled in non-participating Chicago inner-city schools.

Another project for culturally deprived students in all grades of elementary school was conducted in Flint, Michigan. Parents were involved in discussion groups which emphasized (1) the important of school achievement in obtaining employment in a technological society, (2) the importance of the home in providing encouragement for school work, and (3) parents setting a good example for their children to model after. Parents read daily to their children, listened to them read, and provided a regular time in the home for reading and studying. They continued throughout the summer to encourage reading by going to the library and providing books for their children. Children in the two participating schools gained 5.4 months in reading compared to a 2.7 month gain for children in a control school. The success of the project was attributed to home-school cooperation and a real commitment from the school staff to involve parents in important ways in order to utilize parent interest in increasing student performance (Smith & Brahce, 1963).

The degree to which parents are involved in meaningful ways is an important factor in the effectiveness of parent involvement programs. Gillum, Schooley and Novak (1977) compared three school districts involved in performance-contracting programs under a special grant from the state of Michigan to serve educationally disadvantaged children. All three districts had parent involvement components. In two of the districts, parent involvement was left to the discretion of the school principal or included one or two large group meetings which were poorly attended. The third district specified more intensive parent involvement. Parents attended inservice workshops where they learned about how to help their children accomplish curriculum objectives. Parents received individualized help in working on program goals and shared in the profits earned as a result of pupil achievement. It was found that students in all three districts scored higher than would have been expected without the special reading program. However, the group with a high degree of meaningful parent involvement showed the largest gains.

Boger, Richter, Paolucci, and Whitmer (1978) report Walberg's findings that students whose parents were actively involved with teachers "gained twice the grade equivalents on reading achievement scales as students in classes where parents and teachers were less intensively involved" (p. 22).

Other studies have shown that student achievement is influenced by parental involvement but are of more limited value because they fail to take into account possible differences between parents who volunteered to participate and control parents, who did not volunteer (Irvine et al., 1979; Woods, Barnard, & TeSelle, 1974). Still others are reported as project descriptions, with a positive tone, but lacking in statistical data to substantiate the effectiveness of the programs (Breiling, 1976; Gifford & Summerell, 1978; Hoskisson, Sherman, & Smith, 1974).

Parents as decision-makers. Parents have become increasingly involved with the schools in an advisory capacity, as members of Parent Advisory Councils mandated by Title I regulations, and as change agents who have banded together on the local level to effect changes in the schools. The effects of parent involvement in this capacity have not been comprehensively evaluated. It is difficult to measure the effect of parent participation in an advisory capacity. Often the groups are established to satisfy federal requirements but have little or no meaningful input on any level (Hightower, 1978; Steinberg, 1979). A major weakness of these councils is "that they have been initiated at federal and state levels with little involvement of parents or administrators at the local level and rarely provide resources for implementation or monitoring" (Steinberg, 1979, p. 57).

Schools must recognize that citizens, not educators, own the schools and consequently have a right to help shape policies. But parents are also individuals, with differing skills, expertise, and interests. Consequently, many options should be available to allow them to become involved in meaningful ways (Gordon, 1979; Della-Doro, 1979).

When parent groups form at the local level, it is because of the identification of a problem or need which is important to them. These groups, initiated by local schools or by independent parent groups, are more likely to be effective than those mandated from a state or federal level. Lightfoot (1980) reports on parent involvement in the King School in New Haven, where parents negotiated with teachers "for more structured and orderly classrooms, and emphasized the rigors of academic work" (p. 13). Berlin and Berlin (1973) report their study results of a group of parents whose children were near expulsion. They began observing in classrooms, collecting data to be presented to the school board, and were eventually effective in changing school administration and teaching personnel.

Summary of Major Problem Areas in School-Family Research

There appears to be universal agreement that improved school-family relations are beneficial and that increased parent involvement in the schools is a worthwhile goal. However, in reports of programs with this general goal, specific objectives are rarely stated. Consequently, evaluation results are sometimes vague and unclear (Anselmo, 1977; Filipczak et al., 1977; Nedler & McAfee, 1979). Filipczak et al. (1977) conclude that communication between the home and school requires an increased emphasis on measurable outcomes to assess program effectiveness. Without this kind of information to determine which programs are effective, programs may not succeed. Schools will become more alienated from a child's family rather than more involved.

In a needs assessment of Appalachian families, Spriggs (1980) reports that "teachers and parents do not seem to be coordinating and communicating well about student learning" (p. 9). She further states that "parents feel teachers are not interested" (p. 9), that parents are typically excluded from schools, and that parent-teacher conferences are dreaded rather than seen as a useful and helpful process. Lightfoot (1980) attributes this sense of distrust between parents and teachers to misperceptions. She contends that both lower-class black parents and middle-class white teachers value education. However, they have misperceptions of one another which do not allow them to recognize this shared value system. Because of this distrust, parents and teachers rarely come together to try and work out their problems and conflicts. Moreover, they miscommunicate.

Teachers will require specialized training to work effectively with parents (Gotts, 1979; Nedler & McAfee, 1979). This new role cannot be assumed without careful planning, training, and evaluation of results. Teachers will not be enthusiastic and supportive of programs involving parents unless they have shared in developing the programs. Likewise, parents will not support home-school programs unless they feel that an important need is being met (Nedler & McAfee, 1979).

From surveys of parents' attitudes toward schooling, it has been demonstrated that parents care a great deal about their child's performance in school, and are interested in learning more about ways in which they can help and support the local school program. They also are willing participants when they are given the opportunity to become involved in programs which are personally rewarding, or in which they can see evidence of improved child performance. It is also apparent that parents generally do not feel a part of their child's school program unless the school or the district places special emphasis on involving parents. This is especially true of lower income parents who may feel threatened by schools in which *they* did not experience success (Lightfoot, 1980).

Thus, there appears to be much to be learned in the art of communication skills on the part of both school personnel and parents before school-family relationships can be more meaningful and effective. The preceding literature has identified some promising but largely untested and/or unreplicated practices. The results of research presented in later sections of this chapter suggest ways that some of these practices can work to improve school-home communications.

Additional literature and topics

The preceding selective review focuses on areas in the literature that most clearly mirror attempts to learn about and affect school-time communications. However, there are several tangential bodies of literature that we estimated would prove to be particularly useful to efforts to better understand school-home communications. These we will not present in great detail but will merely introduce and cursorily describe at this time under the headings of (a) theoretical perspectives on families and school-family relations and (b) families with special needs.

Theoretical perspectives. This section considers three topics: network theory, developmental issues in relation to parenting, and working with families of older children and teenagers.

Network theory. Network theory provides a systematic way of conceptualizing and analyzing the relatedness of families to schools and to other sources of support and help. A variety of types of data (e.g., questionnaire, interview, agency records, and observations) are amenable to study within this framework. It seems especially *a propos* to our concerns with relations and communications between families and schools. (See Fischer et al., 1977; Leinhardt, 1977; and Lieu & Duff, 1972).

Developmental issues in relation to parenting. It is important in working with families to have clear perspectives on the parental role. Teachers, principals, and other school personnel can more easily relate to parents if they understand what parenting is about. Our developmental view of parenting specifies the nature of the parental role, relating it to "family development" and to the different role demands experienced by parents who have children of particular developmental ages. (See Gotts & Paul, 1981).

Working with families of older children and teenagers. Much of what we know scientifically about school-family relations--beyond a small number of unreplicated model programs and isolated pieces of research--has been studied at the early childhood level. Yet, we clearly need to learn how to improve school-family relations at the upper elementary and secondary levels as well. Unfortunately, what is known about successful school-family relations at the early childhood level may not easily be translated into paradigms, models, and programs for such relationships at the upper elementary and secondary levels. This concern about extrapolating from the early childhood model to the elementary and secondary levels will be further considered by way of findings presented later in the present chapter.

Families with special needs. In order to improve our understanding of school-home relations it is imperative that we recognize and increase our understanding of families with special needs. Although others will hopefully come to mind, let us call attention to six of the more evident family types: (1) families with low socioeconomic status, (2) single parent families, (3) two-job families, (4) families with chronically ill or handicapped children, (5) isolated rural families, and (6) minority families. We do not present reviews of the literature on these six family types vis a vis school-home communications, since to do so would easily double the length of the current review. However, we feel it is essential to alert readers to the importance of not adopting a stereotypic "homogenized" view of the American family when thinking about school-home communications. A technical report which reviews this literature has been prepared by Snow (1982).

Practical Approaches to Improving Relations

The past 15 years have witnessed several federal legislative actions aimed at producing parents' involvement in their children's learning and development. To a much lesser extent and only more recently, legislative initiatives have sought to engender a braodly-felt sense of citizen responsibility for all American children. These themes are explored in a special review paper (Gotts, 1979) that was prepared for an invited conference sponsored by the National Institute of Education.

The above-mentioned review located and discussed: impacts of governmental policies and practices; and emerging literature on family policy; currently legislated parental roles in family and child-oriented progrms (including a small number of state and local initiatives); and a sampling of current school practices (Gotts, 1979).

Together these literatures demonstrate an increased awareness of the interrelatedness of families, schools, government, and other social institutions. Moreover, an appreciation is demonstrated by government officials and social scientists of the need and potential to strengthen and support families by paying constructive attention to the factor of interrelatedness.

Techniques of Communication

Techniques of communication need to be thought of in terms of both a message and a medium for its transmission. In our school-home work we have relabelled these two aspects of technique as, respectively,

1) information-laden focal areas for communication and 2) vehicles of communication. These are considered below.

In order to move beyond awareness and appreciation of interrelatedness, it is necessary to find some focal areas in which the practice of "relatedness" may be conducted. This is especially true if school-home relations is to serve as more than a global rallying point or slogan and is to be translated into concrete actions.

From innumerable sources we have identified the following areas for school-home communications: student academic progress, homework policy and parent role, attendance, special scheduling concerns, credits earned/needed, post-secondary plans, code of conduct/expectations, student behavior, testing for screening/placement, student health, local program emphasis, special events (e.g., open house), extracurricular activities (e.g., music and athletic programs), operation of local schools and school finance, and opportunities to help schools. When questioned about the need for a school-home communications emphasis, we have found it effective to present the preceding list and to ask, "Is it the school's responsibility to communicate about these subjects?"

Our search for practical approaches likewise has led us to identify vehicles or methods of school-home communication. Once more the potential literature citations are too numerous to mention. All of the following are in use as vehicles of communication: newsletter, report card, interim (i.e., between regular reporting times) progress report, phone call, special notice, letter or teacher note, homework to be acknowledged, individual conference, parent-teacher organization (local or district), orientation meeting, open house, information hot line, recorded message, resource center, informal networks, handbook, public media, workshop, parenting class, children, community events, and tutorial guide.

It will be evident, moreover, that the list of "areas" and that of "vehicles" are not fully independent of one another. That is, the practice of communications calls for consideration of functional matches of area and vehicle. This is an alternate form of the familiar communications issue: matching message and medium.

The issue challenges research and practice to seek out optimum matches. Trying out all possible combinations is, thus, an unnecessary and unprofitable exercise in uninformed empiricism. Instead, (a) task analysis can provide insights into possible matches, as can also (b) review of area-vehicle matches currently in use, and (c) assessment of parent preferences for learning about particular areas via various vehicles.

We, for example, have explored with parents the question, "How much would you like to learn about being a parent from: _____? where the blank represents a list of alternatives which were rated by parents (Gotts, Coan, and Kenoyer, 1977). The answers obtained in this way can provide useful guidance.

A Research Paradigm for School-Home Communications

Learning What Parents Are Thinking and Doing

Futurists, trend-watchers, and various bodies of literature proclaim that schools in our society are experiencing a growing need to change their outlook from one of communicating to parents to one of communicating with parents. In matters of change, Naisbitt (1982, p. 87) argues that "...you can't change unless you completely rethink what you are doing, unless you have a wholly new vision of what you are doing." The question is: Where does one start to get a handle on the "new vision" of communication that is appropriate for the information society that is unfolding around us?

Our thinking begins with the observation that, at all grade levels, when parent involvement increases (1) student achievement goes up and (2) support grows for schools (Gotts, 1983b; Henderson, 1981). Next, we recognize that some parents involve themselves, while many others do not. Now the question becomes how can schools go about involving parents who do not get involved? The suggested answer, developed earlier, is that greater parent involvement will follow from more effective Type I and Type S school-home communication.

This thinking appears to catch us in a circular dilemma: greater parent involvement follows from more effective ("new world") school-home communications, which require parent involvement as a precondition. How can we extricate ourselves? Our answer (Gotts, 1983a) is that we have to begin to find out from the parents themselves how to provide for these more effective communications.

More precisely, we advocate the use of personalized (telephone) interviews with parents to find out what they are thinking. Do they have communications as often as they would like? What else do they want the school to communicate and by what means? What can be done to make the school's existing channels of communication work more effectively? Interviews such as these would yield far richer answers to these questions than the typically-used impersonal paper-and-pencil questionnaire. Already, extensive application of this approach has shown that "95 percent or more of all parents contacted agreed to participate in a brief interview" (Gotts, 1983a, p. C-11). Finally, we propose that parent/community volunteers could conduct the phone interviews for the school.

While there is nothing novel about telephone interviews per se, we have found school personnel keenly receptive to using the technique for learning about school-home communications. More often than not the reaction has been one of "Why didn't I think of doing that?" Additionally, this approach provides a personal school-home communication while gathering data on how to improve communications. It is noteworthy that telephone interviews provide the opportunity for the element that is most often lacking in school-home relations--home-to-school communication.

Identifying Levels at Which Action Can Be Taken

Communication issues can be addressed at multiple levels relative to a school system: classroom, department, school, central administrative office (including school board), and community. An overarching objective of both research and practice should be to identify those levels at which particular actions can most smoothly and effectively be carried out. Systems analysis affords one methodology for considering the issue of levels.

In our own research it has been necessary to consider all of these levels in relation to a limited number of topics. For example, we have tended at an exploratory level to inquire of parents, teachers, principals, pupil personnel workers, and central office staff about (a) what kinds of communications are occurring and (b) from what levels they emanate.

This method of investigation later leads to asking questions about which levels locally are assigned the role responsibilities and control the resources which are essential to initiating and sustaining communications within certain focal areas through the use of particular vehicles.

Similarly it is possible to inquire into some new area/vehicle of communication whose use is under consideration--i.e., by asking, "At what level could this communication be most smoothly and effectively conducted?"

Within our research paradigm we have repeatedly arrived at the point of recognizing and studying the principal as the person primarily responsible for providing leadership, even though authority to conduct particular components of an overall communications program should be and are delegated to others. It is, moreover, apparent that the superintendent's office can, with school board backing, support the leadership role of principals by (a) establishing policies that make communication a core function of schools and (b) creating a system-wide expectation of excellence in this function. Thus, our paradigm calls for analysis at the superintendent's level as well.

There is a second sense in which we have concerned ourselves with levels: preschool, elementary, secondary. The predominant model of parents' involvement in their children's schooling and academic learning is based on successful practices at the preschool and primary levels. The practices encouraged by this "primary" model call for parents to be present physically in the school. This is analogous to the physical involvement of parents in their younger children's activities at home. It has long been recognized by educators that the teacher-child relationship in the early years has this same quality and, correspondingly, represents an extension of the parent-child relationship.

It has not generally been acknowledged, however, that teacher-child interaction at the secondary level differs from the former in ways that suggest it is the extension at that level of fundamentally changed parent-child interaction pattern. As children grow older, physical contact of children with parents decreases; they move toward more symbolic and abstract ways of communicating. Parents direct their interest increasingly toward their children's associates, accomplishments, and preparation for eventual economic independence. These changes do not, however, signal a decrease of emotional involvement. To pursue the earlier analogy, we might expect that parents, as a part of their emerging and different ways of relating to older children and teens, would relate less to the school via their physical presence.

In the foregoing we are making a case for a different model of parent involvement at the secondary level in children's schooling and academic learning. This model suggests that parents of older children and teens desire to be involved, but that this desire will not be expressed in terms of physical presence. Surely it would be as erroneous to assume from parents' decreased physical presence at school that they care less as it would be to assume when they allow their children to be out on their own that they are disinterested in their children's dating behavior or physical appearance. Yet we have repeatedly heard educators making this assumption about parents of upper elementary and secondary students, based almost solely on their failure to conform to the "primary" model's call for frequent visits to the school.

A series of comparisons and contrasts will be used to distinguish the primary and secondary models. What we mean by *secondary model* tends to apply from upper elementary onward. Primary relations are proximate or physically close; involvement is expressed by being present. Secondary relations take place at a distance, with parents monitoring progress; involvement means being present when needed. General purpose parent groups are accepted at the primary level; special purpose parent groups function well at the secondary level. Primary parents monitor the school by visiting and reviewing student work. Secondary parents monitor by reading the newsletter and visiting when they are notified of a problem or need. The academic focus for primary is basic skills, adjustment, and social integration; secondary emphasizes graduation credits and progress, plus specialized progress in class and extracurricular programs. Primary discipline problems require parent-teacher negotiation; secondary problems require negotiations by parent-teacher-student-others. Primary special events have a general focus for all parents of a classroom or school; they are to view all children's work--

not only their child's. Secondary parents are drawn by interest or their child's involvement to sports, musical, and dramatic events; their child may be seen here as an independent performer.

The preceding contrasts help to define and distinguish what we mean by the secondary level model. We developed this model early in the research and have used it to guide our strongly secondary-level focus. It has helped us particularly in our efforts to identify appropriate outcome variables at the secondary level—i.e., variables less linked to parent attendance at meetings held by the school.

Selecting Goals and Strategies

In the preceding section we referred to the *who* of research into school-home communications. This section addresses the *what* and the *how*. By this we mean that it is necessary to identify some issue (or set of issues) that is a concern to those who are to be or have been interviewed. Such issues might include, for example, parents not knowing what to do about their children who need to improve their performance and conduct in school, teachers not feeling comfortable about communicating with special-needs families, or the timeliness or effectiveness of certain communications.

Once a given goal has been identified (or set), it becomes necessary to choose some strategy for trying to deal with it. An example of a strategy is the use of academic guidance sheets that have been devised to be sent home to parents along with notices that their child's school behavior or academic performance needs improvement. These sheets can suggest possible commonplace parental responses to specific student deficiencies and, more importantly, suggest that a parent talk to a teacher, guidance counselor, or principal if additional help or under-standing is needed. The foregoing strategy might be adopted by a principal·or a committee if they heard about it beforehand. In this vein, it is noteworthy that the present strategy was created in response to things that we learned from the comments of respondents who had been interviewed as we have suggested earlier.

The point is that an inquiry of any nature into the status of school-home communications in an individual school can reveal whether or not there are any issues in need of attention and what these may be. To a certain extent topics and areas for inquiry in the interview accordingly can be anticipated and prepared beforehand. On the other hand, the use of open-ended questions as a method of inquiry can permit parents to reveal unanticipated concerns and perspectives that may warrant treat-ment.

Schematically, the paradigm we are suggesting here entails identify-ing and stating these goals as clearly as possible, choosing and activating methods for addressing the goals over some reasonable period of time, and then interviewing those involved for their reactions to and perceptions of the effectiveness of the method(s) employed and the extent of attainment of the goal.

Results of Applying the Paradigm

Responses of Parents

As part of a project to study school-family relations at the Appalachia Educational Laboratory, Gotts (1983d) has applied the idea of using telephone interviews to communicate with parents about school-home communications in a number of secondary schools in West Virginia, where the method met with success and was well received. Although this technique has also been applied in elementary schools, we will report only the results of using it in secondary schools here because: (1) relatively greater numbers of studies and information are available on early childhood practices and (2) there are more pressing communication-linked bottlenecks in the secondary schools because of the dynamics of parent-adolescent relations in our society.

Method

Arrangements were made with one larger (around 39,000 students), urbanized and three smaller, more rural West Virginia county school systems to conduct the study as a collaborative activity during 1982. Principals from the schools initially discussed with us their own questions regarding their practices of school-home relations and parents' reactions to them. Although approached individually, there was remarkable similarity of the questions across the various principals. We were, thus, able to construct essentially identical interview protocols for the two groups of schools. They approved final versions of the interview forms, after which they assisted us with sample selections. Within each school (in the larger county) or set of county schools (in the three smaller counties) an oversampling procedure was used to yield an expected final minimum participation rate of 60 or 30 families per school, respectively. Families were selected to represent about equal numbers of 10th, 11th, and 12th graders and equal numbers of boys and girls within grade --e.g., 5 girls and 5 boys in grade 10, etc. Sample selection was performed at random, within the forementioned groupings except that no family was contacted if its telephone number was unlisted to the public. This represents a limitation on inferences that can be made from the study. Emergency locator cards at the schools indicated that virtually all families could be reached by telephone at home or work or through some emergency number.

The interview had been designed to require 15-20 minutes for completion. It sought to document (1) actual school-home communication practices as experienced by these parents, (2) their reactions to these, (3) suggestions for improved practices, and (4) views of what, from

a parental perspective, might work at the secondary level. All custom-
ary "protection of human subjects" procedures were followed, and
families were asked at the interview's termination to indicate any
remaining questions or comments which they might have had.

A technical report containing typical interviews and coding procedures is available from AEL (Gotts & Sattes, 1982). Both structured and
open-ended questions were used. Coding relied heavily on content
analyses. Measures were taken to reduce responding purely on the basis
of social desirability. A separate validity study of the interview with 90
families suggested that it was satisfactory for the present purpose
(Gotts, 1983c).

Results

Final sampling figures for the three smaller counties' schools
combined and the four high schools combined in the larger city were 184
and 198, respectively. The bulk of the parent respondents were females
in both samples: 97.83% (180) in the rural sample and 87.37% (173) in
the large city sample. The sex of the students about whom the
interviewees responded was 52.17% (96) male and 47.83% (88) female
in the rural sample and 56.06% (111) male and 43.94% (87) female in
the large city sample. Actual numbers of respondents varied from
question to question depending upon how many persons responded and the
codability of their answers. Two of the largest schools' samples were
pooled and compared for possible differences in parent orientation as a
function of either child's sex or grade level. Neither factor was
associated with parent orientation toward or experience of school-home
communications. Therefore all subsequent analyses were conducted
without regard to child grade level or sex.

Tables 1 through 5 contain percentages of parents' responses to a
number of questions posed to them in telephone interviews about school-
home communications. The numbers assigned to the questions are
employed here for discussion purposes--they do not represent the order
in which questions were presented in the interview. We will also use the
convention of returning to the three smaller counties' schools as S-schools
and the larger city/county's schools as L-schools.

To begin with, we note in Table 1 that majorities of the two groups
of schools' parents attend extracurricular activities at the schools (S =
76.09%; L = 69.19%). Athletic events account for the larger part of this
attendance, about 60% in both groups of schools. By way of contrast,
although both groups have parent advisory councils and parent meetings
(Q_2), overwhelmingly parents do not attend these (S = 86.96%; L =
80.81%). However, there is appreciably better attendance at PAC
meetings in the L-schools (6.57% vs. 0.54%) than in the S-schools. The
absorbing point, however, in Table 1 is that a majority of parents attend
special purpose extracurricular events, whereas a greater majority do

not attend general purpose parent meetings.

Table 2 shows the percentages of parents' responses to a series of questions about communications received from the school. A significantly greater percentage of L-school parents mention receiving communications (Q_3) from school than S-school parents (S = 69.40%; L = 95.41%). Of the parents who mention receiving communications, further questioning (Q_4) about the types received showed that newsletters are most often mentioned by the L-school parents (81.51%), while special notices have the highest incidence of mention among the S-school parents (38.04%). The differences between the proportions of parents from each group of schools naming the various types of communications are significant for the most part, with newsletters (S = 2.72%; L = 81.51%), special notices (S = 38.04%; L = 18.18%), and report card (S = 14.13%; L = 33.84%) being the most striking.

Table 2 also contains information about how often parents stated they received communications from the school (Q_5). The percentage of mentions by the two groups of parents for categories "never" to "more than monthly" show an inverse relationship between the two dimensions. That is, for the S-school parents, there are higher mentions on the "infrequent communications" end of the scale and lower mentions on the "frequent" end of the scale, with more or less the opposite trend for the L-school parents. Taking Q_4 and Q_5 findings together, we see that not only do significantly fewer S-school parents receive communications (69.40% vs. 95.41%), but for those parents who do receive communications in each group more than twice as many L-school parents receive them "once 6-8 weeks or more often" (63.48%) than S-school parents (27.07%).

Parents' responses to questions about contacts they have with the school are summarized in Table 3. High percentages of parents from both groups reported having contacts with their child's teacher or other school personnel (S = 147 or 80.83%; L = 146 or 73.74%). The groups differed significantly on whether they reported these contacts as being equated with problems their child was having in the school (S = 37.93%; L = 52.03%). This may account for S-school parents having positive attitudes (95.51%) toward these contacts significantly more often than L-school parents (86.36%). On the other hand, twice as many L-school parents (73.40%) as S-school parents (36.88%) feel they are responsibile for making contacts with school personnel, which may reflect no more than the greater need to do so in a larger, more formal system.

Table 4 specifically deals with parents' responses to questions about students' learning and academic performances in school. Q_9 had to do with whether parents took action upon receiving notification from the school about a child performing "below expectations." S-school parents said they took action significantly more often (92.86%) than L-school parents (80.15%). The form of action taken by these different groups of parents (Q_{10}) differed significantly, with S-school parents being much more likely to talk with the teacher (12.82%) or with both the teacher and the child (48.72%) than L-school parents (1.87% and 37.38%, respectively). However, L-school parents are much more prone to talk to their child (60.75% than S-school parents (38.46%) about these matters.

In terms of how serious a problem has to be before the school should notify the home about it (Q_{11}), Table 4 shows L-school parents wanting to "know everything" in the way of a problem their child is having significantly more often than S-school parents (L = 65.45%; S = 49-.17%). Noteworthy here is that virtually no parents said they did not wish to know about any problem their child was having in school! Consistent with their feelings about Q_{11}, L-school parents significantly more often (28.28%) see a need to have direct word from the school about grades than S-school parents (17.93%).

The responses of parents to various follow-up questions related to Q_{11} are presented in Table 5. First, L-parents express a need for prompt notice about problems their child is having in school significantly less frequently than S-parents (L = 53.54%; S = 71.20%). Consistent with that, L-parents significantly more often mention encouraging responsibility for their own behavior in their children than do S-parents (L = 14.14%; S = 2.72%). They also only half as often indicate a need for more discipline in the schools (L = 19.19%) than S-parents (36.96%). This may relate to their: (a) significantly more often feeling that parents can do more than schools regarding difficulties a child is having with school (L = 19.19%; S = 6.52%) and similarly (b) significantly less often that the school and home should work together regarding Q_{11} problems (L = 66.67%; S = 82.07%). (Note, however, that the percentages for Q_{16} and Q_{17} suggest very strong overall support for schools being able to do more than parents and for schools working with parents to solve children's problems in school.)

Reactions and Plans of Administrators

It is noteworthy, first, that each individual principal (n = 12) and all but one superintendent or assistant superintendent (n = 5) whom we contacted was receptive to our study plans and followed through. Our process records of these early contacts revealed that administrators not only participated; they collaborated by adding their own emphases and questions.

After the parent interviews were completed, all data were summarized and presented individually to the participating administrators and any guests whom they invited. The principal investigator was accompanied on each visit by a participant observer who subsequently wrote brief narrative answers about that visit in reply to a series of questions–e.g., How receptive was the principal/superintendent to the findings? Was there any indication of *how* he/she might use the findings of the study?

TABLE 1. Percentage of Parent Responses About School Functions
Attended and Contacts with Parent Organizations.
Where percentages for the two groups of parents differed significantly on an item (individual row under a question (Q) heading, the asterisk is beside the item. Where the entire question
(all rows considered simultaneously) was involved in the Chi
Square test, the asterisk is placed beside the question (Q).

	Three Smaller Counties S-Schools (N=184) %	Larger City/ County's L-Schools (N=198) %
Q$_1$: School Functions Attended by Family Members		
Attended Some Function	76.09	69.19
Athletics	60.33	59.09
Band/Music	18.48	18.18
Drama	7.07	10.61
Community Educ.*	1.09	7.07
P-T Conferences	10.33	12.63
Other Functions*	33.70	10.10
Q$_2$: Contact with Parent Organizations		
None	86.96	80.81
PTA	3.80	2.02
Bank Booster	9.24	14.14
Athletic Booster	7.61	11.11
PAC*	0.54	6.57
Other	3.80	2.02

*Significant at or beyond the 5% level of confidence.

TABLE 2. Percentage of Parent Responses About Communications
Received from the School
Where percentages for the two groups of parents differed
significantly on an item (individual row under a question (Q)
heading, the asterisk is beside the item. Where the entire
question (all rows considered simultaneously) was involved in
the Chi Square test, the asterisk is placed beside the question
(Q).

	Three Smaller Counties' S-Schools (N=184) %	Larger City/ County's L-Schools (N=198) %
Q3: Parents Mention Receiving Communications from School		
Yes*	69.40	95.41
Q4: Types of Communications Mentioned as Received		
None*	30.60	4.59
Newsletter	2.72	81.51
Phone Calls	20.65	25.76
Letters	14.13	11.11
Special Notices*	38.04	18.18
Homework*	0.00	3.03
Report Card*	14.13	33.84
Teacher Talks*	6.52	2.02
Other	7.61	2.53
Q5: Frequency of Communications from School*		
Never	30.39	5.06
Once a Year	22.10	10.11
Every 3 Months	20.44	21.35
6-8 Weeks	13.26	19.66
Monthly	7.73 (27.07)	26.97 (63.48)
More than Monthly	6.08	16.85

*Significant at or beyond the 5% level of confidence.

TABLE 3. Percentage of Parent Responses to Questions About Contacts
They Have With School

Where percentages for the two groups of parents differed
significantly on an item (individual row under a question (Q)
heading, the asterisk is beside the item. Where the entire question
(all rows considered simultaneously) was involved in the Chi Square
test, the asterisk is placed beside the question (Q).

	Three Smaller Counties S-Schools (N=184) %	Larger City/ County's L-Schools(N=198) %
Q6: Are School Contacts Equated with Problems?*		
No	62.07	47.97
Yes	37.93	52.03
Q7: Attitudes Toward Contacts with Schools*		
Negative	4.49	13.64
Positive	95.51	86.36
Q8: Do Parents Feel Responsible for Making Contacts?*		
No	63.12	26.60
Yes	36.88	73.40

*Significant at or beyond the 5% level of confidence.

NOTE: 80.83% S-School and 73.74% L-School parents reported having
contacts with child's teacher or other school personnel. This difference
is not significant.

TABLE 4: Percentage of Parent Responses to Questions About
            Communications on Student's Problems/Grades
        Where percentages for the two groups of parents differed
        significantly on an item (individual row under a question (Q)
        heading, the asterisk is beside the item. Where the entire question
        (all rows considerd simultaneously) was involved in the Chi Square
        test, the asterisk is placed beside the question (Q).

	Three Smaller Counties S-Schools (N=184) %	Larger City/ County's L-Schools (N=198) %
Q_9: Do Parents Take Action Upon Receipt of "Below Expectations" Notice?*		
No	7.14	19.85
Yes	92.86	80.15
Q_{10}: Form of Action Taken by Parent*		
Talk w/Teacher	12.82	1.87
Talk w/Child	38.46	60.75
Talk w/Both	48.72	37.38
Q_{11}: How Serious a Problem Before School Notifies Parent?*		
Limited to Certain Problems	50.83	34.55
Wants to Know Everything	49.17	65.45
Q_{12}: Sees Need to Have Direct Word from School on Grades*		
No	82.07	71.72
Yes	17.93	28.28

*Significant at or beyond the 5% level of confidence.

TABLE 5: Percentage of Parent Responses to Various Follow-up
Questions to Q_{11}
Where percentages for the two groups of parents differed
significantly on an item (individual row under a question (Q) heading,
the asterisk is beside the item.   Where the entire question (all
rows considered simultaneously) was involved in the Chi Square
test, the asterisk is placed beside the question (Q).

	Three Smaller Counties S-Schools (N=184) %	Larger City/ County's L-Schools (N=198) %
Q_{13}: Mentions Need for Prompt Notice on Q_{11}*		
	71.20	53.54
Q_{14}: Mentions Encouraging Responsibility in Child on Q_{11}*		
	2.72	14.14
Q_{15}: Feels Schools Need More Discipline on Q_{11}*		
	36.96	19.19
Q_{16}: Feels Parents Can Do More than the Schools on Q_{11}*		
	6.52	19.19
Q_{17}: Say School and Home Should Work Together on Q_{11}*		
	82.07	66.67

*Significant at or beyond the 5% level of confidence.

In this small experimental component of the study, the information transmitted to administrators about parents' views was the independent variable. Dependent measures were based on the observer-generated narratives noted above, plus on a similar set of questions answered by the administrators several months following the meetings in which findings were discussed. Data from these two points in time were used to assess immediately the potential impact of the information and then to determine later what the administrators attempted and what actual results they accomplished.

There were several notable findings. As the parent views were initially presented, all principals showed their interest in multiple ways. All gave immediate indications that the interview data were properly targeted and presented for their comprehension. All spontaneously offered ideas of ways that they might be able to use the findings. Particularly often they mentioned plans to use the information for in-service training of staff. Principals also appreciated having data to support some of their own "personal touches" (i.e., things not required by their school systems) to which some staff were resistive because of the added effort required to carry them out.

Later, eight of twelve principals completed the questionnaire, and the remaining four commented to us on the same questions in person or by phone. Eleven of the twelve (p less than .01) indicated one or more specific actions that they had taken that same school year, based on the new information provided about their schools' parents by the interview.

Upon initial presentation of findings, the superintendents' observed reactions were uniformly similar to those of the principals. Two superintendents later returned the questionnaire and two more incidentally volunteered verbal reports during informal contacts. Every county administrator acted decisively on aspects of the information provided. Two encouraged increased use of newsletters; four used the information with their school board members; and one arranged for the addition to his central office staff at the start of the following school year the new position of school-family relations coordinator.

What is also interesting is that, though we received follow-up information from four of the five administrators on what they were doing, none of them directly communicated to us the above important decisions/changes. Even though they were uniformly appreciative of our help, the typical administrative style was to adopt innovation and "run with it" without undue concern for its source. This is an essential point to recognize in the research community, where often a reverse ethic applies: give profuse credit for ideas, but do little to put them into practice. Thus, the researcher seeking to impact at the level of the superintendent's office must be prepared--as fortunately we were--to gain perhaps the most telling data regarding impact through informal channels.

Responses of Teachers

Interviews paralleling those administered to parents were used with a random sampling of teachers from each school system. Teachers, thus, were asked in effect to comment on what they knew about what their respective schools were doing by way of communicating with parents and with what results. At this writing results had been analyzed for teachers from the large, urbanized school system. The following results are based on analysis of their responses.

Secondary teachers' responses to the standard interview questions, coded in the regular manner, by and large matched those of parents. Two differences of perspective are, nevertheless, important to note regarding comparisons of teacher responses with those of parents from the same schools. First, teachers were not generally aware of how parents feel about receiving notification if their child is having problems or difficulties at school. Teachers underestimated parents' (self-reported) desire for information and how likely they were to make use of it.

Second, teachers and parents each tended to assign responsibility to the other party for initiating contacts when needed. It seems clear, however, regarding children's problems and difficulties at school, that school personnel almost invariably are in a better position to recognize that a student is having problems. Thus, logically, the teacher, counselor or other school staff member who knows of a problem should initiate the contact. We have since shared this finding and reasoning with four local groups of school administrators.   The point has been well received, without significant exception being taken by those in attendance.

Recommendations

Goals in Home-School Communications

First, the school principal needs to exercise a central leadership role in home-school communications, and then to entrust others with individual assignments. Before commencing anything new, however, it is necessary to learn what parents' views are regarding the job that the school is already doing. Thus, we recommend conducting brief telephone interviews with modest-size, randomly drawn samples (i.e., 20 percent samples in smaller schools and somewhat decreasing percentages as school size exceeds 600 students) of parents, following the general pattern of questions and coding illustrated in a technical report by Gotts and Sattes (1982). Questionnaires are not a satisfactory substitute for personal interviews for many reasons.

Although the interviews were initially administered and coded by our staff and part-time personnel whom we trained, we have since experimented with the use of volunteer groups to perform these activities. We have as yet reached no final conclusions on this approach. We can say already, however, that administrators generally accept volunteers from responsible organizations; volunteers come forward to conduct and code interviews in their communities; and volunteers learn from standard interview training to perform the job of data gathering and coding. Further reports will be forthcoming on these portions of our work.

In any event, we recommend the use of volunteers as a practical solution to the problem of how to staff up to interview numbers of parents. Moreover, we are convinced that parents will give more forthright answers if they are assured of anonymity—a matter about which some parents understandably experience lingering doubt and concern when data are requested directly by a member of the school staff.

Once the interviews have been coded and the results tabulated using simple descriptive statistics, the principal and key staff should analyze and discuss the findings and list their implications. Next they should establish both immediate and longer term goals for improving their school-home communications. Progress toward achieving the goals can often be evaluated by readministering all or selected parts of the interview to another modest-sized random sample of parents from the school. Results will then be compared with those from the sampling completed previously.

Schools should communicate with parents regarding many of the focal areas identified earlier in the chapter. At a minimum, two types of communication efforts are needed: (1) schools need to share information with all parents in a timely manner about their program, accomplishments, activity schedule, and needs, and (2) school and home need to have established, mutually-understood ways to consider together the progress, needs, and problems of individual students.

To communicate with all parents we recommend that the school issue a regular newsletter. It should emphasize upcoming events with a concise but comprehensive activity calendar on its cover page. It should be informative, well organized, easy to scan, with to-the-point writing. The newsletter can be highly effective at both primary and secondary levels. Also for all parents, a well-planned and coordinated open house can succeed at either level—but never plan for more than one per year at the secondary level. Hold it at a time of low schedule conflict and with much advance planning, preparation, participation, and publicity (the four P's). Dress and conduct codes should be published for secondary students and their parents. Elementary schools should prepare and periodically update home-school-community handbooks.

Parents want to be assured that they will be contacted early if their child is having a problem or difficulty which is or may become significant. Schools should commit themselves to providing such early notice and opportunity for discussion whenever there is an academic, attendance, personal or conduct problem. The older the child, the more parents feel dependent on schools to provide them with early notice. A goal is for the school to initiate such communications.

All of the foregoing areas are ones for which schools already monitor and document how individual students are doing; schools also notify parents eventually about serious difficulties in any of these areas. Our findings, on the other hand, recommend a more preventive approach: involve parents before the problem becomes serious. One exemplary practice we found is sending home "interim" grade reports, about half-way through a grading period, if there is a problem, before anything is recorded in the student's cumulative record. Parents express enthusiasm and optimism about the value of this approach.

Finally, we recommend that the superintendent's office, in consul-tation with the school board, issue policies and guidelines that will encourage and promote action at individual schools in the above areas. The superintendent's office can, furthermore, with the help of quality volunteers, conduct its own public information campaign directed toward the broader community made up of parents plus a growing majority of adults who do not have children in school.

Needed Research

In our work we have identified a number of exemplary practices and have studied a limited group of these. While we have concerned ourselves with parents' wishes and preferences, we have also sought answers to the question of what school personnel and parents may do differently as a result of the particular kinds of communications they receive.

In our estimate, too little of this kind of analysis has been done. Instead, analyses have been attempted of the effects of rather global programs intended to increase parent involvement in multiple ways. Two major problems are inherent in these usual "program study" approaches: (1) no independent variable can be isolated, but many possible indepen-dent variables are present and confounded; and (2) global programs often demand unacceptable levels of school effort--an almost certain guaran-tee that they will not survive the loss of outside funding or the departure of some charismatic program leader.

What we have attempted to examine are extremely simple-to-use and efficient arrangements and vehicles of communication--ones that require the same amount or only slightly more effort than educators already expend--and vehicles that permit schools to communicate more effectively in areas for which they already accept responsibility to communicate with parents. Such practices should be singled out for study. That is, study practical practices.

Where we find less impact than expected, this does not always signal that it is time to abandon the cause or find a new one. For example, we were impressed with interim grade reports; parents were too. Many parents took action on these notices, but the action tended to be stereotyped and extremely constricted, i.e., they talked to the child, talked to the teacher or talked to both. They seemed not to analyze why the child was having a problem, nor did they engage in imaginative problem solving.

It seemed apparent to us from the foregoing combination of facts that they needed guidance. Yet that could be a prohibitively costly service. Our solution was to develop a one-page guidance sheet that accompanies the interim grade report. It seeks to engage the parent in the guidance process by asking the parent to consider a short list of simple questions, each of which can be answered *Yes* or *No* If the parent concludes upon reflection that *Yes* is the more likely answer, then the sheet offers a corresponding suggestion about (a) a corrective action or (b) a kind of help to seek or (c) how to engage in further exploration to get an answer. We are still in the process of studying the impact of interim grade reports with guidance sheets added, further discussion awaits those findings.

It is true that we developed something new, but it was not a program, nor was it complicated or expensive to use. We see this as evidence that we are following some of our own advice. We believe that further research needs to follow a similar course of studying the impacts of exemplary practices (and if people can agree that they are exemplary, including the parent recipients, they probably are exemplary). If results are below expectations, the researcher should analyze why or how the practice is malfunctioning and try to refine it. If it does not require refinement, the researcher may find a way to potentiate its effect by some simple innovation.

These suggestions for further research call for the gradual building of a repertoire of validated exemplary practices, each of which has something to recommend it to school personnel in its own right. A related task for future research is to articulate optimum interfaces of focal areas and communication vehicles, and to provide guidelines for the selection of these interfaces in order to meet commonly-encountered, local objectives.

FOOTNOTES

1. The work reported herein was supported through the Appalachia Educational Laboratory (AEL), Inc., by various grants and contracts from the National Institute of Education, U.S. Department of Education and by a sabbatical study award from the University of Rhode Island. However, the opinions expressed herein do not necessarily reflect the position or policy of the Appalachia Educa-

tional Laboratory, the National Institute of Education or the University of Rhode Island, and no official endorsement by any of these agencies should be inferred.

REFERENCES

Alden, J. W. (1979). A broader definition of citizen participation. In R. S. Brandt (Ed.), *Partners: Parents & Schools.* Alexandria, Virginia: Association for Supervision and Curriculum Development.

Anselmo, S. (1977). Parent involvement in the schools. *Clearing House, 50*(7), 297-299.

Barth, R. (1979). Home-based reinforcement of school behavior: A review and analysis. *Review of Educational Research, 49*(3), 436-458.

Berlin, R., & Berlin, I. N. (1973). *School's training of parents to be effective teachers of their own and other nonlearning children,* (ERIC Document Reproduction Service No. ED 099 110.)

Bittle, R. G. (1975). Improving parent-teacher communication through recorded telephone messages. *Journal of Educational Research, 69*(3), 87-95.

Boger, R., Richter, R., Paolucci, B., & Whitmer, S. (1978, November). *Parent as teacher: Perspective of function and context.* Paper presented at the Parents as Educators Conference, National Institute of Education, Washington, DC. (ERIC Document Reproduction Service No. ED 175 576)

Breiling, A. (1976). Using parents as teaching partners. *Reading Teacher, 30*(2), 187-192.

Budd, R. W., Thorp, R. K. & Donohew, L. (1967). *Content analysis of communications.* New York: MacMillan.

Cherry, C. (1966). *On human communication: A review, a survey, and a criticism.* (2nd ed.). Cambridge, Massachusetts: The M.I.T. Press.

Collins, B. E., & Raven, B. H. (1969). Group structure: Attraction, coalitions, communication, and power. In G. Lindzey & E. Aronson (Eds.), *The handbook of social psychology.* (2nd ed.). Vol. 4. Reading, Massachusetts: Addison-Wesley.

Combs, A. W. (1979). *Myths in education—beliefs that hinder progress and their alternatives.* Boston: Allyn and Bacon.

Criscuolo, N. P. (1979). Activities that help involve parents in reading. *Reading Teacher, 32*(4), 417-419.

Della-Doro, D. (1979). Parents & others citizens in curriculum development. In R. S. Brandt (Ed.), *Partners: Parents & Schools.* Alexandria, Virginia: ASCD, 67-74.

Dickerson, D., Spellman, C. R., Larsen, S., & Tyler, L. (1973). Let the cards do the talking: A teacher-parent communication program. *Teaching Exceptional Children, 5,* 170-178.

Dobson, R., & Dobson, J. S. (1975). *Parental and community involvement in education and teacher education.* Washington, DC:

ERIC Clearinghouse on Teacher Education. (ERIC Document Reproduction Service No. ED 100 833)

Duncan, L. W. (1969). *Parent-counselor conferences make a difference.* (ERIC Document Reproduction Service No. ED 031 743)

Edlund, C. V. (1969). Rewards at home to promote desirable school behavior. *Teaching Exeptional Children,* 1(4), 121-127.

Epstein, J. L. (1983, October). *Effects on parents of teachers' practices of parent involvement* (Rept. No. 346). Baltimore: The Johns Hopkins University, Center for Social Organization of Schools.

Epstein, J. L. & McPartland, J. M. (1977). *Family and school interactions and main effects on affective outcomes.* Baltimore, Maryland: Johns Hopkins University Center for the Study of Social Organization of Schools, Report No. 235. (ERIC Document Reproduction Service No. ED 151 713)

Etheridge, G. W., Collins, T., & Coats, B. (1979). *Home-school relations: Together we stand or divided we fall.* Paper presented at the International Congress on Education (2nd, Vancouver, British Columbia) (ERIC Document Reproduction Service No. ED 175 144)

Fairchild, T. N. (1976). Home-school token economies: Bridging the communication gap. *Psychology in the Schools,* 13(4), 463-467.

Filipczak, J., Lordeman, A., & Friedman, R. M. (April 1977). *Parental involvement in the schools: Towards what end?* Paper presented at the Annual Meeting of the American Educational Research Association, NY. (ERIC Document Reproduction Service No. ED 143 104)

Fischer, C. S., Jackson, R. M., Steuve, C. A., Gerson, K., Jones, L. M., & Baldassare, M. (1977). *Networks and places: Social relations in the urban setting.* New York: Free Press.

Futrell, M. H. (1983, November). President's viewpoint: Parents as allies. *NEA Today,* p. 2.

Gallup, G. H. (1980). The 12th annual Gallup poll of the public's attitudes toward the public schools. *Phi Delta Kappan,* 62(1), 33-48.

Gifford, I., & Summerell, S. (1978). *Interdisciplinary approach to failure prevention.* (ERIC Document Reproduction Service No. ED 185 510)

Gillum, R. M., Schooley, D. E., & Novak, P. D. (April, 1977). *The effects of parental involvement on student achievement in three Michigan performance contracting programs.* Paper presented at the Annual Meeting of the American Educational Research Association, New York City. (ERIC Reproduction Service No. ED 144 007)

Goffman, E. (1967). *Interaction ritual. Essays on face-to-face behavior.* Garden City, NY: Doubleday.

Gordon, I. J. (1979). The effects of parent involvement on schooling. In R. S. Brandt (Ed.), *Partners: Parents and schools.* Alexandria, VA: ASCD.

Gotts, E. E. (1967). *Affect, language, and behavior control.* Unpublished doctoral dissertation, The University of Texas, Austin.

Gotts, E. E. (1979, December). *Legislated roles of parent involvement and current school practices.* Invited paper given at National Institute of Education Conference, Washington, DC.

Gotts, E. E. (1983a). Home-based early intervention. In A.W. Childs and G. B. Melton (Eds.), *Rural Psychology,* New York: Plenum Press.

Gotts, E. E. (1983b). Home communications needed. *Alabama Community Education Parents and Learning News, 1*(2), C-11.

Gotts, E. E. (1983c, September). Parent involvement helps... *Alabama Community Education Parents and Learning News, 1*(2), C-7.

Gotts, E. E. (1983d, April). *School-home communications at the secondary level.* Paper presented at the meeting of American Educational Research Association, Montreal.

Gotts, E. E., Coan, D. L., & Kenoyer, C. (1977). *Developing instructional products for effective parenthood.* Paper presented at the American Educational Research Association Annual Convention. (ERIC Document Reproduction Service No. ED 136 788)

Gotts, E. E. & Paul, K. (1981). *Manual for rating indirect parent interview. Revised.* Charleston, WV: Appalachia Educational Laboratory.

Gotts, E. E. & Sattes, B. D. (1982). *Interviews and coding procedures for assessing school-family communications.* Charleston, WV: Appalachia Educational Laboratory.

Gotts, E. E., Spriggs, A. M., & Sattes, B. D. (1979). *Review of major programs and activities in parenting.* Charleston, WV: Appalachia Educational Laboratory, Inc. (Appears as an Appendix to ERIC Document Reproduction Service No. ED 183 293)

Gotts, E. E., Spriggs, A. M., & Snow, M. (1980). *Childhood and parenting research program: Final report.* Charleston, WV: Appalachia Educational Laboratory, Inc.

Greene, J. (1972). *Psycholinguistics, Chomsky and psychology.* Baltimore, MD: Penguin.

Hayes, E. J., Cunningham, G. K., & Robinson, J. B. (1977). Counseling focus: Are parents necessary? *Elementary School Guidance and Counseling, 12*(1), 8-14.

Henderson, A. (Ed.) (1981). *Parent participation—student achievement: The evidence grows.* Columbia, MD: National Committee for Citizens in Education.

Herman, J. J. (1972). Communication: The systems are all go. *Clearing House, 46*(6), 370-375.

Hightower, H. J. (1978). *Educational decision making: The involvement of parents: Myth or reality.* Paper presented at the American Educational Research Association Annual Meeting, Toronto, Canada. (ERIC Document Reproduction Service No. ED 154 086)

Hofmeister, A. M. (1977). *The parent is a teacher.* Paper presented at the 56th Annual Faculty Honor Lecture in the Humanities, Logan, Utah. (ERIC Document Reproduction Service No. ED 161 541)

Hoskisson, K., Sherman, T. M., & Smith, L. L. (1974). Assisted reading and parent involvement. *The Reading Teacher, 27*(7), 710-714.

Hubbell, N. S. (1979). Some things change--some do not! In R. S. Brandt (Ed.), *Partners: Parents & schools.* Alexandria, VA: ASCD.

Imber, S. C., Imber, R. B., & Rothstein, G. (1979). Modifying independent work habits: An effective teacher-parent communication program. *Exceptional Children, 46*(3), 218-221.

Ingram, J. E. (1978). *The relationship between school-community relations and student achievement* (Technical Report No. 463). Madison, WI: University of Wisconsin Research and Development Center for Individualized Schooling.

Irvine, D. J., Flint, D. L., Hick, T. L., Horan, M. D., Kukuk, S. E., & Fallon, E. (1979). *Parent involvement affects children's cognitive growth.* Albany, NY: The University of the State of New York. (Available from State Education Department, Division of Research, Albany, New York 12234)

Jason, L. A., & Soucy, G. P. (1977). *Home-letters as a technique in behavior management.* Paper presented at the Midwestern Association of Behavior Analysis, Chicago. (ERIC Document Reproduction Service No. ED 146 533)

Keeves, J. P. (1975). The home, the school, and achievement in mathematics and science. *Science Education, 59*(4), 439-460.

Kifer, E. (November, 1976). *The relationship between the home and school in influencing the learning of children.* Paper presented at the pre-convention Conference on Research of the National Council of English, Chicago. (ERIC Document Reproduction Service No. ED 133 073)

Lahey, B., Gendrich, J., Gendrich, J., Schnelle, L., Gant, D., & McNee, P. (1977). An evaluation of daily report cards with minimal teacher and parent contacts as an efficient method of classroom intervention. *Behavior Modification, 1*(3), 381-394.

Leinhardt, S. (Ed.). (1977). *Social networks: A developing paradigm.* New York: Academic Press.

Lieu, W., & Duff, R. W. (1972). The strength in weak ties. *Public Opinion Quarterly, 36*, 361-366.

Lightfoot, S. L. (1978). *Worlds apart.* New York: Basic Books, Inc.

Lightfoot, S. L. (Spring, 1980). *Exploring family-school relationships: A prelude to curricular designs and strategies.* Paper prepared for "Toward Being At Home in School: Parent Involvement in Curriculum Decision Making." Symposium sponsored by the American Educational Research Association.

Mager, G. M. (1980). The conditions which influence a teacher in initiating contacts with parents. *The Journal of Educational Research, 73*(5), 276-282.

McAfee, O. (1979). Parent education: Needed characteristics and necessary concerns. In *Families and schools: Implementing parent education.* Denver, Colorado: Education Commission of the States. (Available from ECS, Suite 300, 1860 Lincoln Street, Denver, CO 80295)

McKinney, J. A. (1975). *The development and implementation of a tutorial program for parents to improve the reading and mathema-*

tics achievement of their children. (ERIC Document Reproduction Service No. ED 113 703)

Mize, G. K. (1977). *The influence of increased parental involvement in the educational process of their children.* Madison, Wisconsin: University of Wisconsin Research and Development Center for Cognitive Learning, Technical Report No. 418, (ERIC Document Reproduction Service No. ED 151 661)

Myers, E. J. (1971). Counseling the parents of sixth grade underachievers. *Journal of Education, 154*(1), 50-53.

Naisbitt, J. (1982). *Megatrends—ten new directions transforming our lives.* New York: Warner Books.

Nedler, S. E., & McAfee, O.D. (1979). *Working with parents: Guidelines for early childhood and elementary teachers.* Belmont, CA: Wadsworth Publishing Company.

Parker, F. C., & McCoy, J. F. (1977). School-based intervention for the modification of excessive absenteeism. *Psychology in the Schools, 14*(1), 84-88.

Rich, D., VanDien, J., & Mattox, B. (1979). Families as educators of their own children. In R. S. Brandt (Ed.), *Partners: Parents and schools.* Alexandria, VA: ASCD.

Schaefer, E. S. (1971). Toward a revolution in education. *National Elementary Principal, 51*(1), 18-25.

Scheflen, A. E. (1978). Communicational concepts of schizophrenia. In M. E. Berger (Ed.), *Beyond the double bind. Communication and family systems, theories, and techniques with schizophrenics.* New York: Brunner/Mazel.

Seeley, D. S. (1981). *Education through partnership: Mediating structures and education.* Cambridge, MA: Ballinger Publishing Co.

Sheats, D., & Dunkleberger, G. E. (1979). A determination of the principal's effect in school-initiated home contacts concerning attendance of elementary school students. *The Journal of Educational Research, 72*(6), 310-312.

Shelton, J., & Dobson, R. L. (1973). *An analysis of a family involvement-communication system in a Title I elementary school.* Final Report, (ERIC Document Reproduction Service No. ED 082 091)

Smith, M. B., & Brahce, C. I. (1963). When school and home focus on achievement. *Educational Leadership, 20*(5), 314-318.

Snow, M. (1982). Characteristics of families with special needs in relations to schools. Charleston, WV: Appalachia Educational Laboratory.

Spriggs, A. M. (June, 1980). *Children and families in Appalachia: The status, needs and implications for R & D Activities.* Charleston, WV: Appalachia Educational Laboratory.

Steinberg, L. I. (1979). The changing role of parent groups in educational decision making. In R. S. Brandt (Ed.), *Partners: Parents and schools.* Alexandria, VA: ASCD.

Stitley, R. P. (1978). Behavior contracts: A home-school cooperative effort. *Peabody Journal of Education, 55*(4), 318-322.

Toffler, A. (1980). *The third wave.* New York: Bantam Books.

Trovato, J., & Bucher, B. (1980). Peer tutoring with or without home-based reinforcement, for reading remediation. *Journal of Applied Behavior Analysis, 13*(1), 129-141.

Valentin, C. S., & Alston, H. L. (July, 1978). *Survey of parents' expectations of public schools and aspirations for their children's education.* Project Report, Houston Independent School District. (ERIC Document Reproduction Service No. ED 162 442)

Walberg, H. J., & Marjoribanks, K. (1976). Family environment and cognitive development: Twelve analytic models. *Review of Educational Research, 46*(4), 527-551.

Woods, C., Barnard, D. P., & TeSelle, E. (1974). *The effect of the parent involvement program on reading readiness scores.* Prepared for Mesa Public Schools, Curriculum Center, Mesa, Arizona. (ERIC Document Reproduction Service No. ED 104 527)

FOCUS FOR EDUCATION REFORM: BUILDING THE HOME-SCHOOL

SYNERGISM

Dorothy Rich, Ed.D.

President, The Home and School Institute
1201 16th Street, N.W.
Washington, D.C. 20036

Part I. The Scene Today

Two major questions to be addressed in this chapter are these:

How can the mounting research on the relationship of the home to children's school success be translated into practical action?

How can we involve the community--all families--meaningfully in the education "action"?

The National Commission on Excellence in Education Report (1983) included parents in a postscript: "As surely as you are your children's most important teachers, your children's ideas about education and its significance begin with you...Moreover, you bear a responsibility to participate actively in your children's education."

But what is this responsibility?   And what is expected of schools in working with parents?

With due respect to the recent reports on the state of our nation's education, this author finds that the perspectives and solutions in recent reports such as those of the Education Commission of the States, 1983 and Twentieth Century Fund, 1983) are overwhelmingly school-based. They do not focus on actions that need to be taken by schools and those who govern schools to work with the community, the home, and with today's family.

The education reform actions outlined in this chapter are based on the research and the experience of the Home and School Institute in 20 years of work with thousands of teachers and families across the country.

To facilitate use of this section in professional training programs this discussion utilizes a question and answer format. Documentation references supporting the answers are indicated at the end of the chapter.

What are Appropriate Roles for Today's Families and Schools?

It's been traditional to talk about the need for family support of the school. And that has traditionally been defined through such activities as voting for the school budget and baking cookies for the PTA event.

This is out of date and ineffective as an approach for home-school relations today. It's now known that the home is a vital education institution. What's needed now is *not* old-fashioned support of the school, but new and different support for the educational role of the family (Organization for Economic Cooperation and Development, 1981).

Schools depend upon the input from the home. But overall, schools have not worked yet with the home or with other community agencies in a concerted, systematic manner (Home and School Institute, 1978).

Today, schools must work with a new kind of family. Today's family configuration even looks different. Without going into elaborate demographic detail, it is sufficient to note that the majority of mothers today hold jobs outside the home and that single parenting is on the increase. It is predicted that by the year 2000, 50% of all children will have lived at least for a time, in a single parent household. (Select Committee on Children, Youth and Families, 1983) Working parents may not be able to come to 2 P.M. school events, but they want to help their children. (Epstein, 1983) Even under the constraints of limited time and financial pressures, today's parents care about the value of their children's schooling. After years of heavy dependence on the school to do everything, the public appears ready to assume more responsibility for what's happening to children. In recent Gallup Polls, lack of discipline was cited as a major school problem. When asked for the cause of the school's discipline problems, the public, including parents, laid chief blame on the home (Gallup, 1981).

Research has clearly shown that the effects of schools which do not involve families do not result in lasting achievement for children. The research is clear. What isn't clear is why the focus for educational reform continues almost exclusively on the school when the family is a vital educational force.

Most parents today are better educated than those of previous decades. (National Center for Education Statistics, 1982) It's no secret that parents are asking questions, making demands, and showing concern. Parents are seeking involvement in the education of their children. They may not come to the traditional meetings, but parents are interested in ways to help their own children--ways that are easy, fast, and linked to their children's school achievement (Epstein, 1984).

Over the years several school-home activity models have been identified. They include volunteerism, parent-school communication, policy making, and parent education and training. Briefly, their assets and liabilities today are these: (Rich et al, 1979).

Volunteerism offers extra person power in the classroom. Managed effectively, it can give teachers more teaching time. Volunteerism at its best provides active roles for parents, but volunteers help students in general, not necessarily their own children.

Parent-school communication usually comes in the form of report cards, conferences, and newsletters to keep parents informed. Most of this communication is initiated by the school, and parent play relatively passive roles.

Policy making usually takes the form of Parent Advisory Committees. Relatively few working parents today can participate in such committees.

Parent education and training involves teaching parents how to improve their family life and/or how to work with their children. Of all the models identified, this one offers the most substantive research to date.

What Does Research Support?

It is increasingly clear that priority attention should be given to developing the mode of participation which directly involves parents in the education of their own child. It is often referred to as the "parent-as-tutor" approach.

The reasons for this position are two fold. First, it is the approach which a continuing line of research indicates is most directly linked to improved academic achievement.

The second reason for this position is that it offers the greatest opportunity for widespread involvement and sustained participation. Programs which require attendence at meetings or involvement in school activities during the day will necessarily have limited participation. The need to reach out to single parents and to families in which both parents work is a special concern. Furthermore, this approach appeals to the most basic parental motivation for involvement in the first place--the desire to help one's child do better in school.

In study after study, the home and the community have been identified as vital influences intimately linked with student success.

Synthesizing the work in compensatory education and involvement of parents in training programs, the study, "Parent Involvement in Compensatory Education Programs," assessed the major models of parent involvement. The study considered evidence supporting the hypothesis that parent involvement (in one or more roles) leads to improved child achievement. In general, the evidence supported the participation of parents as tutors of their children. "As a group," say the authors, "the programs involving parents as teachers consistently produced significant immediate gains in children's IQ scores, and seemed to alter in a positive direction the teaching behavior of parents" (Goodson and Hess, 1975).

Studies since the 1970's at all grade levels support the role of families in the education of children. Bronfenbrenner (1974) who reviewed a variety of intervention programs, concluded that the active involvement of the family is critical to program success. It reinforces and helps sustain the effects of school programs.

Ira Gordon (1978) generated much research on parent involvement, especially in the Follow Through program. He concluded that all forms of parent involvement help, but that the more comprehensive the involvement (e.g., the more roles there are in a school for parents to play) and the longer it lasts, the more effective it will be.

The traditional pro forma advisory council as a model for involvement has not been found effective in the major Federal programs. A major study of parent involvement in ESEA Title I, the ESEA Title VII Bilingual Program, Follow Through, and the Emergency School Aid Act presents a cautious picture of parent participation activities. After advisory groups, the next most common form of involvement was communication, mostly from the project to the home. While most projects provided some kind of parent education, usually on a one-time basis, few helped parents teach their own children at home or had arranged face-to-face discussions between parents and staff members. (Burns, 1982) Even in large federally funded programs there was little sustained effort to communicate with parent and help them assist in the instructional process (Burns, 1982).

Various kinds of parent involvement were evaluated by elementary teachers in a six-state regional survey by Williams. Generally, teachers were not enthusiastic about parent participation in curriculum development, instruction or school governance. They did support other forms of parent involvement, such as assisting with homework or tutoring children, but felt that teachers should give parents ideas about how to help. Teachers noted that their own schools did not usually provide opportunities for parents and teachers to work together on such activities (Williams, 1981).

Summary.   How has all of this evidence changed the work of most schools in the way they relate the family and the home?   The answer to date--not very much.   The carnivals, music, and book fairs continue, and so to the bake sales.   These programs take effort and a great deal of teacher time.   They are designed with the best of intentions, but most of them bear little to no relation to what teachers and parents care about most--building student motivation and achievement.

Much has been written about school-parent relations because of its intriguing and often frustrating complexity.   Principal and scholar, Roland Barth, (1978) says: "One might expect that sharing a daily preoccupation with the same children would form a common bond, bringing principal, teacher, and parents together.   Unfortunately, this bond seldom develops naturally or spontaneously.   We school people need help in finding ways to work cooperatively with parents; and parents badly need assistance in translating their basic caring into actions that will improve the situation for their children, the school and themselves.

Part II.   The Changing Scene: What It Means For The School

Schools are on the front lines in a society that is changing all around them.   In the past two decades, over half of the mothers who used to welcome children home after school are out of home working.   (Select Committee on Children, Youth, and Families, 1984)   In many schools the majority of the children are living, at least for awhile, in homes with one parent.   The standard of living in these homes goes down markedly when fathers move out.   These changes that have come upon the schools only recently, and schools are just beginning to respond.   Both families and schools are feeling vulnerable in the face of so many changes today.

In an effort to bolster the relationship between today's family and school, the Home and School Institute in 1983 sponsored a conference in Washington entitled *Single Parent Families and the Schools: Opportunity or Crisis?*   In 1984, the Institute followed up on this program with a conference on *Working Parents and Achieving Children: The Road to Excellence.*

Surveys of research were prepared for these conferences.   These were among the questions addressed:

Do children of working mothers perform less well in school?

No: Two recent reviews of studies sponsored by the National Institute of Education have shown that the school achievement of children of working mothers differs little from that of children of non-working mothers (Heyns, 1982).

Children's development is influenced by many factors. The mother's employment is only one of these and not necessarily the most important.

In addition, employment is not a single uniform condition. It is not experienced in the same way by all parents and it does not affect all children in the same way.

In a National Academy of Science study, the advice is: "Don't ask if working parents are good or bad for kids because the answer is: It depends on the parents, on the child, on the circumstances, and so forth" (Kamerman and Hayes, 1982).

However, two recent national studies of elementary and secondary school students suggest a caution. In two parent white families children whose mothers were employed had lower achievement than those with nonemployed mothers, even after allowing for the influence of various other relevant factors. The size of the effect was directly related to the amount of time mothers worked (Myers et al, 1983).

In addition, preliminary evidence suggests that the sons of middle class employed mothers do not achieve as well as the sons of nonemployed middle class mothers (Hoffman, 1980).

Which children of working mothers do better in school?

There are three groups of working mothers whose children do better in school:

    Professionals
    Low Income
    Black

The children of these groups seem to achieve better in school than their counterparts with mothers in the same groups who do not. It is hard to say whether it is the competency of their mothers, other family and cultural conditions, or factors connected with employment itself which make the difference. (Heyns, 1982; Hoffman, 1980) In addition, daughters of employed mothers tend to achieve more than daughter of nonemployed mothers (Hoffman, 1980).

Do working mothers spend less time with their children?

No: Studies of time use suggest that working mothers spend almost as much time caring for their children as do non-working mothers. (Heyns, 1982) The working mother who is "time poor" seems to work harder at maintaining some level of activity involving child and spouse, eliminating personal leisure time instead (Medrich, 1982).

Does the fact that a mother works limit her involvement in her child's education?

Working poses some limitations on the mother's participation in school activities, but many mothers make significant efforts to maintain close contacts with teachers and schools (Mason and Espinosa, 1983).

There is a decline in parent-school activities that do not include the child or allow for contact with the child. Given time conflicts, working parents may be less visible and active in school activities during the day. In light of the available data, it seems unlikely that work status in and of itself accounts for a significant variance in student achievement or level of parent participation in school (Linney and Vernberg, 1983).

Do workplace policies affect the participation of mothers in education-related activities?

When leave policies are rigid and job stress is high, mothers in dual earner families have lower involvement in their children's education. Among single parents those who are highly involved tend to work in high stress jobs, which seem to energize them, but they less often hold a second part-time job than the less involved mothers (Espinosa, 1983).

Is the intellectual functioning of children harmed in single parent homes?

No: A recent review of numerous studies done for the National Institute of Education shows that when the socio-economic status of families is taken into account, the intelligence of children in one and two parent households is similar. Aptitude and achievement test scores are lower for those from one parent homes, but the differences are not large (Hetherington et al, 1981).

Do children from single parent households perform less well in school?

Yes: This same review of studies done for NIE shows that children from one parent homes do tend to receive lower grades, display more disruptive behavior in school, and have poorer attendance (Hetherington et al, 1981).

In another recent survey of 26 elementary and secondary schools, the family income and the sex of the child were more highly related to achievement than number of parents in the home (Zakariya, 1982).

What circumstances in single parent homes lead to better child functioning?

Several factors seem important:

Conflict between spouses: Conflict between the ex-spouses after divorce is harmful to children, especially if the conflict spills over into the parent-child relationship (Wallerstein and Kelly, 1980).

Time Since Divorce: Many mother-child relationships deteriorate in the year immediately after divorce, especially between mothers and sons. By the second year, parenting improves markedly (Wallerstein and Kelly, 1980; Hetherington, Cox and Cox, 1978).

Children's Responsibilities: Children in single parent families are often expected to assume added responsibilities which can lead to greater self-sufficiency. But too much independence and responsibility can also make youngsters feel overwhelmed, incompetent and resentful (Moles, 1982).

Emotional Support from Other Adults: Support from nearby family and friends, (e.g., grandparents,) promotes positive attitudes toward self. They enhance the parenting role and children's mental health. Positive relations with teachers, peers and neighbors help lessen the impact of family stress (Hetherington, 1979).

Age of Child: Children who are very young when their parents divorce fare better psychologically than their older brothers and sisters. Five years after the marriage broke up, younger children in the study appeared to be more depressed than older siblings. But after 10 years had passed, younger children carried fewer memories of stressful events while older children tended to suffer continued damaging memories (Wallerstein, 1984).

Does becoming a single parent affect family finances and does that in turn have implications for the child's education?

YES: There is an average 35% drop in family income when husbands leave (Hill and Hoffman, 1977). Social isolation following divorce may be intensified for children by a move and the loss of friends, neighbors and familiar schools. The new home is more likely to be in a lower income area with higher risks to personal safety, fewer recreational facilities and schools with fewer resources (Hetherington, 1979).

Does being a single parent lessen home-school involvement?

Single parents are similar to other parents in how often they talk with teachers (Gotts, 1982). Children of one and two parent backgrounds are equally likely to spend time with students on school work. For mothers who do not work, there is a difference between white and black families regarding help in school activities. White mothers help in school less when they have no husband at home. But among black mothers, there is little difference (Medrich, 1982). Across white, black and Hispanic families, over three-fourths of all mothers were judged to be moderately or highly involved in the education of their children (Espinosa, 1983).

How do schools treat single parents?

From the teachers' viewpoint, there are concerns that parents do not provide the information that schools need in order to help children. Quite a few teachers said that they had suspected a divorce but felt it improper and intrusive to inquire. "It is ironic that at a time in our society when parents increasingly hold the schools responsible for their child's well-being, these same parents fail to provide some of the important tools for teachers effective functioning" (Wallerstein and Kelly, 1980).

From the parents' viewpoint, there are a number of concerns such as negative comments by school personnel about one-parent families, including the use of the term "broken homes," the need to take time off from work for teacher conferences, and the lack of information provided to non-custodial parents (Clay, 1980).

At the HSI conference, parents summarized their feelings in this way:

School personnel are insensitive. They stereotype children from single parent families and expect less from them. Schools do not provide the before and after school care that children of working parents need. School functions and parent-teacher conferences are scheduled as if parents do not work and are planned as though there are still fathers in the home. Parents are asking for better communication between home and school and signs that schools understand how today's families live and are provided with the means to work effectively with today's family.

Summary. It does not take a crystal ball to predict that the numbers of working parents will increase and that families will no longer be the traditional model. Schools are being asked to change, but many of the changes asked for are not cataclysmic in nature. They are reasonable, do-able and good for schools. Many of the recommendations don't even involve teacher change. They focus on the use of the school as a community institution, serving the needs of the community in new and needed ways.

Among the priorities identified by HSI conference participants are these:

> More inservice training for teachers and administrators in working with families.

> Parenting, child care, coping and survival skills courses for students, with special attention to those who are already parents.

> Increased awareness of the constraints of working single parents, including scheduling of evening meetings and conferences, discontinuance of parent fees for obligatory school events.

> Revision of the school calendar and lengthening of the school day.

> After-school care in which children do not have to leave the school building.

> Open enrollment policies, in which children can attend schools near parents' work.

> Increased and improved communication between home and school.

> More positive attitudes from teachers about families undergoing separation, divorce and remarriage. This could be assisted through an increase in the number of school counselors, especially at the elementary level.

Schools can be seen as facilitators for various support systems for parents. Among the suggestions: establishment of peer support groups for single parents, use of the schools to match senior citizens and latchkey children, and efforts to mesh services and supports for families from other human service organizations. Opening the school doors is a start. Moreover the school must move to become a needed focus for the community, not as the supplier for all services, but as an important place in the lives of people of all ages. Only in that way will the school be able to educate children and survive as an institution in the 21st century.

How does the new technology affect the home-school relationship?

Technology and the information revolution now and in the foreseeable future demand that schools today play new roles, working in partnership with today's resources outside the school.

"Computers to Revolutionize Family-School Relationship": This is the headline in *American Family Newsletter.* The article continues: "It is not being overly pessimistic to view the microcomputer as the vehicle that may drive a technological and instructional wedge between home and school (Wakefield, 1983).

These facts are cited:

> The computer permits students to work with greater independence from the school and teacher. It shifts the locus of learning from the school to the home as more homes than schools get computers.

> As the cost of the computers drops, home computer use expands dramatically. It's estimated that the majority of families will have home computers or access to them by 1990. These computers will be more powerful, more flexible, easier to use and probably cheaper than today's.

> It is possible that the home educational computer program market will overtake the textbook/AV market by the end of the decade. At a recent seminar on "Implications of the Computer Age" the home computer was described as a tool to bring the family closer together. The technology is already here at affordable costs, to enable families to take over total education of their children at home.

The National Education Association has been working on a study of education in a technological era. As students increasingly gain information from computer, the role of the teacher says Helene Gerstein of the NEA, will be to help students to interpret, and integrate this knowledge into their thinking skills.

Gerstein believes teachers can use computers to deal with a whole range of students' special learning problems. But she is concerned about the possibility of the home computer and home education alienating students and families from the community and society *(American Family, 1983).*

In the same issue of *American Family,* Kenneth Komoski of EPIE suggests four ways for schools to head off a potential home-school collision and help forestall dividing society into information-rich and information-poor:

> Request a district-wide policy to offer programs in computer literacy and the educational uses of computers for all parents.

> Help parents who can't afford a home computer by extending the school discount and encouraging them to buy the same make and model used by the school.

Communicate frequently and clearly to all parents about plans and the purposes and purchases of educational computing hardware and courseware.

Cooperate in establishing and maintaining a home-school cur- riculum software bank. Parents' educational software, would be deposited here once the youngster in the household has outgrown it so more parents may use it.

Summary. There appears to be a growing consensus that attention should be focused on ways to assure access to the technology by those families and schools which need help, and remove some of the barriers that may inhibit this new type of home education.

In view of the increasing numbers of working mothers and single parents, it's questionable how many families will be able to or want to take over their child's education. But, technology is making a new kind of educational partnership possible.

Part III. The School-Community Synergism: Formulas For Change

In the late 70's, the Home and School Institute (HSI) conducted a survey of school and family/community practices for the Maryland State Department of Education. (1978) Also surveyed were the policy-making and administrative structures which support the outreach efforts of schools to family and community at the local educational agency (LEA) level.

Some of the key findings from this survey are summarized below and provide a picture of how school systems have approached the challenge of family involvement in education. Almost all the elements of comprehensive plan for school and family involvement existed some- where in the state, but not together anywhere.

The following findings give cause for concern.

1. Very limited support for parents to be directly involved in the education of their children.

2. A general lack of clear policy guidelines and coordinated planning. Usually parent involvement is treated as an "extra."

3. Understaffing and underbudgeting for family involvement components. If staff time and budget allotments are good measures of institutional and legislative priorities, family involvement cannot be viewed as a commitment of higher order.

4. Proliferation of programs and practices on an ad hoc basis in response to specific needs and problems, with a resulting imbalance in the opportunities available. For example, one school may have a plethora of programs, while another a few miles away may have very little to offer.

5. Preponderant influence of federal programs and guidelines. While federal support has permitted the opportunity for the expansion of activities and experimentation, it raises the question as to what extent practices will be institutionalized and supported at the local level if federal supports are withdrawn.

6. Lack of solid evaluation of family involvement programs and practices. This, of course, is directly related to the limited staffing and budget support available. Much of the data available is the reporting of numbers participating with little attention to quality of program, elements of success, or impact.

7. Pivotal influence of the principal at the building level. What happens with regard to parent involvement in a particular school is in large part determined by the philosophy and the priorities of the principal.

8. Lack of programs at the secondary level. The opportunities for involvement decline markedly as students move up the age-grade ladder.

9. Difficulty in reaching out to a broad segment of the community and in sustaining participation. Involving working parents and single parents was often mentioned as a problem.

10. Widespread perception among school administrators that family involement is a kind of general public relations effort for the school system rather than a meaningful way of sharing educational accountability for the academic achievement of children.

The overall conclusion from these findings is that parent involvement is still seen as a peripheral activity that has not been integrated into the main work of the schools.

It may be unwise to generalize from the experience of one state. However, it should be pointed out that the local educational agencies selected for the Maryland study represent in many ways the diversity of the nation. Rural areas, market cities dominating a rural hinterland, suburban areas, a central city, and areas undergoing rapid demographic change were included in the survey. The results of the Maryland study are scarcely surprising. Family involvement in education, keyed to raising children's achievement, is still at a "pre-scientific" stage of development. Local experimentation has provided a broad base of experience and practice, although it has also produced poorly document-ed efforts and the "reinvention of the wheel" on more than one occasion. It is the author's position that a sufficient data base exists, to place these efforts on a more systematic basis, e.g. setting into place a continuing synergistic action between home and school. Implementing this system offers potential for a quiet revolution in education, one that can substantially raise academic achievement.

How Can the Parent-as-Tutor Model Be Translated into Practical Action?

The parent-as-tutor model poses the challenge of finding a low cost, effective delivery system. Work at the preschool level has often involved the use of home visitors. (Gordon, 1978) While this approach is effective, it is costly. This cost argues against its replication on a wide-scale basis, particularly when the schools are under today's budgetary pressures.

The work of the Home and School Institute (HSI) has been devoted in large part to developing a parent-as-tutor stategy which can be utilized on a cost-effective basis with school-age children.

Basically, HSI has built programs based on assuming family strengths, not deficits. This nondeficit approach magnifies and builds on the strengths inherent in the family. It marshals available family resources and abilities to improve children's academic skills. This in turn increases self-esteem of family members and helps parents feel more secure in their parenting roles.

What is the Non-Deficit Approach? The HSI nondefit approach makes the following assumptions (Rich et al, 1979).

1. All children have had meaningful experiences. However, the disadvantaged child's experiences have been difficult and fewer in number in contributing to preparation for success in school.

2. Home environments, no matter how poor, provide foundat-ions of care and concern for children.

3. All parents intrinsically possess the abilities to help their child succeed in school.

4. Family concern can be readily translated into practical support for children and for schools. Professionals need

only to provide the materials and support to enable parents to become both more active and skilled participants in their child's education.

5. Schools policies should be based on what the family has instead of worrying about what it doesn't have.

6. Schools, no matter how understaffed or equipped, have the capabilities of reaching out and effecting parent involvement by using easy, inexpensive materials, without waiting for what probably won't come: organizational change or massive government funding.

What Occurs at Home Using this Approach?   The nondeficit approach constructs a mutually reinforcing home-school system.   Families are assisted to:

1. Use strategies at home to supplement the school's work. The HSI parent involvement model is built on the basic premise of separate but complementary roles for parent and teacher.

2. Understand that accountability for a child's education can be shared, between school and home. Parents are helped in their role as key people in the student's learning process. It is important to remember that HSI home learning does not take the place of the school--it reinforces and extends the work of the school.

One of the strategies the Home and School Institute has developed is to support parents as educators is called "Home Learning Recipes." (Rich et al, 1979) These are easy, practical, no-cost activities for learning at home. Their goal is to build family interaction and children's academic achievement without duplicating the work of the school.

Since 1965, when the HSI parent programs began, Home Learning activities have been prepared and tested in homes with children ranging from kindergarten through the secondary grades. The activity format outlines at a glance activity objectives, evaluation, and adaptations. The difference between this home learning and typical school work is that these activities are designed to use the resources of the home and the community.   They are not typical school work, even though they concentrate on the basis 3 R's skills.

Over the years, HSI has developed a bank of activities in the basic skills areas so that It Is possible to choose among a variety of them to fit the needs and interests of a particular child or group of children without extensive teacher involvement in the design of the materials.   The approach is self-teaching and perpetuating in that it is relatively easy, once the basic technique is mastered, for teachers and parents to continue to create learning activities on their own. The approach can function on an individualized diagnostic prescriptive level to meet the particular developmental or remedial needs of each child. These activities have been used successfully with handicapped and also with bilingual populations. (Home and School Institute, 1983) Perhaps most important is the finding that families do these activities with their children, voluntarily and delightedly, pleased with themselves as teachers and pleased with their children as learners (Trinity College, 1984).

HSI has initiated a number of such projects with school systems in California, Michigan, South Carolina, and the District of Columbia. Where it has been tried, it has worked: children gain on tests and parents are happier with the schools.

What National Programs Could Be Set in Place Today? A national program to develop and expand this educational partnership could be put into action today--in three major ways that support and reinforce each other:

A. *The Media Campaign* to educate the public on HOME: A SPECIAL LEARNING PLACE. Signs, slogans, Home Learning Recipes through the radio, TV, back-of-the bus signs, messages on grocery carry home bags and on construction fences. In every place and at every opportunity the message would be carried--Home and School Equals Learning. National surveys tell us that parents are ready to help their children to improve their school work. Mothers at home seek greater status and a sense that society values the important work they are doing in child-rearing. Women at work need tested ways to help their children. Through Home Learning, children are helped to better skills and self-esteem, and parents and/or other home teachers (grandparents, friends, neighbors, etc.) are helped to greater self-confidence as "copers" in rearing children--as real partners with the school in the education of children.

B. *Family Learning Centers:* Increasingly with lowered enrollment, schools have some empty classroom space. HSI has pioneered in using this space for Family Learning Centers centered on the theme of *Home: The Learning Place.* Storefronts can also be used for this purpose. These are demonstration rooms, visible how-to models showing how household furniture is used for home teaching purposes. Home learning activities are attached to these objects and self guiding tape recorded messages on home learning will emanate from sofas, sinks, dishes, etc. Visitors to these Centers, which can be kept open past usual school hours so that working parents can attend, are able to see and hear how they can use these activities in their own homes.

Community volunteers, senior citizens or paraprofessionals can staff these rooms, handing out activities, responding to parents' concerns, referring families, when necessary, to other community agencies—in short, establishing a local Home Learning network, with the Family Learning Center as the core or home base.

Another projected "outreach" is a telephone answering service—"Dial a Home Learning Recipe"—so that families can call even when the room is closed and still receive tips. These are changed every few days and emphasize different household rooms and different subject areas.

C. *Home Learning Activity Packets:* Singly or in a group, these materials (one page, easy to read) can be distributed through schools, churches, community centers, gas stations, grocery stores, government agencies. All places that reach families. More can be developed by parents and teachers working together, all over the country.

Among the easy techniques used to foster learning are these: for the young child, such activities as using the clock to teach arithmetic, using the TV schedule to keep to time limits, using the telephone to dial and read numbers. For the older youngster, activities include making "best buy" purchases at the grocery store, using maps to plan family trips.

These activities are done alongside normal household routines. The hurried parent in a few minutes a day teaches science, reading, math or writing in a relaxed, at-home way. The material is presented in such a way the parents know exactly what to do. Families are encouraged to use their own creativity, and they're told that they can do nothing wrong.

What Basic Strategies Are Needed to Make These National Programs Successful?

The school is the pivotal social institution that has contact with students over many years. This fact alone gives schools both the opportunity and the responsibility to reach out to the student and the family beyond the classroom walls. This responsibility must be shared by legislatures and school boards as well as administrators and teachers.

Here are 6 rules, based on 20 years of experience that help ensure successful and realistic parent involvement in education. These were formulated and tested in conjuction with my HSI colleagues, James Van Dien and Beverly Mattox (Home and School Institute, 1978).

1. Link parents' involvement directly to the achievement of their children. An important reward for parents is the

success experienced by their own children. If this is selfish, so be it. But, it is reality.

2. Provide ways for families to teach in complementary ways to home. Emphasize opportunity for families to supplement and reinforce the development of academic skills with work in the home. Home involvement also offers participation to people who cannot attend in-school meetings.

3. Offer various modes of participation. In addition to the traditional advisory councils and volunteer programs, sponsor breakfast meetings and special evenings for single parents. Think about the needs of parents as adults. Schedule events so that working parents can attend, at least some of the time. Involve parents in reaching other parents. In this way, parents help the school and each other.

4. Provide for parent involvement at all levels of schooling. Though research and school-community program development thus far have centered on the early childhood years, continuing support and reinforcement are needed as the child moves through school. A particular need for programs exists in the middle and junior high adolescent years.

5. Build new constituencies for the schools. Schools need constituencies--wider than just parents and children and far wider than specific targeted populations. For example, the Institute has just tested a systematic program for involving seniors as volunteers in the classrooms and as liaisons to the home. These seniors work successfully both with adolescents who need extra help and with their families.

6. Ensure that parent-community involvement is seen as a legitimate, needed activity of the school, an integral part of its delivery of services, not an add on or a "nice but extra" thing to do.

The public needs to understand that schools, to reach the child, must reach the family. This takes time, commitment, and budget. In a major effort to help teachers facilitate working with families as educators, the National Education Association has begun distribution of home learning activities to families in selected districts around the nation. The goal is to provide ways for teachers to reach parents with easy to do activities that build student achievement outside the usual classroom hours. The total community is involved in this Teacher-Parent Partnership Program.

How Can the Home-School Synergism Strengthen the Family?

A unique and really unanticipated result of building good home-school relations is that it bolsters and strengthens the family as the primary nurturing institution. It does this by letting the family know that it is a competent, caring partner in the education process.

When schools help to strengthen families, schools strengthen their ability to educate. In this period of rapid social change, families need to feel important, competent and needed. And schools can help to do this.

Parents have needs that teachers will have to meet. After years of being told that they don't know "the right way" to teach, parents may need to have their confidence restored. Teachers can convince parents to trust themselves and once again regard themselves as their child's primary and ongoing teachers.

Leaders seeking substantive family involvement in education will have to be prepared to exert leadership--with school boards, voters and teachers parents. Working with families requires certain basic attitudes, skills, and behaviors different from working with children alone. School personnel may need retraining--almost retooling--to make this transition.

Policy makers need to hear what educators now need in their work with parents. These four recommendations are but a start in the agenda to build real home-school partnership (White House Conference on Families, 1980):

1.   Educators need and should demand training and materials in how to work more closely and effectively with the family.

2.   "Seed Money" grants should be established to encourage schools, health care and social agencies, institutions of higher education, professional associations, etc. to provide staff development and training in how to reach out to and work more effectively with families.

3.   Information programs including mass media, should be used to increase public awareness of the importance of the family and the many roles and services it provides.

4.   Home activities, in which families learn together, should be developed in such areas as basic functional literacy, nutrition, and health education.

Families and schools might wish that each could do the job alone. But, what is now known is that schools need families and today's family needs the school. In many ways, this is the greatest hope for change.

References

Barth, R. (1978, October). Parents as Helpers, Critics, and Adversaries. *National Elementary Principal Magazine.* 58 (1): 52.

Bronfenbrenner, U. (1974). *Is Early Intervention Effective? A Report on Londitudinal Evaluations of Preschool Programs.* Volume II. Washington, D.C.: U.S. Department of Health, Education and Welfare.

Burns, J. (1982). *The Study of Parental Involvement in Four Federal Education Programs: Executive Summary.* Washington, D.C.: U.S. Department of Education, Office of Planning, Budget and Evaluation.

Clay, P. (1980). *Single Parent Families: How Do The Public Schools Treat Them? A Preliminary Report.* Columbia, Md. National Committee for Citizens in Education.

Education Commission of the States. (1983). *Action for Excellence: A Comprehensive Plan to Improve Our Nation's Schools.* Denver, Colorado: Author.

Epstein, J. (1983). *Effects on Parents of Teacher Practices in Parent Involvement.* Center for Social Organization of Schools. Baltimore, Md. Johns Hopkins University.

Epstein, J. (1984). *Improving American Education: Roles for Parents.* Washington, D.C. Testimony for the Select Committee on Children, Youth and Families. U.S. House of Representatives.

Espinosa, R. (1983). *Work and Family Life Among Anglo, black and Mexican American Single-Parent Families: Executive Summary.* Austin, Tx.: Southwest Educational Development Laboratory.

Gallup Poll and Phi Delta Kappa. (1981). *Annual Survey of the Public's Attitudes Towards the Public Schools.* Bloomington, In.: Kappan.

Goodson, B. & Hess, R. (1975). *Parents as Teachers of Young Children: An Evaluative Review of Some Contemporary Concepts and Programs.* Palo Alto, Ca. Stanford University.

Gordon, I., Olmsted, P., Rubin, R., & True, J. (1978). *Continuity Between Home and School: Aspects of Parent Involvement in Follow Through.* Chapel Hill, N.C.: University of North Carolina.

Gotts, E. (1982). *Summary of Report: Characteristics of Families With Special Needs in Relation to Schools.* Charleston, W. Va.: Appalachia Educational Laboratory.

Hetherington, E. M. (1979). *Children and Divorce.* Paper presented at the annual meeting of the American Psychological Association, New York, N.Y.

Hetherington, E. M., Featherman, D. L. & Camara, K. A. (1981). *Intellectual Functioning and Achievement of Children in One-Parent Households.* Paper prepared for the National Institute of Education, Washington, D.C.

Hetherington, E.M., Cox, M. and Cox, R. (1978). "The Aftermath of Divorce." In J. H. Stevens Jr., and M. Mathews, (Eds.). *Mother Child, Father-Child Relations.* Washington, D.C., National Association for the Education of Young Children.

Heyns, B. (1982). "The Influence of Parents' Work of Children's School Achievement." In Sheila B. Kamerman and Cheryl D. Hayes (Eds.) *Families That Work: Children in a Changing World.* Washington, D.C.: National Academy Press.

Hill, D. & Hoffman, S. (1977). "Husbands and Wives." In G. J. Duncan and J. N. Morgan (Eds.) *Five Thousand American Families: Patterns of Economic Progress.* Vol. 4. Ann Arbor: Institute for Social Research.

Hoffman, L. (1980). *The Effects of Maternal Employment on the Academic Attitudes and Performance of School-Aged Children.* Paper prepared for the National Institute of Education, Washington, D.C.

Home and School Institute (1978). *Survey of Home/School/Community Practices.* Prepared for the Maryland State Department of Education. Washington, D.C.

Home and School Institute (1983). *Final Report: Parent-School Partnership Project.* Washington, D.C. U.S. Department of Education, Special Education Services.

Linney, J. & Vernberg, E. (1983). "Changing Patterns of Parental Employment and the Family-School Relationships." *Children of Working Parents: Experiences and Outcomes.* Washington, D.C., National Academy Press.

Kamerman, S. B. & Hayes, C. D. (1982). *Families That Work: Children in a Changing World.* Washington, D. C. National Academy Press.

Mason, T. & Espinosa, R. (1983). *Final Interim Report: Working Parents Project.* Austin, Tx: Southwest Educational Development Laboratory.

Medrich, E. et al (1982). *The Serious Business of Growing Up.* Berkeley, Ca.: University of California Press.

Moles, O. (1982). *Trends in Divorce and Effects on Children.* Paper presented at meetings of the American Academy for the Advancement of Science, Washington, D.C.

Myers, D. E., Milne, A., & others. (1983). *Single Parents, Working Mothers and the Educational Achievement of Secondary School Age Children.* Washington, D.C.: Decision Resources, Inc.

National Center for Educational Statistics. (1982). *The Condition of Education.* Washington, D.C. U.S. Government Printing Office.

National Commission on Excellence in Education. (1983). *A Nation at Risk: The Imperative for Educational Reform.* Washington, D.C.: Author.

Organization for Economic Co-operation and Development. (1982). *The Educational Role of the Family.* Paper prepared for the Governing Board. Paris, France: Author.

Rich, D., Mattox, B., & Van Dien, J. (1979, April). "Building on Family Strengths: The 'Nondeficit' Involvement Model for Teaming Home and School." *Educational Leadership.* pp. 506-510.

Rich, D. (1983). *Focus For Educational Reform: Building a Home-School Infrastructure.* Paper presented at the National Commission on Excellence in Education Forum, Indianapolis, In.

Rich, D., Van Dien, J., Mattox, B (1979). "Families as Educators of Their Own Children." In R. Brandt (Ed.) *Partners: Parents and Schools.* Washington, D. C. Association for Supervision and Curriculum Development.

Select Committee on Children, Youth and Families. (1984). *Demographic and Social Trends: Implications for Federal Support of Dependent Care Services for children and the Elderly.* Washington, D. C. U.S. Government Printing Office.

Select Committee on Children, Youth and Families. (1984). *Children, Youth and Families: 1983, A Year End Report.* Washington, D.C. U.S. Government Printing Office.

Trinity College. (1984). *Interim Report: Trinity/Arlington Teacher and Parent Training for School Success Project.* Washington, D.C. U.S. Department of Education, Bilingual Education Office.

Twentieth Century Fund. (1983). *Making the Grade: Report of the Twentieth Century Task Force on Federal, Elementary and Secondary Education Policy.* New York, N.Y.: Author.

Wakefield, R. (1983, April). "Computers to Revolutionize Family-School Relationships." *American Family.* National Center for Family Studies, Washington, D.C.

Wallerstein, J. S. & Kelly, J. B. (1980). *Surviving the Breakup: How Children and Parents Cope With Divorce.* New York: Basic Books.

Wallterstein, J. S. (1984). Toronto, Canada. Paper presented at the American Orthopsychiatry Association.

White House Conference on Families. (1980). *National Organizations Issues Resource Book.* Washington, D.C. U.S. Government Printing Office.

Williams, D. L. (1981). *Final Interim Report: Southwest Parent Education Resource Center.* Austin, Tx.: Southwest Educational Development Laboratory.

Williams, D. L. (1982). *Executive Summary: A Survey of Parents Regarding Parent Involvement in Schools.* Austin, Tx., Southwest Educational Development Laboratory.

Zakariya, S. B. (1982, September). "Another Look at The Children of Divorce: Summary Report of the Study of School Needs of One-Parent Children." *Principal.*

AUTHOR INDEX

AAIA, 128, 154
Aquirre, E., 147, 149, 153
Ainsworth, M. D., 8, 23
Alden, J. W., 165, 197
Allen, V. L., 95, 100
Alston, H. L., 165, 202
Alvirez, D., 144, 153
Anderson, R., 17, 24
Andrews, M., 6, 19, 23, 27
Angell, R. C., 87, 100
Anastasi, A., 113, 120
Anes, N., 17, 24
Anselmo, S., 175, 197
Archibald, R., 138, 154
Aries, P., 5, 23
Atkinson, J. W., 93, 100, 101
Bacca Zinn, M., 144, 154
Badger, E. D., 11, 26
Bagchi, J., 29
Bailyn, B., 36, 45, 101
Baker, G., 5, 23
Baldassare, M., 176, 198
Bane, M. J., 36, 45
Banks, J., 139, 154
Barcelo, C. J., Jr., 150, 154
Bargen, M., 113, 114, 121
Barletta, C., 19, 20, 23
Barnard, D. P., 174, 202
Barr, R., 141
Barth, R., 111, 119, 120, 169, 171,
    172, 197, 198, 207, 222
Barton, J., 37, 45
Bartz, K. E., 144, 156
Beady, C., 92, 101
Bean, F. D., 144, 153
Becker, G. S., 6, 23, 109, 120
Bell, H. B., 54, 55, 60
Bell, T. H., 57, 58, 60, 64, 101
Benson, C., 5, 26
Berlin, I. N., 174, 197
Berlin, R., 174, 197
Berman, D. M., 134, 154
Biddle, B. J., 92, 102
Bittle, R. G., 168, 169, 197
Blanchard, E. L., 124, 128, 154
Blassingame, J., 37, 45
Bloom, B. S., 4, 23, 75, 95, 101

Bobbit, N., 52, 57, 60
Bodger, E. D., 56, 61
Boger, R., 4, 7, 9, 19, 21, 23, 29,
    174, 197
Bole, R. E., 18, 28
Bonacich, E., 130, 154
Bond, J. T., 54, 61
Boulding, K., 74, 101
Bowlby, J., 8, 24
Bowles, S., 77, 101
Boyd, V., 6, 27
Boyd-Franklin, N., 136, 155
Bradshaw, D., 73, 105
Braga, J., 54, 60
Braga, L., 54, 60
Brahce, C. I., 173, 201
Brazelton, T. B., 54, 60
Breiling, A., 174, 197
Breivogel, W., 17, 25
Briggs, J., 37, 45
Brim, O. G., 4, 24
Brockway, B. S., 93, 101
Bronfenbrenner, U., 3,
    4, 6, 9, 10, 11, 16, 24, 45, 46,
    58, 78, 206, 222
Brookover, W. B., 92, 101
Broussard, E. R., 8, 24
Bubolz, M., 6, 27, 69, 70, 105
Bucher, B., 171, 202
Budd, R. W., 160, 197
Bumpass, L., 83, 101
Bureau of Census Statistical
    Abstract, 133, 154
Bureau of Indian Affairs, 129, 154
Burks, B., 119, 120
Burns, J., 206, 222
Cahoon, O. W., 56, 58, 60
Camara, K., 209, 222
Carew, J. V., 5, 24
Carro, G., 81, 101
Carter, T. P., 144, 145, 146,
    147, 154
Castenada, A., 125, 157
Chan, I., 5, 24
Chemers, M., 138, 154
Cheng, C. W., 139, 154
Cherlin, A. J., 82, 84, 86, 101
Cherry, C., 160, 198

0